NOW ACT!

NOW ACT!

Vol. 1
Insight, Advice, and Preparation Processes
from Actors, Coaches, and Casting Directors

Edited by LAURIE LAMSON

JAZZYMAE MEDIA
Oceanside, California

NOW ACT!

Volume 1
Insight, Advice, and Preparation Processes
from Actors, Coaches, and Casting Directors

Published by JaZzyMaE Media

© 2025 by Laurie Lamson
All rights reserved. No part of this book may be reproduced, scanned or distributed in any printed or electronic form without permission. Available at quantity discounts for bulk purchases.

Contact: info@jazzymaemedia.com
Website: Now-Act.com

pages 338-340 constitute an extension of this copyright page

"Now Act" logo and spotlight illustration by Victoria Lamson Chavez
cover and book design by Laurie Lamson

Special thanks to Megan Sarnacki for help with inviting contributors and some of the transcriptions.

ISBN #979-8-9997047-2-6
First Edition

Table of Contents

Editor's Note ... ix

GET STARTED

Chapter 1. Explore the Acting Life

Stanzi Potenza	The Hill of Embarrassment	5
Thaine H. Allison, Jr.	An Actor Prepares – The Boy Scout Approach	10
Dioncio Virvez	Diversity in Hollywood	19
Christopher M. Allport	Craft, Career and Content	23

Chapter 2. Do Research

Michael Savage aka Sirtony	Real-Life Preparation	31
Cindy D'Andrea	Do It Because You Love to Act	34
Tim Carr	Choosing Material	40
Michael Genet	Master Classes, Tony Bennett, and How Many Levels Have You Got?	46

Chapter 3. Understand the Script

Thomas Gumede	How to Read a Script	55
Laurie Lamson	A Writer's Perspective for Actors	57
Stephen H. Snyder	Make It Work with Five W's	60
Clea DeCrane	What Would It Be Like if You Really Meant It?	66

Chapter 4. Be Present and Trust Your Instincts

Donn Swaby	Being in the Present Moment	73
Mackenzie Barmen	Talk to Yourself	80
Bruna Bertossi	Embracing the Moment: Techniques for Presence in Acting	84

Jack O'Halloran	Relax and Be Yourself	88
Malcolm McDowell	Yes, I'm Acting – Believe Me Anyway	96

BUILD UP YOUR ACTING CHOPS

Chapter 5. Develop a Character

Katherine Waddell	Learn Your Character's Skills	109
Price Hall	Subtext	113
Bryan Chesters	Acting is Living Truthfully Under Imaginary Circumstances	117
Jayce Bartok	How Could You Play That Part?!	123

Chapter 6. Practice Tools and Techniques

Kimmy Robertson	The Little Brain in Your Heart	131
Diana Jordan	Emotional Personal Touchstones	139
Leigh McCloskey	The Art of Getting Out of Your Own Way	143
Devorah Cutler	Dueling Animal Opposites… Creating the Electric Moment on Stage or Screen	150

Chapter 7. Learn Your Lines

Sarah Rush	Memorization and Stage Direction	159
Crystal Carson	Learning Lines by Heart	163
Cindy Marinangel	Eleven Memorizing Tricks and Tips	168
Allison Bergman	Methods and Strategies for Learning Your Lines	176

Chapter 8. Prepare a Scene or Performance

Leandro Taub	Mind, Body, Emotion & Spirit	183
Ali Cheff	Click In, Click Out	185
Jennifer Allen	Preparing a Character for the Stage	190

Kim Krizan	Save It for the Camera	193
Josh Margulies	Let's Get Physical	196

PUT YOURSELF OUT THERE

Chapter 9. Audition

Holly Powell	The Six Audition Tools	205
Crystal Carson	No Schm-Acting, Please	216
Paul Guay	Audition Notes	224
Danielle Eskinazi	Casting Directors Do Care	228
Joy Osmanski	Let It Go	235

Chapter 10. Get Outside Your Box

Alan Angelo	How Acting Can Help You Help Others	241
Vinnie Langdon III	But They Don't Make Movies Where I Live!	245
Caryn Ruby	How to Create a Showcase for Your Acting Through Collaboration	250
Winter Bassett	So What?	254
Stanzi Potenza	Comedy Is a Necessity	259

DEVELOP A SUSTAINABLE CAREER

Chapter 11. Understand Your Medium – The Craft and The Business

Mark Pellegrino	Life, Luck, Law, and Logic in Art	271
Paul Barry	Stage vs. Screen	278
Christopher M. Allport	Acting is Technical	288
Roxanna Lewis	Casting with Diversity and Authenticity - I'm Looking for You, So Be You!	295

Chapter 12. Collaborate and Play Well with Others

Lynne Burnett	What I Learned from Martin Sheen	305
Mara McCann	Creative Collaboration	308
Lisa Sawicki	How to Cope with Difficult Personalities	310
Kevin E. West	Processing Direction	314

Chapter 13. Be Safe and Take Care

Brionne Davis Davel	Agreements	323
Benjamin Easterday	Making Space for Safety	328
Giovanni Trimble, PhD	Navigating Intimacy in Acting – The Importance of Intimacy Coordination	331
Ali Cheff	Mantras for Actors	334
	Permissions	338
	About the Author / Editor	341

Editor's Note

If you're called to be an actor, I believe you provide an important service to society.

Let me explain what I mean. It may be evolving, yet we live in a culture that has long associated emotion with weakness. As a result, it is common to deny or repress feelings, or get stuck in one go-to emotional response. Yet to deny one's feelings is to deny an essential part of one's self. Our ability to learn from experiences is stunted when we can't feel.

For actors, a big part of the job is accessing and experiencing the full range of feelings, with all of their subtle nuances. That takes a particular kind of skill, and a whole lot of courage. By doing this, you help audience members access their own feelings, remind them of their connection to humanity, and demonstrate that 'what doesn't kill you makes you stronger.' I really believe your work involves sacred service.

As you may guess by now, I have tremendous respect for actors. It can be difficult enough sharing an original story or screenplay or film. Still, as a writer, you're a step removed – it's like your child, it's not you. For an actor there's no buffer, since your instrument is yourself, your own body and voice.

Even though many of the "Nos" an actor receives are not personal, as several contributors in this book discuss, it takes a lot of getting used to, combined with a strong sense of purpose and commitment to keep going.

I know what it feels like to be an artist who has trouble pursuing their calling: it eats away at you from the inside, like a soul sickness. I have great compassion for anyone in the same painful predicament. Part of my own mission is to empower creative people and I got to do that working on the *Now Write!* series of creative writing anthologies started by my aunt, Sherry Ellis. That experience inspired me to create this similar compilation for actors.

Now Act! is a book about both the craft and business of acting, with a "many voices under one roof" approach that includes insights, advice and techniques from diverse working actors at every career stage, along with teachers, casting directors and other industry pros. May it inspire and assist you on your journey, wherever it may lead.

"Some sort of creativity is within everybody; I think that's just a part of the human spirit. I think there's no human being on earth who is not creative in some way, because I think it's just a part of our genetic makeup."

- AUDRA MCDONALD

GET STARTED

"Acting is not about being famous; it's about exploring the human soul."

- ANNETTE BENING

Chapter 1.

Explore the Acting Life

"Overcoming a lack of talent will make you unique."

- STEVE MARTIN

STANZI POTENZA

The Hill of Embarrassment

Stanzi Potenza is a Boston native now based in Los Angeles. She is a trained actor, comedian, and digital creator with a rabid fan base of over five million. Stanzi is known for her viral sketches and comedic commentary, and she is the co-host of the popular weekly podcast Late to the Party. Her other piece in this book is "Comedy is a Necessity" in Chapter 10.

There is a kind of "Hill of Embarrassment" I think you have to get over in order to be successful at this acting thing.

Going into an audition, I definitely used to have a feeling that anyone involved in casting was looking for a reason to not like me. A lot of comparison kind of gets in your head.

Then I took an acting class with Jane Jenkins, who is a Hollywood casting director – she worked on BEETLEJUICE and THE PRINCESS BRIDE and a ton of other big movies. I told her I feel like they're nitpicking me as soon as I walk in the room, looking for a reason why I'm not right for the role.

She said it's actually the opposite. In casting, they <u>want</u> to like you, because if they like you, that means their job is done for that role. They're looking for every reason to like you and choose you, because that makes their lives a whole lot easier.

That was very important for me to hear. Every time you get rejected; you may think that it's because you did something wrong. But not getting a role is <u>not</u> synonymous with you doing something wrong. There could be a lot of different reasons.

In the same class, Jane had us listen to some podcasts, and one of them was with the casting director of *Modern Family*. He talked about when they were casting for that show, a big part of the process was searching for actors who looked like they could be related. You could have had a really great audition, but you just don't look like you could be a member of the Dunphy family, whom they had already finished casting. It's not because you aren't a great actor or you didn't crush your audition. There are different reasons why you might not get chosen for a certain thing.

I was doing some stand-in work and was asked to potentially stand-in for Melissa McCarthy. The only reason they didn't pick me was because we didn't have the same shoe size.

Jane also told us about a lot of celebrities who, before they were famous, did some auditions and didn't get a part because they just weren't right for it. But casting kept them in mind for other things because, if you establish a relationship with casting people, if you get your foot in the door, if you have the ability to show up and show off your skills, they will keep you in mind for something else. That's what happened with those actors who eventually started getting cast.

Missing out on a role isn't a failure. It's not a loss. Nowadays I think every rejection is something that gets you closer to your inevitable acceptance into a role. We all have to go through the process.

Having a likable personality helps, because people don't want to work with someone they don't think is going to mesh well with the rest of the cast or the crew. Especially for things where you're going to be working with the same people for a long time. I saw the documentary about creating of the LORD THE RINGS and how they had all the people playing hobbits spend a lot of time together, because they were going to be working together for years, in close proximity, for months at a time. If they didn't all mesh well together it could really cause a lot of trouble for the production.

Acting is a collaborative art form. That's why you want to go into everything putting your best foot forward. For the type of person who isn't that comfortable with other people, one-person sketches might be the way to go.

I work a lot more with other people now, because I'm surrounded by a lot more creatives than I used to be. But at the beginning of my online thing, I spent a lot of it just working on my own. If the idea of working with a lot of other people makes you anxious, you might find you're better suited creating videos by yourself, at least to start.

I grew up doing theater and going to a multimedia theater camp. I had some very challenging and intimidating experiences like being the youngest kid in an acting class. Over time, I got comfortable being on stage, being in front of an audience, and making a fool of myself.

But when I first started acting in theater, I wasn't great. Then when I thought I was doing a really good job, a teacher told me, "This isn't enough."

I had to learn what it takes to make it enough. I had to learn how to be bigger. You develop along the way.

So I had a lot of stage experience, but when I went to Esper Studios, it was my first time in front of a camera. In college I started doing background work on film sets, because I wanted to get comfortable in that arena. But being in the background isn't the same as really working in front of a camera.

At Esper, they could tell I had a big personality and was good at acting, but I was holding back when I was in front of the camera. Part of that is because going from theater to television, the rules are a little different. There's this natural element that needs to come across when you're working in front of a camera. That doesn't mean you necessarily have to make yourself smaller, but I surely was making myself small for the camera.

I also didn't like the idea of being filmed, because I had all these insecurities about the way I looked. I didn't like seeing myself onscreen – not something you typically have to worry about when you're doing theater.

Then when I started doing TikTok videos I was by myself, filming myself, and acting with myself, which is not necessarily the best thing for acting – it's a lot better to work off of someone else. So it was very uncomfortable, and my first batch of videos are a little awkward. I filmed everything on my phone. I didn't have a green screen. I didn't know how to edit. The quality was a lot worse than it is now. Plus, like I said, I wasn't comfortable in front of the camera.

See, you have to just put yourself into that uncomfortable position, whatever it is for you. The more you do whatever that it, the more comfortable you'll become.

Eventually I made friends with the camera. It's almost like a person you're spending time with – you just have to get to know it better. It took me a while to get here, but now I get in front of the camera and just do my thing.

PREPARATION

You have to start somewhere, and the place you're starting from is not necessarily going to be great. You have to accept that going in.

That is perfectly fine. That is your starting point. You have to allow yourself the grace to grow and develop your skills. Along the way, you're going to learn new things that enhance what you were doing before.

A lot of actors know that maybe their earliest work isn't their best work. There are interviews with amazing respected actors who are embarrassed about some of the earlier things they've done. (You might want to seek some of those out – it's reassuring.)

All you have to do is take the initial steps. I know so many people who don't allow themselves to take the first steps forward because they're embarrassed, or they don't feel like they're qualified enough. You will become qualified, but you have to take those first initial steps. They are the hardest steps to take, but you just have to pull the trigger and begin. If you play video games, it's the same thing. You try to defeat a character and you lose. If you keep playing, you get better at it and progress to a new level of the game.

As an actor, you have to develop your skills and your familiarity with the world, whether it's content creation or doing theater or film or television. If you keep at it, you will become better, _if_ you allow yourself the time and space to do that. You will build up skills and confidence along the way, exactly like progressing in a video game.

I wasn't necessarily writing sketches at first, I was just trying things out. You have to try things out and pivot if you don't like the result, or the audience response. You do have to take those first initial steps, and that takes getting over the hill of embarrassment.

Your first step might be an acting class. Creating your own short content, and posting it, at least as an experiment, is a great first step to help you climb over the hill of embarrassment. Start writing things you want to perform, start making short videos and posting them.

THE HILL OF EMBARRASSMENT

How to start? Explore ideas for what you want to do, what you might want to say. (See my piece "Comedy is a Necessity" for ideas on finding inspiration.)

Most people come up with all kinds of excuses as to why they shouldn't take the first step. No one is telling them they shouldn't do it, they're afraid of embarrassment.

You are the only person who can get in your own way. You might come up with scenarios that are preventing you from starting the journey. Please do get out of your own way and just start moving forward, and going down the path.

That is probably the hardest thing you're going to have to do. So make life easier for yourself: get out of your own head, move out of your own way, and start the journey, knowing there is a hill of embarrassment every actor and artist has to climb.

Once you get past that hill, it will get easier. Along the way, you will learn more skills, and develop more confidence.

You will also learn more about yourself as an artist, and that helps replace embarrassment with the joy of doing the work.

THAINE H. ALLISON, JR.

An Actor Prepares – The Boy Scout Approach

Thaine H. Allison Jr. is a Los Angeles-based actor with numerous screen credits. He wrote, directed, and co-starred in the short, *Chance Meeting,* produced a documentary in Morocco, and has produced the on-line series Show Talent – Talent Show for four years. He also wrote, produced, and performed a solo show, *Raizing Kids, It Ain't Easy,* and has published short stories and poems. Prior to becoming an actor, Thaine was a professional economist, teaching, consulting and doing research, with a specialty in rural health development.

The biggest criticism an actor will ever get from a casting director is, "He wasn't prepared."

As a Boy Scout, I learned the motto, "Be Prepared." As a scout, it became a way of life for me: to develop the right skills and acquire the right tools for the tasks at hand. I learned to anticipate the various contingencies that can be present in a given situation. It is important to map out a plan and ask, *Where am I going? And why? What is my strategy, the shortest route, the fastest route, or maybe the most scenic route?* Incorporating these skills into my life has guided me, and sometimes protected me, along the various paths I have chosen, especially as an actor.

So what is this thing we call "preparation"? My dad used to say, "Before you criticize that person, walk a mile in their shoes."

I do my best to get and read the whole script before I start to understand the character I've been given the privilege to bring to life through the words written on the page. Acting Coach, Clay Banks, taught me, "The black lines on the page belong to the writer, producers

AN ACTOR PREPARES – THE BOYSCOUT APPROACH

and the lawyers. The white lines on the page belong to you as the character."

I once heard writer and showrunner Shonda Rhimes say in a radio interview something like, 'I expect an actor to use my exact words as written. However, I do not tell an actor how to say those words. It's an ironclad deal we make.'

As an actor, I honor the writer and their written words as precisely as I can.

Many young and or new actors want to live in the emotion of the moment, live in the character's truth. "Be true to one's self and the moment, the emotion will follow."

This is particularly true on camera. Today's cameras can see deep into your heart and soul. My dad was not a 'Hum diddle diddle, um diddle aye' guy when it came to expressing himself in the moment. When his first grandson was born, it was pretty much an 'okay' kind of moment, as he failed to communicate verbally. But in his eyes you could see pride, excitement, and joy shining through like the headlight of a hundred-mile-an-hour locomotive. He couldn't express his joy verbally, but his truth radiated out of his eyes and body.

As an actor, I realized that finding that inner life for my characters is as important as the words and actions on the outside. My computer can read the words on the page, it cannot, not yet anyway, give an emotional life to the character's being. Stoking that internal furnace is incumbent upon the actor in their preparation process.

Recently I had the privilege of playing an aging Nazi in a film. That character is about as far away from my personal value structure as I could imagine. It would have been easy to judge this man and dismiss his value as a human being. I could have judged him, mocked him, or made him a cartoon character, but he is a major underlying figure in the story, so I had to find some reason to care about this character, to make him come alive and move the story along for the film. I had to make him real and contribute to the overall arc of the story.

He is an aging anachronism in today's world, but he sticks to his principles to the end. Tenacity is a rare quality in the quick-turnaround, situational ethics world we live in today. He had to be understood in the terms that he lives by in his, many would say, misguided life. Let the audience judge the characters and their character. Give the audience a reason to be part of the show.

Too many times I have heard an actor describe his/her part in a film as a small role. No role is small. What would a football game look like if it didn't have fans, or a fancy restaurant with no other diners in the place? I have to ask: *How does this role move the story along?* The writer created the character and wrote the line for a reason. It's my job as the actor to bring that character and that line to life. That's why there is all that white space on the page.

At my age, I've traveled a lot of miles in a lot of places. Along the way I've encountered people either going my way or coming back from where I'm heading. There are four roles I either played or auditioned for, that I think reflect observed or lived experiences in my life.

My last job with a salary and benefits ended when I was fifty-four years old. I spent months trying to find a similar position. In the play *Death of a Salesman,* Willy Loman walked home from the subway sixteen blocks after he was laid off as a salesman. As a man, Willy Loman was defined by his job, his ability to support his family, to build his long-term dream of retiring comfortably with his wife. Walking those sixteen blocks with the dark secret that he wouldn't or couldn't tell his wife and sons might as well have been sixteen hundred miles. When I hit that stage as Willy Loman, finding his disappointment, his shame and his failure, were informed by my own experience as a person who was laid off. I heard echoes of the sound of my dad's toolbox as he pulled it along the sidewalk when he was laid off from jobs as a carpenter. Understanding what it's like to lose a way of life helped me to create my Willy Loman on stage.

In the movie version of AUGUST, OSAGE COUNTY, Chris Cooper played Charlie Aiken. This is a movie about family dynamics in a time of crisis. Charlie's wife of thirty-eight years is Mattie Fae Aiken, a powerful woman whom he loves very much. Yet he's paid a price for the relationship; there is a huge cultural difference between his and her respective families' approach to life's challenges, and in all their time together, he never stood up to her and her family. After his father-in-law's funeral, he finally has the courage to confront his wife.

AN ACTOR PREPARES – THE BOYSCOUT APPROACH

I had the opportunity to play this role onstage and, as an actor living Charlie's life, I came to realize this has been festering for a long time, deep in Charlie's soul. He acknowledges his pain, he realizes he has shrunk from the consequences many times. He realizes that he can no longer take the abuse. He risks everything to confront her. He lays it all on the line, either she changes or they are not going to make it to their thirty-ninth wedding anniversary.

His courage had to come from somewhere. Others in the family find it in their entitlement, alcohol, or mind-altering substances. My courage as Charlie came from the realization that I was going to die the same way my father-in-law died if I didn't resolve this unspoken conflict between myself and Mattie Fae. We've all been in a power-struggle relationship, or observed someone who has, with a parent, a lover, a spouse, a boss, a teacher or some authority person.

Living in other people's lives helps me to prepare. Becoming Charlie Aiken was facilitated from the first read of the script, by learning the lines and building a life around him. It is my secret what life I have created for my character. It informs me of my journey as the character. No one else on the outside has to know what is informing my character's life.

A few years ago, I had the honor to audition for a role in the movie NEBRASKA. I was thrilled to have the opportunity to be considered. I grew up on a farm, with a dad born on a farm in Iowa and a mom born and raised on a farm in Kansas during the depression. No matter the time, even today, there is never enough capital to do the farm justice. At fourteen, I leased sixty acres of land and planted corn. Around the fourth of July the well caved in. Without irrigation water, I had to watch my crop die, along with my dream of a college fund. Every dime I had saved had gone into seeds, fuel and electricity to make that crop. Every leaf that curdled and turned brown hurt my young and helpless soul.

There is a scene in the film NEBRASKA where the guys are at the local bar talking about why they aren't farming anymore. My character says, "I needed a new combine to harvest my crop. When I went to the equipment dealer, he wanted five hundred thousand dollars for a new one. My banker wouldn't loan me the money. I had no choice but to rent out my land to the corporation and take up a rocking chair."

He can't borrow the money, he can't harvest his crop, he can't pay his taxes, he can't feed his family and he can't maintain his lifestyle. What choices does he have? Being boxed in a corner with limited options is an all-too-common theme in twenty-first-century America; the cluster of men in that bar were all in the same boat. And I had lived in this man's life for a few hours and understood his reasoning, his feelings, his state of being.

In a short piece, *Into the Fire,* I play a serial killer locked up in jail with a wannabe young punk. After reading the script and wondering, *How do I become a serial killer?* – it came to me that my real role was to school this young kid and set him on a different track, to not follow my path. Now before I began to prepare for this role, I did not go out and become a serial killer. I don't have any experience at killing people. However, I have played Macbeth, a Scottish general who, with his wife, goes on a killing rampage.

In preparation for both of these roles, I reflected that while in the eighth or ninth grade I worked on a turkey farm. Every morning in the weeks leading up to Thanksgiving and Christmas, my job was to herd off approximately two hundred turkeys into a separate pen, then feed the rest. At the beginning of the season there were approximately five thousand turkeys on the ranch. We did not name every turkey, but they each became familiar and each was a living being.

After feeding the rest of the flock, I would collect turkeys from the pen to take to the slaughtering shed. At the shed I would kill about two hundred to two hundred and fifty turkeys before going to school every day.

At age fourteen, there is a certain thrill in killing an animal. The power; the finality of it. The first few times anyway. After the first week or so the thrill wore off and it became a terrible job to me. I began to look for a way to avoid going to work but I needed the money (seventy-five cents per hour,) and if I quit mid-season I would forfeit a big bonus: twenty-five cents for each hour worked, and a free turkey for my family's holiday meals on both Thanksgiving and Christmas.

These memories helped me find the desperation and insight into the characters to understand who they are and what they want. They find some kind of thrill in what they do and maybe some insight into how they might have done it differently. As a serial killer, I took on the role

AN ACTOR PREPARES – THE BOYSCOUT APPROACH

of a teacher who wanted to steer the young punk away from a life of crime. As a serial killer, I found a socially-redeeming quality that may have gone unnoticed by another actor applying for that role.

Opportunities to prepare are all around us. Every character has a way of walking, talking, a voice, maybe an accent, a geographical location and personal history, and a time in history. I, as the character, have to SEE the other characters in the scene, LISTEN to the other characters in the scene and be ALIVE in their world. As I enter a scene, I have to know where I'm coming from, both the actual location, and the attitude and burden I am carrying into that next moment. When I am on stage, or set, I move with purpose. Every movement has to be justified by the character.

I've experienced this conversation on set before between an actor and the director: "Why did you walk over there?"

"Oh, I don't know, it just felt right."

"Why did you stand up?"

"I wanted to."

"Well guess what, you just walked out of the scene," (or "the light.")

Or, "We have a nice shot of your belly but we have no idea what your face was saying because you didn't tell the camera operator what you were going to do."

Move with purpose. When you leave a scene know where you are going. An actor takes action, fill the space.

It helps to know the world and experience different cultures to understand the point of view of various characters. Imagination and creativity also contribute to understanding the character.

For example, I once played a mother. I had to understand her view as a woman, a wife, and a mother. I had to walk in her life, which was definitely unfamiliar to me. But as a Boy Scout, I had learned to plan for contingencies as the moment unfolds. Every play and film has moments that were not strictly planned by the writer and director. As an actor, I have to be prepared to deal with those moments, when things change and make it a part of my character's life in the moment.

Preparation requires attention to detail and perseverance. I look forward to the next opportunity I'm given to bring a character to life from the words on the page. Once you hit the stage, film or live, forget about the preparation and be the character and play.

PREPARATION

<u>Prepare Yourself to Be an Actor</u>

I think there are some fundamentals to get out of the way. An actor has his/her body, face, intellect, creativity, memory and experience to draw on. I do not abuse it. My body is my instrument – some say a temple. I can spot a smoker by the wrinkles around his/her mouth, the fading eye sockets, and the weakening or raspy voice. I can spot a dancer by the way she walks and carries her body. Some carry their life as a burden, some as a celebration. A finely tuned body is a premium asset.

The actor needs to train and have discipline. I admire dancers who train for years and practice for hours every day. Few actors have that kind of discipline.

Get competent training. At my age especially, I meet new actors who say, "I have a life of experiences, why should I waste my time in class?"

Because it is a craft, a skill, a technique. Doctors spend their whole life practicing medicine. When I worked at a medical school (not as a doctor,) the mantra was, "See one, do one, teach one."

We as actors have to gain the experience and skills to become a journeyman actor. Watching other actors work, honing with practice, performing and working with less experienced actors, all help me to be a better actor.

<u>Prepare Your Mind, Body and Spirit</u>

It may not be obvious, but acting requires physical stamina. Most of us are not going to be chasing "bad guys" over fences or down the river bank. Stunt actors are required to get extra training, but we are often on set for sixteen hours straight.

I have a solo show that runs sixty-five minutes. Add to that a question-and-answer session afterward, and it requires me to be "on" for close to two hours. And every audience deserves the best show I ever performed. They paid their money, showed up, found parking and made their effort to be entertained and informed. It is my duty to deliver on their dreams and expectations. If I am too tired or distracted to do that, I am cheating them, and myself, out of a grand experience.

Physical stamina and emotional stamina are part of the process of being in shape. I am told that actors who have done *Street Car Named Desire* are emotionally drained for weeks after the show closes. Think of the emotional and physical stamina that the actors use in a show like *Hamilton*, eight shows a week. Many television series run twenty weeks. Be prepared for the physical and emotional strength that you will be asked to rely on.

Which leads to getting enough rest and the right food into your body. Along with this go issues around alcohol and other foreign substances. A welder cannot get a job on a commercial project if he/she tests positive for marijuana (legal or not,) the liability is too great for the pipeline or construction company and their insurers. Why should an actor be tolerated who is high, or stoned, or hung over?

In one of my early experiences in a play on opening night, one of my fellow cast members came to the makeup mirror, set a six-pack of beer on the dressing table, and popped a beer open. When asked what he was doing, he said, "I need a little buzz to go on stage, loosens me up."

If that's your source of courage to go up there, I would say, find another occupation. An actor needs to be one hundred percent present. In the case of the beer-drinking actor, things went well, until the sword fight scene, when he lost the cadence of the choreography. The scene was out of balance and awkward. It did not work. Luckily no one was injured.

If your character's life, and sometimes your own physical wellbeing, is dependent on an actor who has a buzz, you won't feel safe, and vice versa. You will react in ways that may serve the actor but not necessarily the character's place in the show. It's the same thing if you get on a bus or in an Uber and the driver has a beer on the dash. You want out.

Prepare a Character

As an actor, I have to walk a mile in my character's shoes, get to know him from the inside out and I encourage you to do the same.

What is the character's journey like? What burdens does he carry, and how well do his shoes fit you based on your own experiences? What are the impediments on the road and journey that he has chosen?

There are some technical givens for you as the actor to understand about your character. As soon as I read the script, I begin to seek, imagine, and interlace the answers to these questions:

Where was my character the moment before the scene begins?
Where am I in the scene, physically and psychologically?
What am I experiencing in that scene, and in the story?
Who are the other characters in the scene?
How do they make me feel?
What do I want from them?
What will they appear to look like when I get what I want?

Prepare for a Career

Prepare, prepare, prepare. Every actor should be studying every day. If you don't have a script, there are plenty of free ones around, or pick up a newspaper and read anything out loud. Learn to see the line and deliver the line eye-to-eye to a partner. Coach Banks taught me to have five monologues prepared at all times, and to be able to deliver each one in three different ways.

Over and over, I hear casting directors say, "We live in a very fast-paced environment."

It's essential to be prepared for any career opportunity, by always having resumes and headshots with you and available online, so you can send electronic copies at a moment's notice.

"An actor has to burn inside with an outer ease."

- MICHAEL CHEKHOV

DIONCIO VIRVEZ

Diversity In Hollywood

Dionicio Virvez is Vice President at The Multicultural Motion Picture Association and writer/producer of the annual Diversity Awards. As an actor he is known for his performances in the television series Is it Real? produced by the National Geographic Channel. He appeared on the second season of HBO's sci-fi/Western television series Westworld as a Ghost Nation warrior. He also appeared in *Sons of Anarchy,* the Marvel television series *Echo,* and the movies PREY and KILLERS OF THE FLOWER MOON.

The Diversity Motion Picture Association is a nonprofit organization that started in 1992. They were looking for a press coordinator, and I got the job because they wanted someone who was bilingual in Spanish and English. I wanted to get involved in the industry and I didn't care what it was.

The president of the organization, Jarvee Hutchinson, said, "Why don't you hang around with the producers and see what you can learn?"

I would sit at the table and see what they do. I was a fast learner and being an actor struggling to get into film and television, I would give them a lot of input.

The whole idea was to pay tribute to diversity in cinema and I had a lot of ideas, so it was easy for me be creative. We did our first awards show, and Jarvee made me an Associate Producer of the show. The first year it was called the Minority Motion Picture Award Show. People didn't like it, because in the general population, we're not actually the minority, we're the majority. So, the second year, it was called the Diversity Award Show.

After all this time, there are a lot of opportunities, there are a lot of diverse projects, but there's still a long way go. Diversity in the industry is still way behind. In casting, for example, Latinos make up seven percent, Native Americans only one percent. Asians are also way behind. African Americans are ahead of Latinos, but not by much. The numbers haven't even moved at all in the last couple of years.

To me, it starts with the writer, and then it's everyone else coming in to the project after them. For example, NIGHT OF THE LIVING DEAD. Everybody wanted to change the story and the characters, but George Romero stuck to his guns. He said, "No, I'm going to stick by the writer and I want the African-American character as the hero. That's the beauty of my movie."

For the remake, the studios again wanted to change the character. But the writer said, "No, you want a remake, take it the way it is in the first film, because it was groundbreaking."

Yes, from the late 80s to now, the industry has changed a lot. Back in those days, there were just a few casting agencies and studios. Now there are hundreds. So why is it we haven't even come close to what we're aiming at, as far as seeing more diversity on screen, and being well-represented?

There are tons of organizations that advocate for minorities in film but, in my opinion, they're sending the wrong message. Yes, we're trying to let the public know that Latinos are not just maids, African Americans are not just gang members, Chinese people are not just doctors and computer whizzes. We have so much more to offer, of course, but we all kept getting stuck in stereotypes and narrow-casting.

The diversity advocates say that the only way we can change the stereotypes in Hollywood is to turn down those jobs. If they offer you a part as a maid, or a killer, or an inmate, they say not to take it, because that's denigrating. It's not good for diverse representation.

Here's what I see that is wrong with this approach: the only way we can change the status quo is to participate, at whatever level we can.

My advice is to take the role, no matter what it is.

The most famous actors, from every culture, when they were starting out, they took those roles. Any role. And thanks to that small role giving them an opportunity, they're big now.

That's how you're going to change Hollywood. By refusing roles and not becoming part of the process, you're never going to make it as an actor, and you won't be able to have an impact on the status quo.

If you're Native American you may be offered a job as a Mexican, or as an East Indian rather than a Native American. If you're offered a job that is different from you – miscasting – I think you still have to take it, because that's your opportunity. Of course, do it in a way that honors both the culture and the character you're playing.

I've seen a lot of projects where actors literally walked off the set because they didn't like how things were going, or the two-dimensional stereotype-ness of their character, and I think, *Man, this is wrong. I know how hard it was to get this opportunity.* But that's them.

On *Westworld*, it was February in Ridgecrest, California, about forty or fifty degrees. The actors playing the settlers all had jackets, hats and gloves, and they looked pretty happy. We who were playing the Nation were practically naked; we were literally shaking from the cold. But inside, I was the happiest man in the world. Why? Because I was living my dream as an actor.

If you are a "minority" actor and believe there's a lot of discrimination out there, you're right, there is. But there are also casting agents right now who may not tell you so, but they're advocating for you. There's a lot of good people in Hollywood who embrace diversity. They want to give you an opportunity. It happened to me.

There's another reason why we lag in diverse casting: too often, we're playing small by only going for student films, short projects, micro-budget indie films. I can understand why we don't go for the big stuff; it can seem like the big roles and movies are for Caucasian actors only. If you're Latino, if you're Native American, if you're African American, if you're Asian, you might be limiting your own idea of what you even want to accomplish, because you think it's impossible. (See my other contribution to this book: "Face the Giants and Go for the Big Fish.")

That's internal. That's about changing our mental game. We have <u>got</u> to overcome that.

From the start of my career, I was put in front of the big guys. I experienced so much rejection that I became resistant to trying out with huge companies. *Westworld* was HBO. We're talking about hundreds and hundreds of actors auditioning, and I just assumed I didn't have a chance. Ever felt like that?

One of my daughters pushed me to try out, and after a long audition process, somehow I was cast.

Now I know a couple of casting companies that have hundreds, if not thousands of Native American actors in their files. So I wonder, *Why is it that Native Americans didn't get the opportunity to play a Native American character, while this Native Mayan guy got the part?* I still don't know why they took me. But being an actor in the film and TV industry is all about accepting the opportunities that are offered to you. So, *yeah, I'll take it.*

PREPARATION

If you really want to be an actor, take every opportunity you can. Don't limit yourself to only small projects – go after big fish too.

Getting in the game, in whatever way you can, is the only way you are going to make your mark as an actor, and make a real difference in Hollywood.

So, instead of following the current reigning wisdom to refuse a stereotypical role – a maid, a drug dealer, a killer, a computer whiz – just take it. Now you're getting inside the system instead of sitting on the outside.

This is your chance to shine and prove yourself. The biggest actors in the world started with a small role, and they shined in it. They made it their own. They did something different. They were charming, they were funny, they were weird. They transcended the limitations of the role.

I think part of the job of the actor is to bring your own uniqueness to whatever you're cast in. My advice is to embrace who you are and what you look like. Love yourself. Overcome your own internal "No" and go for it.

CHRISTOPHER M. ALLPORT

Craft, Career and Content

Christopher is a Hollywood native who performed in movies including HOCUS POCUS and PIRATES OF THE CARIBBEAN 3, the series *Peter Pan and the Pirates,* and the short film *The Man Who Would Not Shake Hands.* He has also performed extensively on stage and as a recording artist. Christopher penned the novel *Senja Chronicles* with co-author Fansu Njie, and wrote, directed and starred in the award-winning feature film EMILY OR OSCAR. He is completing a feature rock-u-mentary chronicling the legendary Gold Star Studio from 1950 to 1984, and composed the orchestral suite, *Song of Solomon.* (His other contribution to this book is "Acting Is Technical" in Chapter 11.)

Acting came to me by way of singing when I was really young. My mom was a pianist, and she taught me music from age two or three years. By the time I was four, I was singing in Japanese and English. I remember standing on top of a grand piano singing "Sakura" in Japanese and "America the Beautiful" in English at a Japanese piano bar in Northridge, California – for a bowl of green tea ice cream and twenty bucks, which was a lot of money for a four-year-old.

A former Radio City Rockette, Madilyn Clark, happened to see me there, and she said, "Look at that kid with the red hair and freckles, he should be in the pictures. He's going to be in my acting class."

My mom was not too sure about that, but my grandparents kind of supported it, so I got into acting, dance and vocal workshops. Three weeks later, I was signed with a big talent agency with a good youth department. That's how it began.

Fast forward a few decades and you will find that I recently finished writing, directing, and co-starring in a feature film called EMILY OR OSCAR? — a love letter to the Golden Age of Hollywood. Because I grew up on the tail end of it, many of my coaches and mentors were really cool people from that era. I had the chance to study with Debbie Reynolds, Donald O'Connor and Alan Young, (voice of 'Mickey Mouse'), and even work with Jeanne Russell ('Margaret' in *Dennis the Menace*) and Paul Petersen (*Donna Reed Show*.)

I was lucky to be a golden-era grandchild. A lot of folks are gone now. I'm fortunate that many heavyweights took the time to share their knowledge with me and ensure that I was on a good path. I even had that chance to work with Steven Spielberg on HOOK, who dubbed me "One-take Allport!" Later we collaborated again, when I was chosen to direct behind-the-scenes footage associated with BAND OF BROTHERS.

"Dare to fail gloriously," was a big take away from one of my coaches. You have to be willing to take a risk. Audiences don't come to see you not taking a risk. They want to see you be vulnerable. What makes a performance interesting is when you are emotionally vulnerable, physically vulnerable, and remain strong within those qualities in your performance. Vulnerability does not equate to weakness. It is actually a strength.

So, yes, I've been around many Hollywood celebrities of yesteryear who were really at the top of their game. They've done many things in their lives – not just acting, but also writing, producing, advocacy. I'm part of a team that successfully changed the laws in California and New York to protect child actors. We still have 48 other states to go.

Successful actors have a truly broad set of interests and skills. The best are people who have broad life experience. I knew an actor, Ed Gilbert, who did *Peter Pan and the Pirates* with me 35 years ago. He was an entomologist – he studied bugs. I can't tell you how this influenced his performance, but I can tell you that I remember his performance. I also remember thinking, *Wow, there's other things to do outside of acting.*

For me, I was fascinated with electronics and not just consumer electronics: the micro components, how things work, taking them apart, designing circuits. Today, I love restoring antique cars and international travel. I have lived in multiple countries around the world while working on different productions. The more you engage with other people around the world, in different fields, the broader sense

CRAFT, CAREER AND CONTENT

you have about what you can do with the experience, and subsequently bring those familiarities into a strong performance.

When you see how people actually are, you can incorporate those insights into your work. Then you can exaggerate those characteristics just a little bit for theatrical effect. You are necessarily making something up that is completely new.

This is what Aristotle teaches in his *Poetics*, which he wrote around 600 BC. The most successful devices developed in modern screenwriting actually stem from the teachings of Aristotle. What he declares about characters is that the ingenue just has to be a little bit prettier than a regular person. The antagonist has to be just a little bit nastier than somebody you may know who's causing you trouble – you add just a little bit more, rather than an over-the-top caricature. That's what makes a character an interesting, dimensional, theatrical representation. That 'little bit more' than a person would normally be like is what works – not a major embellishment.

Another thing about pursuing outside interests is that the psychology of being an actor is that we always must be perky, tuned up and turned on – or so we're taught. Really, we should not constantly be performing for our friends. You just have to turn on at the <u>right</u> moment.

I think it's really important to figure out a way to build a psychological switch in your head to turn it off after showtime and just be real. Then be able to turn it on again, yet modulate yourself to mix an augmented reality with being <u>present in the moment</u> – at the right time. That right time means being prepared and ready when you're supposed to give a performance for a casting director, on stage, in front of a microphone, or on camera.

As a teenager, I was working for a plumber, crawling under houses to install pipes and all sorts of technical stuff – but I knew I had to stop at four o'clock no matter what, because I had to get scrubbed up and get in costume to go sing opera at the Dorothy Chandler Pavilion. It was very exhilarating, because I was making this Clark Kent-style transformation from coveralls to a Mozart opera costume with heels and a powdered wig, since that's what noblemen wore in 1785. Being forced to make that extreme transformation helped take my mind off the idea that *I will be in front of 3,500 people tonight.*

PREPARATION

Explore all life has to offer, be a well-rounded human with diverse experiences and friendships. All of this will enrich your work as an actor and can help your career, sometimes in surprising ways.

The Current Moment

The best advice I have to offer is to respond to the current moment. Yes, you have to have your lines memorized. But if you're only memorizing your lines and only able to respond with that line, you might not be listening to what your scene partner is giving you, (or in a monologue, what the moment is giving you.) If you aren't listening, you are not giving an authentic performance.

It's easy to say, "Be present, and stay in the moment," but what does that mean? Part of it is the maturity to realize that empty space is okay, in fact it's glorious – if you are listening. Empty space only becomes awkward if you say your line and don't know what to do next because you're thinking, *What was my next line again?*

Other people are there, giving to you and helping inform what you're doing. What are you giving to them? If you focus on giving rather than getting, performance becomes less about you and you realize you don't have to carry a scene all by yourself. In fact, you should not be carrying anything all by yourself. Performance, scenes in films and TV are integrated. If you hear what other people are saying, you'll know how to respond. So memorization becomes far less technical and much more organic. You are working in an ensemble relying on others – and they're relying on you.

Auditioning

Casting directors are there to help you succeed. If you can play in the moment and give them something, you're helping them succeed. They need you, but they need the right you. It's more than just being able to give a great performance. Are you easy to work with? Do you follow direction? Can you go with the flow?

A lot of times, after you give a performance exactly based on the script, a casting director will give you a redirect in a completely

CRAFT, CAREER AND CONTENT

different direction. Some actors will think, *But that's not what's in the script.*

That's the wrong thing to think. The thing to do at that point is drop what the script says, drop your preconceived notions, and give the casting director exactly what they're asking for. The casting director is playing with you, testing you, seeing what you're capable of, or how flexible and adaptable you are – or how much imagination you bring to a redirect.

What happens in the audition room is separate from what happens in performance. Those are two different performances: winning the audition and then doing the performance. In auditions, you almost have to take more of a risk than you would in a booked performance.

You have to realize casting directors are there to do a job. They're there to narrow down the pool.

There are a lot of incredible actors. The supply and demand reality of it is that there is a much larger talent pool than there is quantity of jobs available. So that puts the hiring advantage on the production side. Yet it says nothing about the quality of talent available. You are likely already super talented, and you wouldn't be pursuing a career in the arts if you weren't completely passionate about it. The stuff that we have to do and put up with is crazy.

So, I think you have to go into that audition to <u>give</u> something rather than to get something. If you go into an audition with the attitude of trying to 'get the job' or 'get something out of this,' you are there for the wrong reason. You don't have to <u>get</u> anything. But you can give a maximum amount. You can give one hundred percent or more of yourself without being attached to the outcome. Then your chances go from being one in a thousand to maybe one in fifty. Just give your honesty and intention. That will get their attention, and maybe you'll get hired for another project if not this one.

Create Content

You have career dreams and aspirations. Those dreams will not be fulfilled unless you turn them into specific actions. What actions can you take besides studying, practicing and auditioning? Create content! You can implement your craft through content you create, all while staying within your means.

I do see it as three C's – Craft, Career, and the creation of Content. What you can do on a limited budget with your talent is more valuable than what you can do with a big budget.

An actor said to me one time, "We have to have three million dollars for a proof of concept."

I've got news: NO, you don't! With a smart phone, you can start now. There are many pro-level cameras and editing tools available at reasonable prices. If you learn how to use them properly, you can start with the basics and expand beyond the craft of acting. Learn how to correctly light yourself to craft the image you want to portray. Learn how to make sure you're not overexposed. Learn how to mic yourself and set audio levels. At minimum, learning how to record yourself well will help you with remote auditions.

I'm not saying to ignore the finances. I'm saying they're a separate piece to support the craft. Stay focused on the craft, and you <u>can</u> build a career by creating content.

Chapter 2.

Do Research

"My favorite place to get to is when like a specialist says something and I say, 'I don't care.'"

- JOAQUIN PHOENIX

Chapter 2

Do Research

MICHAEL SAVAGE AKA SIRTONY

Real-Life Preparation

Michael Savage aka Sirtony is an award-winning actor, and was a popular star on *General Hospital.* An award-winning filmmaker, he is skilled in all aspects of the craft, he has written, directed, edited and produced thousands of short films. Michael was an honor graduate at S.U.N.Y Purchase with a BFA in Theater/Film, and is an alumni member of The Acting Company created by John Housman and Margot Harley in 2003. He received an honorary Tony award for his contribution to the culture of the nation, and thus the brand name "Sirtony" was born. In 2021-22 he was inducted as a member of Marquis Who's Who in America. You can see his bio film, *Sirtony History Promo* on YouTube.

Will you be able to survive as an actor? Maybe, maybe not. Cowards are all around. You can NOT succeed if you are a coward.

In order to be a great actor, you must be a Tiger. It is difficult for anyone to survive in the jungle, or in Hollywood. Only Tigers survive.

You must get up and do the work. It is always about the work. Never be lazy. Always know your lines. Be prepared.

Make your own play, your own films. Take your career into your own hands – you can do what could never be done before, so just do it.

Don't waste your life thinking that if you can't afford to be in a workshop or be around other actors, that you cannot drill what it is you need to drill, meaning actual scenes of life. You can do it all day long. You must stay motivated, stay active and prepared, so when you do get a phone call, when you do get an opportunity, you can go in knowing you've been staying in shape.

Stop auditioning... do it as if you've already been cast.

An audition is an opportunity to learn the lines, wear the clothes required, and use any necessary props. If you need a gun for the scene, get a toy gun.

Show the producer and director what you would do if you already had the role. Do it like you have already been cast, and don't do the least, do your very best. If they don't like it, move on. At least you will know you did your best for what that character is, and gave a <u>performance</u>, not just an <u>audition</u>.

If you can't afford to be in a workshop it doesn't mean that you're not an actor. There are things you can do on your own that can keep you in good shape. People who can't afford gym memberships work out at home. Do what you can with what you have to get to the next level.

Observe how people interact. Observe yourself in your own life. That's where you can draw upon details that you can include in your work in film, in television, or in the theater.

The classics can inspire, enlighten, and give you an inner confidence. Working in theater is much more of a luxury for an actor, because you get weeks of rehearsal, you get to work on one role, and then, hopefully, you get to do many performances of that role.

It's very different from television, where you get a script a week, they don't have a lot of time for rehearsal, you shoot, it's over, it's done, and you move on.

In movies and TV, you're mostly playing roles in which you are typecast. Actors are told that typecasting isn't a good thing, but if it helps you earn a living, it's a very good thing. If you're able to make enough money to afford to pick and choose jobs, it's a very helpful thing.

You want to offer as much quality as possible, but in television especially, it's about "fast" and you have to move quickly in order to succeed. Understand that it's like when you meet someone and you talk to them in real life. You met them, you talked with them, you might even tell them about something that upset you, or vice versa, and you might even cry. You shared a moment.

If you can think like that in your everyday life, you can practice moving through emotions very easily and comfortably. Then just apply that same technique – what you do in your own life, living it fully – to a role. Don't overwork yourself thinking you have to over-prepare. The truth is, you've been preparing your whole life.

I wish you all the good luck that anyone can wish for YOU, and blessings forever!

PREPARATION

Spend time with people. Every situation you're in, that's a scene in your life. Whoever you meet, it's an opportunity for you to be available instead of not being interested in the moment.

Embrace interactions with strangers as well as people you already know. Every encounter is a chance for you to exercise your spontaneity, your interest level, your listening ability, your emotional capacity, your passion, your compassion… through interchange with other human beings.

Don't waste a day not being interested in people, when you could have been interacting and exercising your emotional and mental capabilities the whole time. If you get in the habit of being present with others in your real life, you'll find that you're in great shape when it comes time to audition or take on a role.

CINDY D'ANDREA

Do It Because You Love to Act

Cindy D'Andrea is an actor, writer, producer and award-winning solo performer. Her one-woman show, *Cat Shit Crazy*, attracted rave reviews at the 2023 Edinburgh Fringe Festival. Cindy has studied acting at the William Esper Studio in New York and was a prominent member of The Actor's Gang in Los Angeles. A veteran fitness trainer, Cindy is writing her memoir as well as her fourth solo show which will debut at the Hollywood Fringe Festival 2024.

"Acting isn't a real job."
"You should think of your family first, not your dreams."
These were the responses I received when I announced to my parents that I'd be moving from New York to Los Angeles to pursue my dream of becoming an actress. Okay, I may have suggested something to the effect that I would be famous, and *maybe* it slipped out that an Academy Award would be swell, but still… why crush a young girls' dreams?

As a twenty-something living in New York City, I learned about the art and craft of acting and what lies at its core: Listening and Responding. I never learned that better then when I studied at the renowned William Esper Studio, in which I completed the two-year Meisner program with one of the most dynamic and hardcore teachers at the studio, Maggie Flanigan. Maggie was a four-foot 11-inch ninety-pound spitfire of a woman, and her work ethic and constant search for her actors to find the truth in every moment was both awe-inspiring and terrifying.

When I graduated, Maggie wrote me a letter of congratulations on my achievements. And as par for the course for Maggie, she gave me her somewhat abrasive words of advice if I wanted to continue to pursue my career as an actress.

The first was, "Every scene does not have to bring you to tears."

I cried A LOT in class, before, during or after a scene, sometimes all of the above! The second nougat of advice was: "You MUST work on your voice."

I had been an aerobics instructor for several years, sometimes teaching six classes a day to make ends meet, and this was before we had microphones. I put a lot of pressure on my voice, yelling and screaming out dance and aerobics moves over blaring Paula Abdul and Madonna songs. My vocal cords had polyps and I was even told by my doctor to stop teaching aerobics. Maggie was right. I needed to address my vocal issues.

Sometimes you do things to survive, and pursuing a career in which there is much more demand than supply has its drawbacks. So, for an actress like me who was just starting out in a big city like New York without much money, a survival job was a necessity. Waitressing was one option, but for me, it was teaching aerobics and personal training. Full disclosure: I was waiting tables too, I was just really bad at it! So, I couldn't address my vocal issues without imposing upon my livelihood and I am now, many years later, seeing the repercussions.

"Better late than never," as the saying goes and the lesson here is that, as actors, we have to be proactive about our instruments. And our instrument is our physicality and yes, that includes our voice.

It's being strong in body, mind and spirit. It's practicing our vocal trills and our monologues and our self-tape auditions and our scenes. It's reading plays and scripts and going to the theatre and watching movies and TV shows and reading the *Hollywood Reporter*. It's getting a good nights' sleep and eating foods that give you energy. It's abstaining from taking things that bring you down, or bring you up and then bring you down. All of this requires money, time, patience, focus and discipline. And what do you get in return? A job? Perhaps. An acting gig that you love? Maybe. Money? Sometimes.

So, I always ask myself, "Why am I pursuing this dream of acting? Is there something else I could be doing? Why do I want to be an actress?"

Every time I ask myself this question, a different answer emerges. But the number one consistent answer is that I LOVE IT. It brings me so much joy and pleasure to entertain people. It gives me great depth and understanding of myself and how I fit into the world by working on a character, by learning about how someone else handles themselves and others in a given circumstance, how they get along in their job, with their spouse, their children, the world. How do *they* see themselves, and how do others see them? How am I a better person because I am doing what I love?

When my parents warned me not to move to Los Angeles to pursue my dream, for the first time in my life, I went against their wishes. I packed my bags and flew across the country to pursue my Hollywood dream. I had saved some money from my personal training business and knew one friend who lived in Los Angeles. Yes, it's been a bumpy road, to say the least, but all that I have learned as a person, an actress, a businesswoman, an entertainer, an activist, and a fleshed out human being, I learned from pursuing my dream.

When I first got to Los Angeles, I was bright-eyed and bushy-tailed, *Wow, I'm in Hollywood, I've really made it!*

I hit the ground running and immediately signed with a commercial agency through a friend of a friend in New York. I got work as a commercial actress quite quickly. People even recognized me as the "Bull's Eye BBQ" mom. I'll never forget going to my favorite coffee shop in West Hollywood, where I went pretty much every day before I taught a client or a class (yes, I still had the survival job.) As I was waiting for my coffee, a cute young man turned to me and said, "Hey, aren't you the Bull's Eye Barbecue mom?"

"Yes, I am," I replied.

"That's my favorite commercial!" he exclaimed.

I thought to myself, "Well, mom and dad, look at that. I made it! I was recognized in a coffee shop in West Hollywood!"

All good things must come to an end. And thus, commercials did for me. There was a strike in the 90's and after the commercial strike, something changed. I was no longer getting callbacks on my commercials, and I certainly wasn't booking. I thought, *That's it. I guess that's all I'm going to get.*

I began to resent going to commercial auditions. There was no joy. It got me so down that I quit pursuing my acting dream. I thought maybe my parents were right, maybe I should focus on finding a boyfriend and getting married, maybe Los Angeles isn't my place. I went back to what I felt comfortable doing, which was my personal training and teaching. I traveled and checked out other places I might want to live. But there was something missing in me, in my spirit.

Thankfully, I never stopped studying the craft of acting. I stayed in acting class, taking a three-month intensive Actors' Studio/method class for seven years. I even got asked to do two Italian Vogue spreads because of the emotional work I had done in class. But it wasn't enough. I always saw the glass as half empty. I never had real confidence in myself and I let things get to me.

So much of acting is about how you feel about yourself. You can study, as I did, for twenty plus years; some teachers break you down, some pull you up, but it is up to you to take power and stand up for yourself. Work on your instrument like you would practice the piano or a sport or a new language, surround yourself with like-minded people who support you, and you support them. And for those who want to dim your light, run as far as you can from them.

Acting is the only career where you can follow all the rules, go to college, get a BA or MFA in theatre, study, audition, get beautiful head shots, pound the pavement, write your letters, make your own content, put yourself in what you think are the right places with the right people who can advance your career, set up your business contacts and network. And still, you might not get anywhere near where you want to be. So, you go back to the question: "Why do I want to pursue an acting career? Why do I want to be an actress?" And if the answer satisfies you, you keep going.

Back in the 80's and early 90's we didn't have the internet or cell phones or TikTok or Instagram or Facebook. We had pagers and answering machines, DVDs and VCRs. We had black-and-white headshots and pounded the pavement to stop by at agents and managers offices just to drop off a headshot and resume.

Now, the world is your oyster. You can make whatever content you like. All you need is a smartphone. You can post that content and get followers and become an influencer. You can create a fifteen-second video, write your own solo show, enter contests and competitions. There's storytelling everywhere. There are opportunities to do what you love everywhere. So, do it because you love it. Not because you want to get something back. All of the acting techniques and classes and books and tutorials might make mention of this, but probably not.

I've studied with some amazing teachers. I've been in theatre companies and written, produced and starred in three solo shows. I've been in national commercials and done photo shoots and films. And only now am I tending to the business aspect of, well, the business. And only now am I certain that I am doing this because acting, performing, entertaining people is what I've always wanted to do and always will do. It's in my DNA, it's a part of how I think every day. It's why I study characters and am curious about people and ask so many questions about them. I will often be slightly annoying, especially on a date. "Tell me more about you."

"No, how about we talk about you?"

"No, I still have more questions about you."

Believe in yourself no matter what anyone says. Take care of your instrument and be kind to your fellow artists. Enjoy the ride and try not to expect too much in return. *Do it because you love to act.*

This Farmer's Market exercise has helped me whenever I get in my head about a character I'm playing, or a scene I'm doing. It keeps me curious about people and characters, and reminds me that there are so many specificities about people that make them unique.

PREPARATION

Go to your local farmer's market with a notepad and pen and have a seat on a bench with a cup of coffee or tea.

Part One is to simply observe people.

Watch how they walk, how they talk, how they interact with the vendors, other people at the market and people they know. How do they speak differently to each one and how do others respond to them? How is their voice and body posture different? Do they seem to be agitated? In a hurry? Patient? Enjoying the experience?

Take notes and write down everything you observe.

Part Two is to choose one person to study more intensely.

Ask yourself, *What might this person do for a living?*
Are they married, divorced, single?

Do they have children?

Are they happy, sad, angry, scared?

What might have happened before they got to the market? Did they have a fight with their spouse?

What will they do when they get home? Make dinner? Have friends over? Go back to work?

Continue to be curious. What did this person have for breakfast? Are they a vegetarian? A meat eater? Then ask yourself why you have come to those conclusions.

Why do you think he/she might be a vegetarian? Were they hanging out at the petting zoo more than shopping for produce?

Write down everything you "made up" about this person.

Then, go home and look at what you wrote, and see if you can apply that process to your character/the character you're working on at the moment. You might find that you have a fresh new outlook and your mind has opened up to many possibilities you previously hadn't considered.

Oh, and don't forget to buy some blueberries – support your local farmers!

TIM CARR

Choosing Material

Tim Carr is an American writer, actor and director, known for roles in the movies ROCKY BALBOA and SAFE, and TV series The Grounders, Homicide: Life on the Street, and All My Children.

There are many reasons to be an actor, but the main motivation <u>as</u> an actor? To be of service to the story. That is the beginning and end of everything an actor needs to do before tackling any material. Whether it's a play, TV show, film, musical, or commercial, ask yourself, *What is the story? How does it start, how does it end, and how can I do my part to tell this narrative?*

As an actor, you will always have options to display your talents. You will always have some say in choosing what you work on. You have more creative control than you think. Don't think so? You do. Of course, not everyone may have the opportunity to meet with enormous studios who offer you studio projects and huge money and creative control, but actors will always have some say in the material they choose.

For example, I love auditioning. I love every step of that process. Why? Why would anyone want to be in a waiting room where people, probably brought in for the same role as you, sit in silence, with everyone giving each other dirty looks?

Then, why would anyone want to walk into an audition room where there's a possibility that no one will talk to you, or even look up at you? Where the camera is pointed at you and it's implied that you have to just get started on the material?

Why do I love it? Because it's creative. It may be the only time we get to read the material in the way that we see it, the way that we feel it, or even dress the way that we think that character would dress.

CHOOSING MATERIAL

Say we book that job. There will be direction, there will be other opinions on how we should deliver the lines or play the role. But that audition room? That may be the one and only time we get a chance to use our own ideas. I love that. That very first line read is the time where we, as actors, get to try something. We get to interpret the character the way we see fit. It's beautiful.

When I go into that audition waiting room and everyone is busy giving one another the stink eye, I say hello. I wish everyone good luck. When I leave, I wish everyone good luck again. I'm feeling great, because I just had the chance to do something creatively fulfilling.

When it comes to choosing material, I take that exact approach. Of course, in this business we all want to have a hit, we want our work to be seen, we want audiences to appreciate what we're doing.

So, how? How do actors get to choose that material, even if marquee film directors are not knocking on your door? (Yet. Keep working. There will always be the "yet.")

Even at the beginning of your career, keep an eye out for opportunities. There is always a student film being done, or maybe there's an indie film being made somewhere. ("Indie film" is short for independent film, meaning it may not have full studio funding. Some indies have no funding, and your pay for being in those films is pizza and beer.) There may be a play or a musical happening locally. See where you can be of service to these stories, because whether you're a brand-new actor, or have been in this business forever, the goal is always the same, to tell the story, to serve the writing to the best of your ability.

There is a wonderful actor, the late, great Matt Myers, who would quite literally take every single opportunity that would come his way. Matt was in movies that many have seen, some smaller films or some smaller parts... and he would also take background or extra roles. Background roles are roles where you wouldn't be the main focus of the scene – maybe you'd be walking by in the background or seated at a back table in a restaurant scene. Please remember, these roles are also incredibly important to the story, and taking these roles also allows you to serve the story. Remember the deli scene in WHEN HARRY MET SALLY? Everyone in that restaurant was a part of the iconic,

"I'll have what she's having" scene, and all served that scene incredibly well.

So Matt took every role that came to him. Studio films, television, short films, indie films, big theater productions, dinner theater, background roles in projects where maybe he was just a "blur" in the background. Matt Myers is the purest actor I have ever worked with. Because there was no ego there, no role was ever too big or too small for him, Matt just wanted to put in great work, he just wanted to be of service to stories. That's how he chose his material, and it was beautiful, and there was never a time when Matt wasn't working on something.

I think about his approach all of the time. Even in those background scenes, we have a chance to be in the story in our own way. Does our character have a limp? Does our character keep looking at their watch? Even what may be considered the smallest roles are a part of the story.

There is an incredibly large and diverse theater and musical theater community out there. Choosing a theater project can be a big-time commitment. There are rehearsals for months leading up to the premiere of the show, and sometimes those shows can perform anywhere from two to twelve shows a week. So, no matter how big or how small the show is, you will want to think about the time commitment, the material, and the demands of your role. Musical theater has additional demands, as you will also need to make sure that your singing voice can hold up for the run of shows.

Sometimes, a project comes our way that takes up a great deal of our time away from home. Another incredibly talented actor I've been fortunate to work with, just finished a role in a theatrical production in Indianapolis, Indiana. He was away from his family for three months. That is something to consider when choosing your material: where will this production be? How long will it be? Will this interfere with other roles I'm involved with? Does it suit my lifestyle to be away for this long? Sometimes locations are more exotic than Indianapolis and some locations are closer to home. All of these scenarios should factor into your decision on what project to select.

In musical theater, there are main roles and ensemble roles. Main roles are when your character is more of the focus, ensemble means you may play multiple parts, maybe you'll be a character in the

CHOOSING MATERIAL

background, maybe you're one of several singers. But the ensemble is incredibly important too. Many in musical theater audition for a main role but are offered an ensemble part. This never means that anyone is a bad actor, it means there are many talented people reading for one main character.

Ensemble roles often require an equal time commitment, so it makes sense to establish if this is something you want to spend a great deal of time and energy doing. Some actors won't accept ensemble pieces, which is their choice, but many do. I spoke with a musical theater actor just this week and asked what would encourage her to take an ensemble role. She told me it's the material and the cast – sometimes the joy of the ensemble is singing great songs with cast members you enjoy working with. Again, her intent is to serve the story.

So far we've discussed traditional acting material, but it doesn't stop there. There are additional ways to select material. There are ways to post monologues or perhaps share an acting scene online. There are commercials, there is performance art – more of an experimental, less traditional way to perform or do a monologue, which could be a performance in a public park or even on the street. There are Shakespearian festivals and Fringe festivals. There's spokes-modeling – a company hires you to hand out t-shirts or a product and you interact with your audience. That is, no doubt, an acting job, because you're serving that company's narrative.

There are corporate and government videos (formerly known as industrials) which might be training videos for their own employees, or part of a public awareness campaign. These projects are oftentimes an incredible acting opportunity because the scenarios can be quite dramatic or humorous, the money isn't bad, and it can be an interesting exercise for an actor, as some companies and industries use so much jargon you may be saying words and delivering lines you not only have never said before, you may never have even heard them before.

Since I just brought it up, money can also be a factor in selecting material. Some acting jobs pay well, some pay minimally, some don't pay at all. This doesn't mean any project is better than any other. It does mean that, depending on the situation, money can be a factor in how we choose our material. A paying or non-paying role for a project does not make anyone less of an actor, it simply means that the actor may have had additional reasons for selecting to participate.

Personally speaking, there have been times where I just wanted to work with a great storyteller, a great director or great actors, or be involved with a great script. To the dismay of many in my life, who focus on the business side of things, I have taken on projects that were low in pay but high in creativity and collaboration.

These are all things to think about when you have the opportunity to select your material.

How our choices and material is perceived when the project is finished and presented to audiences, is out of our hands. All we can do is serve the material, collaborate with the cast and crew, no matter how big or how small, stay inspired, work with the direction and writing and feedback, and give the best performance you can give.

Please remember, there is no one on this planet who can give your performance. These are your thoughts, your ideas, your visions, your reasons for selecting your projects.

I wish you tremendous success.

Success can mean so many things. For me, acting success is being able to tell the story to the best of your abilities. It's that simple. I wish you that success, I wish you strength to take some chances with your choices of material, I wish you inspiration, I wish you fulfillment, I wish you creativity, I wish you continued passion and joy in your craft.

PREPARATION

Read anything, read everything. Read books, short stories, essays, and ask yourself, *Would this make a good project? How would I be able to approach this story in my own way?*

Your neighbor may have a story, your relative may have a story, is there a project there? Is there a personality trait that you can incorporate into your interpretation of a character?

Never stop listening, never stop observing, never stop researching – you will always be able to mine for characters with this approach. About fifteen years ago I heard a gentleman say the word "barbecue" in a very unique, almost pompous way. I never forgot it and have always wanted to find a way to use that.

CHOOSING MATERIAL

Did you just hear a song? Did it inspire you? How would you tell that story in your own voice, with your own words?

Is there a window nearby? Please have a look out of that window. What's there? Are there people? What's their story? Is it the woods? What happened there? What kind of characters would roam around there? Is that a story? Is that a project? Is it something you can use?

There is potential for a story in anything. Everyone has a story, everyone has personality traits, everyone is fascinating. Did you go to a store recently? Was the store empty? Was it crowded? How did people interact with one another? Did you see a behavior you could include in your character? Everything is something that can be mined. All of it can be used for ideas and applied to your acting craft.

Have fun with this. You know how you can try on clothes and feel like a different person? Try a different speech pattern that you overheard, try a different look with your eyes.

Pay attention and play with everything that sparks your imagination. You never know what you can incorporate into your acting style, or use for a character in the material you've selected.

MICHAEL GENET

Master Classes, Tony Bennett, and How Many Levels Have Your Got?

Mr. Genet appeared in *Wicked* on Broadway from 2015 thru the beginning of 2017, and the national tour from 2022 to 2023. His work includes starring turns in additional critically-acclaimed Broadway and Off-Broadway hits, such as the original production of Aaron Sorkin's *A Few Good Men*, the Tony award-winning *Choir Boy*, *The Prom*, *Hamlet*, *Elton John*, Anne Rice's vampire seduction, *Lestat*, the Off-Broadway smash *Is God Is*, and *American Son*, *A Soldier's Play*, *Fences* and *The Whipping Man*. Film credits include TERRIFIER 3, ONE FINE DAY, 25TH HOUR, BOOTY CALL, and SHE HATE ME. His numerous TV credits include *Best Man: The Final Chapters*, *Billions*, *Blue Bloods*, *The Affair*, *Bull*, *Fosse/Verdon*, *Dr. Death*, *The Mysteries of Laura*, *Ugly Betty*, *The Following*, *Law & Order*, and *Tyler Perry's House of Payne*. Mr. Genet was also a contributor to *Now Write! Screenwriting*.

Upon sharing his thought on acting, Academy Award winner Gary Oldman is reported to have said that on any platform, be it stage, screen, or TV, "Every scene has ten levels. An average actor should be able to reach Level four or Five on a consistent basis. A good actor, Level Six. A really good actor, Level Seven or Eight. And a great actor, Level Nine or Ten. Consistently."

This struck me as a profoundly succinct guideline for the intricate art and discipline of acting. Far too often, actors, young ones especially, are eager to settle on the first or second choice they make with regard to their character's overall arc, their line delivery, or a

MASTER CLASSES, TONY BENNETT, AND HOW MANY LEVELS HAVE YOU GOT?

particular scene looming before them. Choices, that when measured against Gary Oldman's Ten-Level paradigm, consistently leave them sitting at a paltry Level Two, or maybe a Level Three at best. Which leaves only one relevant question to be asked… how many levels have you got?

I know at first glance this may sound silly, overly simplistic, or even a tad bit arrogant. But trust me, if an actor really wants to be recognized for producing outstanding work, wants to ascend to the rarified heights of Level Nine or Ten craftsmanship, then that question is all-important, and quite frankly, straight-up legit.

Like a dance studio bar to a ballerina, or that secret how-to manual that some writers keep hidden beneath the desk, the question of "How many levels have you got?" is the beacon to which every actor must periodically return, if only to refresh themselves once in a while, so they can keep their feet planted squarely on the path that leads to acting enlightenment.

In fact, "How many levels have you got?" is arguably the most important question any honest actor will ever face. Particularly after enduring another seemingly endless round of brutal disappointments and industry rejections from complete strangers sitting behind audition room tables, who, for a brief moment in time, hold total sway over whether or not you work today. Or after one of those long stretches where you could be No. 1 on the FBI's Most Wanted List, and still can't get arrested.

How do you put enough fuel back in your tank so you can get up the next morning and go knock on another door? How do you find the will to step into yet another acting class, trying to fix what may or may not be broken in the hopes of getting a gig? The answer: You return to the beacon and face the almighty question: How many levels have you got?

Way too often, artists get caught up in the shiny presentation of their craft. You know, the graceful lines of a dancer, the chill-inducing vocal runs of a singer, or the complex, colorful brush strokes of a painter. We get so enamored by the sparkle of what we do, that sometimes we forget that a first, second, or even third pass at anything is still just surface work. In order to reach the heights; in order to reach the pantheon, the Nirvana of Level 10 excellence, actors, in particular, must be willing to dig deeper in order to find their characters' inner truth and learn how to tell their story.

Each word an actor speaks, each note an actor sings, and each bit of movement an actor's body generates has its own uniquely coded rhythm weaved deep into the sinews of his or her soul. But if that actor gets too comfortable, or – let's keep it real here – becomes lazy to the point of thinking they're "all that," and settles for the colorful eye candy lying on the surface; those easy, low-hanging fruit pickings will produce anemic Level One, Two, or Three performances, and whatever magic they ultimately find will be minimal at best. Whatever rhythms you unleash will be barely felt, if they're felt at all. And whatever words you speak, no matter how poetic or profound, won't be heard; certainly not to the point of touching an audience's heart, and encouraging them to think.

Reaching Level Ten begins with talent. But it's fueled by how much water an actor is willing to pour into their own personal soil to make their talent grow. An artist can pray all day for their big break or a great review. Prayer is a wonderful and powerful thing. It works in church, at the dinner table, and at the side of your bed at night. I pray all the time.

But in acting, prayers only work if you're good. And in the end, the actor who's willing to keep digging, keep climbing, keep searching – like a jazz musician – for a deeper, richer way to embody a role, say their lines, and tell their character's truth, is often the difference between the actress who becomes Meryl Streep, and the one who becomes Mary What's-Her-Name. Mediocrity or greatness? They're both sitting right there, lying in the cut. And which one you achieve will largely depend on *how many levels have you got?*

Master Classes

I'm always struck by how whenever I'm introduced to a young actor, and sometimes a not-so-young one; our initial conversation nearly always begins with them enthusiastically telling me about a new acting class they're taking, or one they've just signed up for. This

MASTER CLASSES, TONY BENNETT, AND HOW MANY LEVELS HAVE YOU GOT?

is usually followed by them telling me, with a furrowed face, how much the class costs. And believe me, it's never cheap.

Apart from college tuition, since leaving school I've never paid for an acting class. It's not that I don't believe in them. I think acting classes, some of them, are wonderful tools to help actors shape, hone, and in some cases, re-invent their craft. But in taking inventory of myself a few years back, I suddenly realized that I'd been enrolled in an acting Master Class every day of my childhood, and I didn't even know it! Every time I turned on the TV, or went to see a movie, or took in an occasional play at the Kennedy Center, Arena Stage or Warner Theater, I was given a front row seat to some of the best acting classes on Earth. I realized that I'd learned the art of timing by intently watching the comedic genius of greats such as Abbott & Costello, Jackie Gleason, Lucille Ball, Dick Van Dyke, and yes, The Three Stooges, who my mother was fiercely against me watching as a child; but from whom I learned so much.

I learned how to <u>move</u> (not dance, MOVE!), by watching the likes of (again) Dick Van Dyke, Charlie Chaplin, and the sublime Fred Astaire. I watched in awe, every move the great Sidney Poitier ever made, because he moved like a graceful panther, silent and strong. And I'd laugh while watching arguably the greatest "moving" actor of all time… Art Carney. If you don't know who this man was, look him up. Study him. Drink in every subtle and grandiose gesture his body made. People take "actor movement" for granted. But an actor who can move takes his or her character, and whatever production they're in, to a whole other level. And in this, Art Carney was an absolute master. Watching him move is like watching an acting ballet. Pure genius!

For intensity, commitment and pure drive, I watched and studied the likes of Charles Laughton, Jimmy Stewart, and Paul Muni, an actor few people ever talk about anymore, but who was so good at his craft that he completely disappeared into every role he ever played.

Then there's DeNiro, Pacino, Bette Davis, James Earl Jones, whose power still blows me away to this day, Cecily Tyson, and the amazing Viola Davis. The traits of all these amazing Level-Ten artists, and more, live within the recesses of my mind. I keep them stored there like a microchip, so that I can call on them whenever I have a new acting mountain to climb.

This is just my opinion of course, but I will suggest to you that the greatest performance ever given by an actress on film, thus far, was given by Marion Cotillard in the French feature, LA VIE EN ROSE. Her performance in that film is a master class of master classes, for in my opinion, her work sublimely shatters the ceiling of Level Ten, and reaches the acting stratosphere. Any actor or actress longing to be great, would be wise to watch her work in that film. It's like standing on the Yellow Brick Road. Her performance will definitely lead you to the Wizard!

FINALLY.... when I was 17, I bought a ticket to see the great Tony Bennett in concert. I didn't tell my friends at school I was going because I knew they would laugh. I mean, it wasn't like I was going to see The Jacksons or Earth Wind & Fire. It was Tony Bennett. So I kept it to myself, and with my own money, bought an orchestra seat so I'd be somewhat close.

Tony Bennett walked out on stage. He had to be in his 50s then. He only had a jazz quartet with him, which scared me. I remember feeling disappointed that there wasn't a full orchestra, and wondered if I'd wasted my money. I needn't have worried, because Tony Bennett sang thirty-three songs that night. Thirty-three songs! I counted every one of them. And with every song he sang... in his 50's... the man got better and better and better! His voice became richer and richer, like a 200-year-old Scotch being poured over butter. The bend of his musical phrasings went deeper and deeper, as if he was trying to convey a more profound feeling with every new lyric he sang.

He was so good that by the time he finished his performance, the entire sold-out crowd, myself included, enthusiastically leapt to our feet. I walked out of there literally on a cloud, knowing that I had just been in the presence of greatness. I had witnessed an artist who wasn't satisfied with just coming out on stage and singing a few tunes. Tony Bennett kept digging and digging for a more fulfilling way to give his talent to the lyrics at hand, and to the stories that each song told. Tony Bennett kept searching through his music for a deeper way to tell his

MASTER CLASSES, TONY BENNETT, AND HOW MANY LEVELS HAVE YOU GOT?

story. To tell each song's absolute truth. Level Ten doesn't even begin to describe that kind of commitment.

When the show was over, I went home with a life lesson embedded in my soul. The lesson was... If you're not always getting better, get off the stage! Because the great ones keep digging. They never stop. They're always asking themselves, *How many levels have I got?*

When the movie WAITING TO EXHALE opened, Oprah Winfrey had the cast on her show to discuss their experiences in making the film. It was the late Whitney Houston's first venture into acting. When Oprah asked her what was the most important take-away she'd learned about acting versus singing, Whitney Houston pointed to her fellow castmate, Angela Bassett and said, "I'm trying to be like Angie."

When a curious Oprah followed up by asking, "Whitney, why?"

Whitney replies, "Because Angie can bend a line the way I can bend a note."

To this day, that's one of the greatest takes on acting I've ever heard.

PREPARATION

In preparing for every role you do, think about identifying three Level Nine or Ten actors that you admire. Actors whose rhythm, drive, and overall commitment to the embodiment of their characters is so pronounced, that they speak to your particular artistic essence. Not every actor will, so choose wisely here.

Find a project for each of those actors that fits in line with, or is somewhat similar to, the role you now have before you; be it a play, film or TV; a drama or comedy, etc. You're looking for a similar type of role, or it can be a completely different role that's played by an actor you identify as having sensibilities and "actor instincts" that gel with yours.

Examples would be: if you're cast in a role of a cold-blooded, completely heartless human being, you might want to look at Ralph Fiennes in Schindler's List. Or if you're an actress trying out for the role of a woman put upon by society or people she loves, that are destroying her self-esteem... you might want to look at Bette Davis in NOW VOYAGER, or Ingrid Bergman in GASLIGHT.

Watch it. Study it. Study their performance like you'd study for a midterm. Study their eyes; their every glance. Study every word they speak, loud or soft, and the variations of their inflections. Study every move they make. Even the stillness of the ones that don't. Look for all their subtle nuances. A smirk, a sigh, the raise of an eyebrow, or the length of an exhale.

Study the way they shift their body from one side to the other. The way they smile, or how they shed a single tear, as opposed to a full out cry. Look for all the little things the general public never sees, for these are the essential tools in transforming a performance from a Level Five piece of work into a Level Ten, and will help you carve out a performance that will leave audiences electrified and maybe a little breathless by what they've just seen.

Do NOT watch any of these actors with the intention of copying them. There are no absolute ways to success. But trying to copy another artist is a sure-fire way to failure!

After you've completed your study session, it's time to go back to the beacon. You've just watched Level Ten actors at work. So now you must face the question. Opening up your script, look at it and then ask yourself, *How many levels have I got?*

Then start saying your lines. You can say them out loud, or whisper them softly to yourself. But say each line a <u>minimum</u> of ten times.

The trick here is that each time you say a line, say it differently than the time before. Say it with a different inflection or a different tone. Try using a different speed. Maybe even pause in between a word to break up the phrase, and see if that gives it a deeper meaning.

What you're looking for here are the true depths at which the roots of your lines are buried. Any prospector will tell you… gold is never found on the surface. The gold of a scripted line is the same way. You have to dig for it.

So get out your shovel and start digging. Keep digging. Because that's the only way you'll ever find out HOW MANY LEVELS YOU'VE GOT.

Chapter 3.

Understand the Script

"I understand pain very well, so I look for that in a role. If the characters are well-written, don't tell nobody, but I'll do the damn thing for free. I'm serious. It's the writing. I love beautifully flawed characters."

- MICHAEL K. WILLIAMS

THOMAS GUMEDE

How To Read a Script

Thomas Gumede is a South African actor known for his work in MANDELA: LONG WALK TO FREEDOM, AYANDA AND THE MECHANIC, GOMORA HUSTLE, THE GOOD MAN, BACK OF THE MOON and other feature films. He has also appeared in the TV series *Silent Witness, Bay of Plenty* and *Single Guys*. He directed the movie KEDIBONE, and produced and directed the reality TV series, *Uthando Lodumo*.

When I was learning how to act, I tried every technique and method. It allowed me to work out exactly how I would perform the character's voice, personality, and physical mannerisms and behaviors.

However, this over-preparation left no room for improvisation on set. I found it extremely difficult to make any decision about my character on the spot. What I learned was that being overly-prepared or stuck on one technique creates blocks.

Yes, prepare for a role. Being ill-prepared will also create blocks and other challenges on set, but what you must learn is that every moment requires a different technique. Some moments require Method. Some moments require improvisation. Some moments require you not to act at all and just be yourself. What helped me grow most as an actor, was realizing that all these techniques are correct in their own ways. Everybody is right. Nobody is wrong. We just need to know when to use those methods, and when to throw them out. We must use our flexibility to stretch ourselves.

We, as humans, all display our emotions. There is no difference between showing emotions right now and displaying those emotions in front of a camera. What matters most is honesty. Being honest with yourself, to the next person, and to what you hear or smell in that very moment allows you to transcend into another being. You start to be aware of the smallest things happening. You almost become psychic because you are so in tune with the moment.

When I'm acting in a scene, I feel the most connected to life. Even though those are supposed to be the moments where everything is fake, it is that real moment where I release everything and I no longer feel as if I am acting at all.

To understand these honest moments further, I recommend watching people and really listening to them. See how they behave when they don't think they are being watched. When you are at the airport, do not wear earphones and listen to music. Instead, listen to what people are complaining about, what tone people use, and take life in as it happens.

Then, when someone asks you for that moment in a scene, you can refer to your memory, learn what your subconscious can teach you from that past moment, and bring that into your character.

Always be curious about yourself, humanity, and your own vulnerability. Keep practicing and learning each day.

PREPARATION

When reading a script, read the whole script as an audience member first – not as your character. Use this time to see if and how the story entices you.

The second time around, read the script as the character who is the furthest from the role you have been assigned. If you are the main character, try reading it from the antagonist's point of view, or if you are a supporting role, try reading it from the main character's perspective. Find out how you would speak as this character, or what motivation you are feeling as this character.

Reading the script from multiple perspectives and learning from their points of view will help you understand the script and the story better. It will even help you elevate your own role when performing, because not only will you have gained flexibility, you will also have gained knowledge about what makes each character special.

Having an extensive understanding of each point of view in the story is a crucial responsibility, and your duty as a storyteller.

LAURIE LAMSON

A Writer's Perspective for Actors

Laurie has written over 100 produced film, video and audio scripts, including the indie feature film GUITAR MAN which earned twenty festival awards. She has directed internationally well-received shorts: the metaphysical romance *Eternal Waltz*, the comedy *Family Values in the Goddess Years*, and the reggae music video, *Live and Learn*. A true "anthology lady", in addition to editing this book and several *Now Write!* anthologies, Laurie produced the scripted audio compilation/podcast series, *Anti-Heroine*.

I've learned some movie actors don't read a whole script. They want to be surprised by the events of the story as they unfold, to respond as genuinely as possible, so they only know about their own character, and, I assume, their dialogue cues. This is not for that kind of actor.

If you're interested in your character's role in the story, and another lens through which to explore a script, you may find this helpful, or at least interesting.

I think for most actors, the better you understand the context of the story or the scene, the more freedom it gives you to experiment while staying in the ballpark of serving the overall story.

When I say 'role,' I don't mean the character as an individual. From a writer's perspective, a character doesn't live alone in a vacuum. Each character serves a function, a role within the story, and in relationship to other characters. Possible roles in an effective narrative:

PROTAGONIST (traditionally, the "Hero"): the one who drives the story in pursuit of a goal, and overcomes a personal blind spot/moral flaw (or fails to overcome it, if the story is a tragedy or satire.)

MAIN CHARACTER: usually the Protagonist, but sometimes an Ally or other character, and we're viewing the Protagonist's adventure through their eyes.

For example, Dr. Watson is the one reporting on Sherlock Holmes' adventures. In SHAWSHANK REDEMPTION, Andy drives the story, but Red is the one telling it, and he's the one who is changed by it.

ALLY/ALLIES: helper/s to the Protagonist in achieving their goal.

Usually in movies and TV series, at least one Ally will also be the Main Character in their own subplot, which, if done well, serves as a comparison or comment on the main story. The Ally may have a more extreme, silly, or opposite approach, but ideally both the Protagonist and their Ally are dealing with a version of the same issue or challenge.

In FORTY-YEAR-OLD VIRGIN, the main character has three Allies helping him lose his virginity. They each have subplots that compare and contrast how they approach their own sex lives.

ANTAGONIST (the "Villain" or "Bad Guy"): one or several characters in conflict with the Protagonist. Often, the primary Antagonist either pursues the same goal as the Protagonist, like competing for a job or championship, or the opposite goal, as in, they want to kill the Protagonist and the Protagonist wants to survive.

In a romance or romantic comedy, the focus may be a little more on one of the "lovers", but it's as if they're both the Main Characters, and serve as Antagonists to one another. In a buddy comedy there's a similar dynamic. These genres are often combined with another genre, like action or science fiction, in which the potential couple or buddies join forces to go up against an outside Antagonist.

ALLY-ANTAGONIST: one who behaves like an Ally, but switches sides, or was secretly an Antagonist all along.

ANTAGONIST-ALLY: one who behaves like an Antagonist, but switches sides, or was secretly an Ally all along – like the Witch's guards in WIZARD OF OZ.

HENCHMEN: Allies to the Antagonist, who help with their goals.

Naturally, each character feels like they're the main character of their part of the story, and that is how the actor should view their own role while embodying it. I just think it may be helpful to have this context.

For example, an Ally usually calls out the Protagonist on a blind spot or moral failing, so, at times, they can look like an Antagonist. But they are trying to help, not harm, even if it's with brutal honesty.

Side note: in the book *Audition*, author Michael Shurtleff suggests love as the underlying motivation for every choice, even if it doesn't seem like it on the surface. Worth considering, I think.

PREPARATION

Determine Your Character's Role

See if you can identify your character's role from the above list.

It's part of the writer's job to put in clues for actors to be able to understand their characters. That's what you're seeking.

If you can't figure it out, the writer might not be sure either. In that case, choose the most logical role, because it can inform your execution, and will serve the story better than leaving it unclear.

Look for Clues About Your Character

If the dialogue seems very on-the-nose, meaning the character says exactly what they think and feel without any apparent subtext, it could be the writer's shortcoming, OR it could be that you haven't yet figured out the subtext.

Either way, it is up to you as the actor to look at the scene in the context of the whole story, if you have access to it, and then make decisions about what might really be going on in a given scene. Get curious and dig deeper.

If you can't find clues in the script, it becomes even more important to use your imagination to figure out how your character thinks, feels, and behaves in any given scene.

STEPHEN H. SNYDER

Make It Work with The Five W's

Stephen Snyder has nearly three decades of casting experience working with over fifty independent films, and collaborating with esteemed directors like James Cameron and Cameron Crowe. His portfolio includes casting iconic rock music videos by artists such as Kiss, REM, Cheap Trick, Nirvana, Tom Petty, George Harrison, and Bob Dylan. He cast the indie movies SKID MARKS, POWNED featuring Eric Roberts, the TV pilot series *Fifty and Over Club* and multi-award-winning plays by Neil LaBute. With his diverse casting expertise, Stephen Snyder continues to make a significant impact in the world of film and music.

Jack Nicholson said that the bottom line is this: there are many methods, and as an actor you have to beg, borrow, and steal from a variety of methods to create one that works for you.

We learn by failing, it's all trial and error. In order to know what works, you have to learn what doesn't work. You have to be willing to fail in order to succeed. As Joe Walsh says, "You can sit in a studio all day long and play, but if you really want to play, go play in front of people. Then you learn how to play."

My first job I ever had as an actor was three lines in a movie. I got fitted into a tuxedo, I showed up on the set, and there's Gene Hackman. I was pissing my boots but he acknowledged me as an actor, and that lifted me up.

He said, "Hey, are you in the movie?"

I answered, "Yeah, I'm playing 'Guy Number Two'."

"What's your dialogue?"

"'Show me the way to the bathroom'."

He says, "Wow, you're doing the scene with me. You want to rehearse?"

I only have three lines.

He says, "I always like to play, let's play."

I was so touched by that. He must have thought, *We have to act together, so let's make it the best we can.*

True artists are the actors and filmmakers who make it work, no matter what. I had the great pleasure to collaborate with L.A. Casting and James Cameron for a couple of weeks on THE ABYSS. The studio wanted to change the ending, and they did, because he was not yet "THE TITANIC" James Cameron.

We were scrambling because we only had one day in a parking lot in Long Beach to shoot the ending of a twenty-million-dollar movie. And there's James Cameron with a staple gun, hanging what looks like a big coffee saucer from a crane as the spaceship. Watching true artists make things happen is quite inspiring to me.

I got into teaching so that I could make it affordable for actors and help keep them positive, because I believe everybody has a right to be an actor, and everybody needs plenty of chances to fail. If this is what you want to do, I'm here to support you. If you're willing to do the work, I'm willing to stand beside you and push you up the ladder. I'm the guy who goes, "Yes, you can do this, if you're willing to work hard."

The overall goal is to find the truth. Every actor's journey is to find the truth within the character and the material.

Whether it's a cold read, a prepared audition, a scene, a play, or a movie, how do you maximize your preparation time? With any acting technique, it all comes down to the five W's: Who, What, When, Where, Why… and also How.

Based on the information you have, even if you only have one scene of dialogue without any additional context, these are the basic imperatives, the questions you need to ask and answer for yourself to be able to prepare.

PREPARATION

WHO am I?

This is the easiest one. You are YOURSELF – within the given circumstances. The character can never not be you, it has to be an extension of you, a version of you.

What are the parallels in your life? What is the character going through that you've gone through? All human beings have the same emotions and the character you know best is yourself, so how would you feel if you were in the situation?

WHAT Is the Tone? WHAT Is the Genre?

One of the jobs of an actor is to find the tone in the scene – it gives us a path to follow. First, look at the material and figure out the genre, because that will help you set the tone, and answer some of the other questions.

The same scene with the same dialogue can be interpreted differently, depending on the subtext that comes out of the genre and tone, and the choices the actor makes about their character and what the character really wants.

For example, my character gets a message that his wife has been kidnapped. If it's a drama or thriller, my point of view might be: *My beloved wife is in danger and I'm desperate to save her.*

But what if it's a dark comedy? You might figure out from the text, or make your own choice, that you don't really like your wife. In that case, regardless of the dialogue, your attitude may be, *Go ahead and keep her.*

WHAT'S My Objective – What Do I Want?

What do I need? What obstacles are in my way?

Desire plus obstacles plus conflict creates tension. Tension is what holds the audience's interest. As an actor, it's your job to create tension, even if the writer didn't spell it out for you. Exploring the "Whats" given in the script will help you do that.

Desire: What's my objective – do I want to save my wife… or not?

Obstacle: What is in my way of getting what I want? If the kidnapper demands a million dollars, I have a big obstacle to rescuing my wife, because I need a million dollars that I don't have.

If I don't want to rescue her, what obstacles are stopping me from telling the kidnapper, "Please keep her." Am I afraid she'll be killed? Am I afraid of what her parents will do if I don't do all I can to get her back?

Conflict: in my example, the conflict begins as soon as you find the message and have to call the kidnapper. You just learned your wife was kidnapped, so you ask yourself, *How does that make me feel?* How does this news affect me emotionally – as if this is indeed happening to you, because it is.

If you like your freedom and believe your wife took it away, you might feel relieved that she's gone.

If you adore your wife, you're afraid for her and desperate to get her back.

If you have mixed feelings, or don't want to save her but have to pretend you do, that creates inner conflict for your character.

As the conflict with the kidnapper, and possibly your inner conflict, escalate/s, the tension in the scene increases, and that is interesting for an audience.

WHEN Is It? What Is the Time Period? What Is the Time of Day?

In my example, I imagine it's the end of the day and I just came home from work, looking forward to seeing my wife.

Depending on the time period and place, there may be different societal expectations, different ingrained, kneejerk reactions, various direct and indirect ways of communicating.

WHERE Am I Coming From, and WHERE Am I Now?

Getting clear on your environment is very important, because we're always somewhere. The actor's job is to create that environment for themselves, so that it's a real place for the audience – we go to that place with you.

Often a scene starts in the middle of something. For example, your wife is being held hostage in an unknown location, and your scene takes place in your living room where you are on the phone talking to her kidnapper. (A different environment than if you were speaking to a kidnapper in your office during working hours.)

Where are you coming from? If you were only provided this one scene, it's up to you to decide that. If you begin the scene just when the dialogue starts, you're usually saying the first line without it having any purpose or meaning.

You could decide that you came home from work, you just got a raise, and you walked in the door eager to share the good news, but your wife isn't there.

You get a message that she's been taken hostage – your life just got turned upside down, and now you're in a conflict with a kidnapper.

WHY am I here? Why do I want what I want?

The tension in the scene is built on the stakes, and the stakes are built on the why: Why, specifically, is what you want important to you? This is how you justify for yourself whatever your character says and does.

Villains don't see themselves as bad. Dr. Evil in AUSTIN POWERS thinks he's wonderful. Every villain does. They justify their actions: "The world's a shithole, I'm doing a good thing by blowing it up."

So even if you want something socially unacceptable, like letting a kidnapper keep your wife, you have to justify to yourself why, in order to play it convincingly.

HOW Will I Get What I Want?

What will you do, and how far will you go, to get what you want?

Much like in life, in a scene we often mask how we really feel and/or what we really want. What are you concealing? How and when and why are you going to reveal it?

Are you trying to be brave and stoic to the kidnapper while you're dying inside?

If you don't want her back, why not? What did she do to you?

If the dialogue reads as if you really want her back, are you just pretending, but you actually never want to see her again? Do you suspect it's a trick and this supposed kidnapper is your wife's lover?

MAKE IT WORK WITH THE FIVE W'S

The script will usually help you figure out a lot of these things. By deciding the answers to all these questions, whether the script provides them or not, you will be prepared to bring your character to life and make the scene believable.

CLEA DECRANE

What Would It Be Like If You Really Meant It?

Clea DeCrane is a writer, director and actor currently working as a showrunner's assistant for Joe Weisberg *(The Americans)* at FX. Her work skews towards the absurd and surreal, often centered on women grappling with obsession, transition, and heartbreak in horrifying and hilarious ways. Her short series *Following Hannah Stone* played Bentonville Film Festival, Stareable Fest, LA Indie Film Fest, won "Best Web Series" at Big Apple Film Festival, and was licensed by Roku for a year. Clea was also a 2022 member of WIF's Emerging Producer Program, and is the founder of Station 26 Productions, through which she produced the short films *Daddy's Girl* (Sundance, SXSW) and *Class* (starring David Krumholtz, also produced by Hank Azaria.) As an actor, she studied at Mason Gross School of the Arts and Shakespeare's Globe in London.

"What would it be like if you really meant it?" was the favorite phrase of an acting teacher of mine. I was studying at Shakespeare's Globe Theater in London, and my classmate and I were doing the scene from *Much Ado About Nothing*, when Benedick says to Beatrice one of the most beautiful lines ever written:

"I do love nothing in the world so well as you. Is not that strange?"

My teacher stopped my classmate in his tracks, paused dramatically, then looked up at the ceiling and said, "Hm. Interesting. Now what would it be like... if you really meant it?"

After a pause, my classmate said, "Better."

WHAT WOULD IT BE LIKE IF YOU REALLY MEANT IT

Actors want to be actors because we want to explore the full spectrum of human emotion in the most vibrant, horrifying, exhilarating and beautiful circumstances. We crave being vulnerable. We crave feeling it all. That's why it's so ironic so many of us stop short of doing exactly that.

It's hard to really mean something. It takes guts. And often, actors – even great ones – get used to stopping just short of that. I believe it's the director's job to push actors that last ten percent, into a space where they mean words more than they knew was possible, and end up surprising themselves, and the audience. This is where magic happens.

And so, when I am acting or working with actors as a director, this is the question I return to: What would it be like if you really meant the text you're saying with every fiber of your being, as if it's the first time in the world you've come across these ideas, these words, these sensations?

What would it be like if I truly looked at my scene partner and discovered that I really do love <u>nothing</u> in the <u>world</u> so well as them? Is that not strange – and terrifying – and absolutely wonderful?

The question itself, "What would it be like…?" is so activating because it forces us to expand into curiosity, which, another brilliant acting teacher once told me, is the most important quality an actor can have. I wholeheartedly agree. If you're curious, actively curious about yourown emotions, and those of your scene partners, you will always be innately compelling to watch.

PREPARATION

Trust the text.

So often, actors can get thrown into their heads by worrying too much about what's happening sub-textually. Often this is not their fault – it could be the by-product of bad directing or bad writing. They can get worried or confused about over- or under-playing a beat, an action, a desire, etc.

One of my favorite exercises to do with actors is to throw all those notions away and physicalize the text. Another way of putting it would be to be literal with the script.

For example, Abigail in *The Crucible*, speaking to John Proctor:

"It were a fire you walked me through, and all my ignorance was burned away. It were a fire, John, we lay in fire."

What would it be like to truly imagine being walked through a fire? Take your body through the burning sensations and connect them with the actor playing John. How badly does it burn? How different do you feel, risen from the ashes? Do this exercise, and then see how much more you empathize with Abigail's passion for John.

This exercise works with Nina in *The Seagull*, too:

"I am so tired. If I could only rest – rest. I am a seagull – no – no, I am an actress."

What would it be like to truly believe you are a bird? Don't play at being confused, or crazy, or sad – physicalize that sensation. To say, and mean it, that you are small, and agile, and able to take flight at any moment. And then, as you switch from seagull to actress, feel yourself transforming from bird to… an actress on a stage, in front of dozens of people. How disorienting is that? If you dive head first into the language, much of the character work is already done.

And, because it's so juicy, *Hamlet*:

"O all you host of heaven! O earth! What else? And shall I couple hell? Hold, hold, my heart! And you, my sinews, grow not instant old, but bear me stiffly up."

Is there anything more active than fighting to keep your heart inside your chest? And demanding your body stay young to keep you from falling down? What would it be like if you really meant it – to believe that if you didn't beg your corporeal form to stay strong with all your might, it would crumple into a quintessence of dust right then and there?

Trust the text – mean the text – it doesn't have to be Shakespeare or the classics to do so.

And when you do, see what happens in your body. I promise it will be more surprising, delightful, absurd and beautiful than you could've imagined over-intellectualizing it inside your head.

And if you are a director, remember that actors, at the end of the day, are players. Offer them this joy and playfulness every chance you get. Pull them out of their heads and into their bodies with direction

WHAT WOULD IT BE LIKE IF YOU REALLY MEANT IT

that ignites their senses. Be it for stage or screen, their performances will multiply in clarity and curiosity, and you will be mesmerized.

Chapter 4.

Be Present and Trust Your Instincts

"Overthinking is the biggest crime in acting."

- ALAN CUMMING

DONN SWABY

Being In the Present Moment

Donn Swaby is a professional writer, musician and actor in film, television, theater and radio. Feature film credits include RAW NERVE, OPEN WINDOW, BUDS FOR LIFE (which he also wrote), NORA'S HAIR SALON, NORA'S HAIR SALON II and Ridley Scott's G.I. JANE. He has appeared on the television shows *Passions, The Sopranos, Judging Amy, Crossing Jordan, The Parkers, Vaughn, Half & Half, Surface, Charmed, Gigantic, Monk, Happily Divorced* and *How to Get Away with Murder*. He wrote and acted in the short films *Wedding, The Two Professors, The Forum* and *Orpheus Star*. He has written for The Huffington Post, *Melt Magazine for Women, Entertainment Voice*, and authored the children's picture book, *It'll be Irie*, published by Cardinal Rule Press.

As any profound and illuminating lesson in any discipline lends itself to also being a great life lesson, so to with acting. When an actor is present in a scene, they are not in their head. They are not thinking about their next line. They are actively listening to their scene partner.

Of course, if their character is absent-minded or daydreaming, then they are doing that and <u>still</u> living within the present moment of the scene.

Being in the present is where the magic happens. It's where we notice all the parts of our environment and genuinely interact with them, where we observe the way in which our scene partner says something or does an action that makes us react in the moment, so our next line or action is not programmed, but rather organically created. If the actor has learned their lines thoroughly, then they can "throw them away," which means they no longer have to think about them and thus be more present in the scene.

In life, the magic also happens in the present moment. We call it "mindfulness" now and it's a great thing to practice. It's so easy to allow one thought to lead to another and then another and soon, we are either dwelling on something from the past or else speculating or worrying about something in the future. Anyone who's ever tried to meditate will tell you how easy it is to get distracted by the endless chatter in our brains, or to dwell obsessively on a particular thought.

The best thing to do is not beat ourselves up for not being present, but just acknowledge it and come back to the present moment. Otherwise, we are still in the past, linking this failure to stay present to all the other times we've "failed," or we're dooming our future, convincing ourselves we'll never be able to stay present.

So better that we forgive ourselves, forgive our brain for doing what it naturally does, and just gently come back to the present moment. The present moment is where we become aware of the synchronicity playing out in our lives, magical "coincidences" that we would have otherwise missed had we been in our head, stuck in speculating about either the past of the future.

This is how we enrich our acting work as well, by finding ways to stop focusing on the chatter and just be, which is easier said than done, hence the art of mindfulness is an ongoing practice.

Whether it's a quick breath exercise, even just one deep inhalation and exhalation, or looking into your scene partner's eyes, noticing something about the way they are dressed or how they hold a particular part of their body (this is from a method known as the Meisner technique), or noticing something within the immediate environment, there are many methods for getting back into the "now" moment.

This is true for both acting and in life. And that's where we want to be, because that's where all the magic is.

PREPARATION

<u>Acting on Stage vs. Acting in Front of the Camera</u>

As a professional actor who started in theater, it took me a while to learn how to modulate my acting when I was on a film or television set. Upon watching my performances, I could see I was "muscling it," simply doing too much in my attempt to convey emotion and thus, indicating.

In theater, acting "bigger" is a practical consideration; you want to make sure the audience in the back row can hear you and understand the emotion you're conveying. But when acting for film there is no need to "broadcast" to that back row. The camera picks up everything, even the smallest eye twitch or the slight raising of an eyebrow. There is no hiding from the camera; it sees all.

In this context, when you try to show how you feel through facial expressions it registers as too much, as melodramatic over-acting and insincere.

I eventually learned how to pull back on my efforts to show what my character was feeling; I learned to simply feel the emotion and trust that the camera would pick it up. The key word was "trust." The more you understand that the camera will pick up everything, the more you will trust it and the less you'll feel the need to push the performance.

Now that doesn't mean an actor can't be big on screen and still be believable. Acting legend, Al Pacino, is known for his bombastic portrayals of larger-than-life characters who "chew up the scenery." The reason he is believable is because the grandness comes from the character, and actors like Pacino commit one hundred percent to the choices they make.

In real life, there are people who talk loudly or who are overly dramatic. The trick as an actor is to make it real for yourself. When the emotion is truly felt, it can either bubble up just underneath the surface or spill out in great torrents, if that is what the character and situation call for. But if it's fake, the camera will see that, and so will an audience.

Try *Not* to Cry

When I was a younger actor, I thought it was my job to get myself worked up to whatever emotion was called for in a scene. If I didn't organically feel it, I would try to force it and think whatever thoughts I needed to in order to produce a specific emotion which would be "displayed" in some physical way, whether it be a facial expression or body language. If I had to cry, I allowed myself to feel the sadness well up inside me until actual tears came.

The thing is, as actors, we're not always emotionally available, and in some performances, you need enough mastery of applied technique that an audience will not detect the artifice, in this case, forced emotion. An actor who forces tears and pushes themselves to cry robs the audience of empathy. Instead, the audience will feel pity, which is an emotion that separates them from the character. They may not even hear what the character is saying, so focused are they on all the sobbing.

A major lesson I learned in an acting class was that real people try *not* to cry. The teacher's example was watching someone on the evening news talking about the loss of a loved one. They are on camera and trying not to cry because they're attempting to communicate something. Despite their efforts, the pain may come to the surface, rendering them unable to speak. But they once again try to rein in the sadness in order to finish what they're saying.

An audience will feel empathy for this person because they see the struggle to maintain composure, and will root for the person to "keep it together" emotionally. If there are any tears, it may be the audience crying themselves, empathizing with the person's grief.

A cinematic example of this is in the film WHALE RIDER, in which Keisha Castle Knight plays a little girl delivering a speech in a school play that she'd dedicated to her grandfather who didn't show up to see the play. When she sees his empty seat, her heartbreak threatens to overwhelm her and she starts crying, unable to continue. Her mother encourages her to finish the speech, and the whole time the audience is rooting for her to finish too, empathizing with her pain.

This is how actors should approach a scene, no matter the emotion. Real people don't always show anger directly, sometimes acting passive aggressively. An actor can choose to indicate they are drunk by swaying and falling down, or they can behave like a real person who is feeling tipsy but trying to walk straight and not to fall. They can play fighting against the emotion or condition rather than playing the effect.

Just like people in real life, characters are much more dynamic, captivating and endearing when we sense their emotions bubbling just underneath the surface, threatening to spill over and overwhelm them. This is because we register there is an inner struggle going on, which can be the hardest struggle there is, worse than any external obstacle.

Never Judge Your Character

An actor should never judge their character or project their own criticism onto their character. Your job is not to condemn, but to portray the truth of a human being within a given set of circumstances. It's one thing for a character to judge themselves and think, for example, that he or she is a horrible person. It's quite another for you as the actor to think you're playing a horrible person.

In real life we judge ourselves and we judge others. We also rationalize our thoughts, beliefs and actions and can sometimes be in denial.

In "real life," judging others reduces those being judged to being only a rigid interpretation of their words or actions. When we feel compassion, we may not condone words or actions, but can still recognize that they, like us, are human, "Born to make mistakes," as affirmed by the 1980's pop band, The Human League.

When portraying a character, you must be able to fully identify with that character's humanity. If you sit in judgment of your character, you cannot see the humanity of that character and thus, cannot portray that character truthfully.

Alleviate Nervousness and Anxiety

Breathe.

We do it automatically but most of us don't realize our breathing is often shallow and we don't breathe deeply enough.

Deep breathing works naturally to slow our heart rate and calm us down. We may begin to notice we were unconsciously holding tension in certain parts of our body, like our shoulders, for example, and can then release that tension with a deep exhalation.

If we're physically stiff, we're blocking our energy from flowing freely in our body. So if we're locking our knees, we can bend our legs. Stretching can loosen your body and allow your energy to flow more freely. Feeling more connected to your body you can more easily act upon impulses, allowing yourself to respond more immediately.

When about to perform or audition, remind yourself that you're merely playing and that it's not a life-or-death situation. That whoever's watching, whether it be a casting director, producer, director or audience, is just as human as you are. That everyone's rooting for you to do your best. No need to fear not "getting it right" – just have fun playing the truth of every moment. Then the nervousness can become excitement; your nerves will still be jingling, but without the accompanying feeling of dread.

Be A Well-Rounded Person

Acting is about playing as if it's real life. Therefore, all real-life experiences become source material to draw from. Acting cannot and should not be the only thing you focus on. Just like in real life, acting is about relationships; about people's desires, fears and emotions.

An actor should not just observe life, but actively engage in it. That could mean pursuing other passions and hobbies, or joining a community or group, creating opportunities to cultivate new relationships. That could also mean opting for day-jobs that offer a chance to learn new skills and gain new experiences.

In truth, every situation, including ever person one interacts with, is a potential learning opportunity. The degree to which one is able to see their life in this way is proportional to the degree to which one is aware and present, which in turn is dependent on one's emotional, psychological and spiritual health.

It's vital that an actor be holistically healthy – balanced in mind, body and spirit. An actor operating from a place of dysfunction due to unhealed trauma, perhaps experienced during childhood, will also be dysfunctional in their inability to access the full range of a character's emotional life. Such an actor will have an "emotional block" they must work through in real life if they are to grow as an actor. It's important to find a means for healing emotional wounds in order to fully "show up" both in real life and in the work.

It's About You and It's *Not* About You

It's true that actors need to bring themselves to the role. Part of making a character seem organic and authentic is doing things in the way only you would do them.

It's also true that as an actor, one has the responsibility of honoring the given circumstances of the character and emotionally going wherever the story requires them to go; they should do no more and no less than the role requires. I

f a character "loses it" via a nervous breakdown, you cannot bypass "going there" because you personally don't feel like it, or are uncomfortable doing it. If you're not comfortable being in the character's skin, then you have no business playing that role. Imposing personal limitations upon a character comes from our egos, the idea that we ourselves are in control, rather than the creative force.

In order to play the character and the situation truthfully, an actor needs to be in service of telling the story. We are but vehicles through which the story is being told. In this way, actors become true modern-day shamans, as we get out of our own way to allow the magic of the creative force to take form and work through us.

In this way, we are able to be of service to our communities by the offering of much-needed medicine for the soul.

MACKENZIE BARMEN

Talk To Yourself

Barmen is a SAG-AFTRA and AEA actor based in Los Angeles. She has starred in dozens of plays and voiced multiple commercials and audio books. She is also a writer, content creator, singer and podcaster. She currently hosts two comedy podcasts: *Bullshittery* and *Smack* (currently in development, co-hosted by Steph Barkley.) Barmen is best known for her original sketch-comedy on TikTok (3.1M followers) and Instagram (~317K followers.) Off-Broadway credits include *Swing* and *The Marvelous Wonderettes*. Regional theater credits include Johanna in *Sweeney Todd*, Cathy Haitt in *The Last Five Years*, Miss Casewell in *The Mousetrap*, Stella in *A Streetcar Named Desire*, Sister James in *Doubt*, and more. She is currently represented by Buchwald Agency, Framework Entertainment and Underscore Talent.

Ever since I got into theater and performing in tenth grade, I've been fascinated by the process from start to finish. I love the thrill of being cast in a new role and the undertaking of getting to know the character, learn the lines, learn my blocking, identify my relationships with other characters, and the micro-expressions and dynamics I can bring into the role by tapping into my real personal experiences – when they suit what I'm working on.

My preparation techniques have changed a lot as I've grown, shifted, and adapted to new settings and stages of my life, but there are a few important things that I always make sure to have a good handle on.

Whenever I approach a new character, whether it be for a play or for a sketch I'm producing for social media, I always try to find the grounding in the character – the relatability and humanity. I'm personally a big fan of making the audience feel so engrossed in a performance that they forget they're watching one. I typically improvise all of my sketch comedy that I do online, but I always prepare by finding their quirk and unique sense of being for whatever world they're in.

For standard acting – film/TV and theater, it's always so important to me to read it a million times before I start trying to memorize anything, so that I can fully understand the world without immediately shoving myself into it. I want to make sure I understand the relationships, the subtext, the dynamics, the power shifts between characters, the relationship I have with myself as the character, the needs and wants of my character and what I'm going to do to get it. I always make sure to start with these basics, so that when it comes to memorizing and learning it, I already have a strong handle on who this person is – without me.

When that work is done, the memorizing and structural work is the next step. I love the rehearsal process and collaborating with other actors to find that give-and-take that works so beautifully in acting.

I live by this: if you are on stage or on camera, the main objective is to make the other character look good. If you can make the other character look good, you'll look good. Active listening is so important, and if you're not fully engaged and IN IT with your scene partners, the performance will fall flat. It won't feel real. And that part is the most important to me.

PREPARATION

It's so important to be loose as an actor, especially with comedy. I love the idea of play and keeping things loose and spontaneous. Here are some of my favorite ways to do that.

<u>Flesh It Out</u>

An exercise that always works for me is something I learned from a New York City acting teacher, Anthony Abeson. He has a phrase called F.I.O. (flesh it out), in which you take moments that are mentioned in the script but not necessarily acted out, and you improvise them privately so that you have that real, physical memory to work with when you're in it.

For example, if I'm doing a scene and my character mentions a memory they have, I will go and act out that memory as if it actually happened. This brings it to life and gives it much more weight than if I just mentioned it, but never lived it.

When you're working on a character who mentions something they experienced off camera or off stage, try acting it out on your own to create your own memory.

Talk to Yourself

I improvise all day long. I have such an active imagination and I find that no matter what I'm working on, it keeps my brain fresh, and fires off the synapses that make me a better performer in the moment.

So I recommend talking to yourself. It's fun, easy and freeing. Try making up scenarios when you're in the shower.

If you're preparing for a role, walk around your apartment and act out an entire scene between two people. Play both parts. Change your voice. Change the way you walk and talk and move. Experiment and don't get locked in to any choices you make during this process. STAY OPEN. Be flexible, and be ready to completely change your delivery on a dime.

Slow Down Your Prep

I think one of the most important things in the preparation process is to make sure you're enjoying it. Make sure that you're having fun with your process. If you find it draining, put it down and pick it up again later.

Oftentimes we feel that we need to be working like mad to hurry the process along and get there faster. In reality, I find that pacing it out, taking it slow, and just trying to be present has a much more positive and lasting effect than trying to cram all the prep work in at once.

Get Some Inspo

Something I'd recommend to anyone working on a role of any kind, is to watch clips of your favorite actors. I'm personally a huge fan of watching *Actors on Actors* and hearing about their processes and experiences.

I love re-watching my favorite comedies to refresh myself on pacing, technique, timing, micro-expressions, rhythm, etc.

Also, whether you're a stage or screen actor, go see live shows, plays, stand-up comedy. As much as you can.

Be Truthful

It's so important to be loose as an actor, and truth is also very important, especially with comedy.

You don't need to overdo it. Keep your actions small and deliberate, unless of course you're doing clowning or something that requires a larger physical energy. As Stella Adler said, "Nothing is too big if it's truthful."

Stay grounded in your work and stay truthful.

Think the thoughts of the character, and have fun.

Listen to your scene partners and make it your mission to make them look better than you. You will shine with your graciousness.

My final word of advice: believe in yourself and your talent – to the point of delusion. It's much more fun that way, and having an air of confidence can take you very far.

BRUNA BERTOSSI

Embracing the Moment: Techniques for Presence in Acting

Bruna Bertossi, originally from São Paulo, Brazil, is an international Actress, Clown, Producer, Writer, and Voice-Over Artist. Her early theatrical pursuits led to a degree in Dramatic Arts from the Foundation of Arts in Sao Caetano do Sul in São Paulo. Bruna expanded her artistry internationally, engaging in clown performances for a humanitarian cause in Angola, Africa and creating the character Kátita Esvairovisk. Her diverse experiences extend from Brazilian stages to Chinese circuses and entertainment companies. Based in Los Angeles, since 2021, Bruna focuses on impactful film production, leading her own company, BBArt Films Productions LLC, and enriching the U.S. entertainment landscape with her Brazilian vibrancy and creativity.

As an actor with a diverse background spanning from the vivid cultural landscape of São Paulo, Brazil, I have always held the concept of presence on stage and screen in high regard. This piece explores that journey, highlighting the nuances of presence I have learned and cherished throughout my career.

Presence in acting is more than just a skill; it's the soul of performance. It brings forth a level of authenticity that resonates with audiences and fellow actors alike. I've found that presence is not just about being seen; it's about truly being there, at the moment, in every breath, gaze, and gesture.

Maintaining this presence has been a challenge and a reward throughout my career. I recall a performance in a small theater in

EMBRACING THE MOMENT:
TECHNIQUES FOR PRESENCE IN ACTING

Brazil, where the intimate setting demanded a level of presence that was profoundly personal and raw.

Conversely, on the international stage, the presence required was expansive, reaching out to touch the hearts of a large diverse audience.

Practicing presence involves a deep connection with oneself and the character. It's a skill that can be honed and mastered through various techniques, impacting not just the performer, but also the audience, in a profound and lasting way.

The art of presence in acting is an ever-evolving journey. The following techniques are not just exercises, but pathways to unlocking deeper layers of performance. I encourage my fellow actors to embrace these practices in their daily routines, rehearsals, and performances, as we all strive to capture the elusive magic of true presence on stage and on screen.

PREPARATION

Mindful Movement

Engage in slow, deliberate movements, maintaining an acute awareness of each muscle and sensation. (This practice enhances body awareness and control, which is crucial for an actor.)

When preparing for a role that demands a profound connection with the character's physical presence, I embark on a journey of mindful movement.

For instance, while rehearsing for a role that involved intricate dance sequences, I adopted a method of deeply conscious rehearsal. Each morning, I spend an hour in a quiet, uncluttered space, focusing solely on my body's movements. I visualized my character's emotions flowing through each motion, whether it was a stretch, a leap, or a subtle shift in posture. This practice wasn't just about memorizing steps; it was about embodying the character's soul through every part of my being.

Emotional Tuning

Connect deeply with the emotional state of your character.

Embrace and embody these emotions, maintaining this connection throughout the performance.

For emotional tuning, I recall a role that required me to tap into a complex array of feelings, some of which were foreign to my personal experiences. To truly embody this character, I created a playlist of songs that mirrored the emotional landscape I envisioned for them. Each track represented a different facet of their psyche. I would listen to this playlist in solitude, allowing each song to evoke and amplify the emotions within me.

Following this, I practiced my lines, letting the music's residue color my delivery. This method helped me access and maintain a genuine emotional connection with my character, ensuring a performance that was both authentic and resonant.

Audition Preparation

Visualize the stage, your character, and the audience.

Imagine delivering your performance with utmost confidence and clarity.

Preparation is a blend of rapid technique and mental visualization. I record my scene partners' lines, leaving gaps for my responses. This simulates the real-time exchange of dialogue, honing my timing and reactive instincts.

These days, it's easier for me to use the app Linelearnerlite to help me with the part. I take a notebook and start writing out my dialogue until I memorize the lines. Sometimes I also record myself, and I listen to it a hundred times until I memorize everything.

To get inside a character, I ask my character questions. I like to go deep inside and understand every single part of the scene.

I also use a detailed visualization process: imagining every step, from waking up on the day of the audition, to the moment of doing it. This mental walkthrough includes the feel of my attire, the weight of the script in my hand, the texture of the air in the room, and the exchange of energy with the casting team.

This visualization culminates in a vivid image of delivering my lines with precision, passion, and presence. I approach each audition and

EMBRACING THE MOMENT:
TECHNIQUES FOR PRESENCE IN ACTING

role with the professionalism, enthusiasm, and authenticity that defines our craft.

Grounding and Centering for Stage Presence

This is another of my favorite exercises for grounding and centering for stage presence.

Stand with feet shoulder-width apart, knees slightly bent.

Inhale deeply, imagining roots extending from your feet deep into the earth.

Exhale slowly, envisioning any tension in your body dissipating into the ground.

JACK O'HALLORAN

Relax and Be Yourself

Remaining undefeated in his first sixteen professional boxing matches, Jack O'Halloran was considered one of the most promising heavyweight hopefuls, and became the California Heavyweight Champion in 1972 and 1973. He was on the verge of a bout with Muhammad Ali when he was knocked out by Jimmy Summerville. Though he knocked out Summerville in the rematch, O'Halloran retired in 1974 with a record of 34-21-2 and 17 knockout victories. He was inducted into the California, Pennsylvania and, New Jersey Boxing Hall of Fames. He also managed and trained the Super-Middleweight WBA World Champion, Frankie Lilies. Jack then launched a successful career as a character actor in FAREWELL, MY LOVELY, KING KONG (1976), SUPERMAN, SUPERMAN II, THE BALTIMORE BULLET, HERO AND THE TERROR and the DRAGNET movie. He is developing his published novel *Family Legacy* as a mini-series.

I had no acting lessons or anything of that nature. In 1967, I was boxing in Boston. Steve McQueen was in town to do THE THOMAS CROWN AFFAIR and he and I became good friends. He said, "You've got to come back to Hollywood with me. I'll put you in the movie."

I said, "No, I'm an undefeated heavyweight and I'm on the brink of fighting for the title, and I don't think I'm ready for Hollywood."

In 1969, I knocked out the number two heavyweight in California, Manuel Ramos, who was the champion of Mexico. Steve McQueen wanted me to do THE GREAT WHITE HOPE with James Earl Jones. It was the biggest movie in Hollywood at the time. I went in to see the producer, who said, "We're shooting in Spain and we're going to give you fifteen hundred a week."

I said, "You're going to give me what? I give that away in tips every week. I'm getting ready to fight Muhammad Ali, and you want me to go to Spain for six months?"

He said, "I thought this was all taken care of and you were coming in to sign a contract."

"Thanks, but I don't think this works for me. If you need a heavyweight, there's a guy named Jim Biddy who just retired from boxing. He's a big white guy, and he needs a job. He's got six mouths to feed."

I get a phone call from Steve McQueen. "What are we going to do to get you to Hollywood?"

He did a picture called THE TOWERING INFERNO and told me his character was Captain O'Halloran. "I like your name, Kid."

It went on like that. Then in '75 I suffered from a pituitary tumor and finally retired from boxing. I had an agent and I started doing a lot of commercials, Royal Crown Cola and a bunch of stuff down in San Diego. My agent called and said, "They want you to do a movie with Robert Mitchum, and I think you really better consider it."

Whoa, maybe it's time I give this a shot. I said, "Okay, set it up. What do I have to do?"

She sent me to New York to meet the director, who said, "You're the guy. You're the guy. We're going to do a screen test, because you're the guy. I know it."

The first day I went to work on the movie, which was FAREWELL, MY LOVELY, Robert Mitchum, who played private eye Richard Marlowe, became my mentor.

He arranged to pick me up and told me funny stories all the way downtown to the shoot. I was getting ready to do my very first shot in a movie and we were standing at the bottom of stairs – about to walk up together for the scene.

He looked at me and asked, "You read the script, Kid?"

"Cover to cover."

"Good. Throw it in the trash. Get it? Don't let me catch you doing what thousands of people do when they come to this town for acting. Just be yourself. If the character walks down the street, you just walk down the street like he's you."

That wasn't hard to do. He taught me about camera angles but he never tried to tell me how to act. He taught me how the industry worked and how to protect yourself.

By the way, Sly Stallone has a small part in the movie. He didn't know anything about Philly and would pick my brain about being this gangster boxer from Philadelphia. I gave him a lot of things about breaking up strikes on the waterfront and Jimmy Hoffa. Believe it or not, his screenplay for ROCKY came from stories about my life!

Back to my first-ever scene. They started moving the camera, and I asked Mitchum, "What's going on?"

He said, "That's it, Kid. That's all there is to this. We're moving on to the next shot."

I said, "Oh man, I'm a star!"

Later that day he was done and I still had another scene. He left the set and I'm asking myself, *How am I going to get home?*

I go down to the motor pool, and there he is standing beside the car, smoking cigarettes, talking to the driver. I said, "Wow man, you're still here."

He said, "I couldn't go home without the star now, could I?"

When Mitchum came on set you could hear a pin drop, but he was a normal person, he was Robert. The FAREWELL, MY LOVELY budget was two and half million dollars, which was a lot at the time. We had four Oscar winners on the crew and they loved to come work for him because he was such a great guy. Plus, everybody had steak for lunch.

The film editor, one of the Oscar winners, had his office right at the studio gate. I was walking out once and he stopped me and said, "You're Jack O'Halloran."

"Yeah, what's the problem?"

"I'm editing FAREWELL, MY LOVELY. This is the first movie you've ever done?"

"Yeah."

"Let me tell you something, Man, you're going to be a star. I'm putting this footage together, and there's one thing about the industry that people never really understand: the camera either loves you or it doesn't, and the camera loves you. You got a home run here."

I told Mitchum, "Maybe I should go to UCLA and take some elocution lessons or acting lessons."

He laughed and said, "Stick with me, Kid. Whatever you're doing is fine. Just keep doing what you're doing."

He was like a father. Everyone was saying FAREWELL, MY LOVELY was going to be very successful and I didn't have an agent at the time. Mitchum pointed to the phonebook. "You think I'm going to tell you who to go to? You don't like the guy, you're going to get mad at me. Ain't happening."

So I found an agent and Mitchum told me, "You couldn't get a better guy."

I said, "Well, thanks. You could have saved me the legwork."

It was Lee Marvin, a wonderful agent, and my new acting career was working out great.

I went from FAREWELL, MY LOVELY to KING KONG… one good movie after the other.

One day I told Mitchum that Cubby Broccoli was waiting in my agent's office – he wanted me to do a Bond movie but I was signed up for MARCH OR DIE with Gene Hackman. What should I do?

Mitchum asked if I had read the Bond script and I said I had. He asked, "You like it?"

I said, "No."

He told me to stick with scripts that I liked. I told my agent to say, "No thank you," to the Bond movie.

During MARCH OR DIE, Gene and I were brought to London to speak with Richard Donner about SUPERMAN. Donner asked me, "How do you feel about playing a deaf mute? The character Non was a major scientist and they lobotomized him because he was working with General Zod."

Jackie Gleason was a friend of mine and had gotten a Golden Globe nomination for playing a deaf mute in a picture called GIGOT. I told Donner, "If I ever get a role where I can do just facial and body expressions to make you understand what I'm saying, I would love it."

I was offered the role and I think it turned out to be a much better move than doing a Bond movie. The character of Non became so iconic, it was a career-defining moment.

So, I've worked with some great actors, like Charlotte Rampling and John Ireland and Sylvia Miles, stalwarts in the industry, and I learned from all of them. Jeff Bridges is a real method actor – he took a half hour to get into the role. It was a lot of fun and I enjoyed going to work.

I was in THE BALTIMORE BULLET with Omar Shariff – a good movie that never got pushed out very well. I liked him a lot and hanging out with him was a trip. One morning we had breakfast and women were standing at the door, they were outside the building and around the block.

I asked, "You got this problem all the time?"

He smiled and said, "What are you gonna do?"

He was a gambling degenerate. Hustlers from around the country would come to backroom card games, ready to take his money. Once we were both getting make-up for a scene, and he was in the chair surrounded by these gamblers wanting him to come to a game. He said, "Guys, I just got off a plane from Egypt."

They insisted they had a game set up and would love for him to come play. He couldn't say no and invited me to come watch. I never saw someone get twenty grand off a bunch of guys faster than he did. He was probably one of the three best bridge players in the world. He was a super guy, one-of-a-kind. A huge movie star who wound up working as a greeter in casinos.

Then there's Marlon Brando. We got on like a house on fire because he knew my father. I went down and watched him work a couple times and I saw him do something I never saw any other actor do. He was in a scene, and the camera guy said, "Oops, got a problem with the camera. We're going to have to come back later."

Marlon said, "No, I'm turning around while you fix the camera. When you tell me you got it ready, I will turn back and finish the scene." And that's exactly what he did.

He had cue cards everywhere. He even had signs on actors' heads. You'd think Marlon Brando, a Method actor, would be so prepared he wouldn't need cue cards. I asked him, with all due respect – didn't he know his lines?

He laughed and recited several Shakespeare speeches off the cuff. It was amazing. "Of course, you must know every single word," he said. "After learning Shakespeare, this stuff is a piece of cake."

Then why all the damn cue cards?

He said he started using them as a device on MUTINY ON THE BOUNTY. "I wanted to make it look like I'm just thinking up what to say off the top of my head, like I haven't been studying the lines for the last year."

I watched a lot of movies, I studied how they were made, and I had a lot of conversations with the director John Ford. Like Mitchum, he was all for actors being relaxed. He told me he'd shoot rehearsals – he found that when actors would just do what they were doing, assuming the camera wasn't rolling, they were more relaxed and had greater performances. The actors would rehearse and then tell him, "Okay, we're ready to go."

He'd say, "No, we're done. We're moving on now."

PREPARATION

My advice for actors is the same stuff Robert Mitchum and John Ford told me.

<u>Relax and Be Yourself</u>

Take the character and become it. Enjoy yourself embodying this character inside this story.

Look at who and what the character is, and put that character inside of you. You will become the character through your body language and your facial expressions and your movements.

If the action is walking down the street, you don't have to "act" or plan it out, just be yourself. Be yourself "as if" you <u>are</u> that character who happens to be walking down the street.

You don't need to overthink it.

<u>Dialogue is Talking to Someone</u>

Who is the person you're doing these lines for?

Think of it as, you're not a character speaking with another character, you're a person communicating something to another person.

You are the one speaking, as yourself, but the character is inside you with something to say to another character, who is the person in front of you, being their character. If that makes any sense.

Consider the Audience

How are you going to come across to the audience? Think about how you want an audience to relate to your character.

With SUPERMAN, General Zod was a vicious killer and Ursa was a man eater. I felt there needed to be a bad-guy character that kids could relate to, because SUPERMAN has a child audience.

I wanted a child to be able to identify with my character. So I took this big British guy and imagined him as a child, learning how to work his eyes and communicate for the first time.

I must have pulled it off, because people thought it was quite convincing. At my first Comic-Con, a guy came up to me and said, "I'm dying to meet you."

I said, "How's it going?"

He was flabbergasted. "My God, you can talk!"

It helps to have a specific idea for the character, like I did with Hon. Whoever the character is, put it inside of you, and then just be yourself. Your actions and movements will come naturally, and the audience is going to believe everything you do is real.

Don't Go Looking for the Camera

Looking at the camera all the time is the worst thing you can do as a movie actor.

Mitchum said, "Never go looking for the camera, let it find you, understand?"

If it's a close up, he said, "Find an eyeline right past the camera. Look at the eyeline and let the camera find you."

So I ignored the fact that there's a camera in my face, because that's what Mitchum told me to do. I would look right through the camera, as if it's not there.

It's Okay to Turn Down a Role If You Don't Like the Script

If you need the money, by all means go ahead. But if you don't feel drawn to a role, it may not be right for you, and it may not be a great experience in the long run.

If you like the story, you automatically start getting ideas about the character, right? You have a better chance of feeling relaxed and natural and sure of yourself, it's easier to get the character inside you, and you'll enjoy it more.

Regardless of the type of role you're playing, if you enjoy yourself, the audience will enjoy watching you – at least that's been my experience.

MALCOLM MCDOWELL

Yes, I'm Acting – Believe Me Anyway

Malcolm McDowell is a multi-award-winning actor, perhaps best known for his iconic portrayal of the lead role Alex in Stanley Kubrick's A CLOCKWORK ORANGE. With 275 film, stage and television credits, he has starred in numerous movies, including O LUCKY MAN, TIME AFTER TIME, GANGSTER NO. 1 and one of his favorites, CALIGULA. He played Rupert Murdoch in BOMBSHELL, Mr. Roarke in the TV movie FANTASY ISLAND, and himself in THE PLAYER. Other movies include HALLOWEEN, I'LL SLEEP WHEN I'M DEAD, STAR TREK: GENERATIONS and his first Western, LAST TRAIN TO FORTUNE.

Mr. McDowell has appeared on-screen and voiced characters in a multitude of TV shows including *Son of a Critch, Pearl, Entourage, CSI Miami, Mozart in the Jungle, War and Peace* and *South Park*.

CALIGULA was very cutting-edge and raunchy, a story about the Roman Empire, which had very different moral values than we do now. It was nothing in those days to sleep with your relations, simply because they were the only people you could trust not to poison you. Caligula's father was a famous general, a brilliant man, but his parents were both murdered. Of course, that left its mark, and Caligula was a very troubled young man.

Everyone knows him as a madman, but I couldn't play a crazy person for two and a half hours. You get bored. I wanted to take the character from one place to another. He's a provocateur, he pokes at Roman institutions, he's one of the original anarchists, because he wants to bring the Empire down from the very top.

I wrote a lot of the script after Gore Vidal resigned. He walked off, and we had to get on with it, so they brought over a playwright friend of mine and we worked on it together. It has a lot of historical fact. When I first worked with Colin Firth, who's some kind of Roman scholar, he said, "That's the most accurate movie I've ever seen on the Roman Empire."

One of the nice things about the new version, CALIGULA: THE ULTIMATE CUT, is to see Helen Mirren's character develop. In the Guccione version her part was seventeen minutes, now it's an hour. She gave a very subtle, beautiful performance. There's a marvelous moment when she started licking my face. I remember at the time thinking how brilliant it was. That wasn't in the script, she just did it, instinctively, I think.

Becoming an Actor

I started acting when I was eleven. The headmaster of my private boarding school loved theater. His sister was the wardrobe mistress at RADA (Royal Academy of Dramatic Arts) and she did all the costumes, so the school production's costumes were very wow.

How I got started is, I did not love church much, I don't think any boy does. To relieve the boredom, I launched into the hymns with great gusto. I didn't know the headmaster was standing behind me. The following Sunday he rang a bell after lunch and announced that everyone's going to church except Malcolm. I thought, *Oh no, I've done something wrong.*

He wanted me to sing the song. I did not sing it very well, but I was given the part, and that's how I started in theater, in a Christmas play.

I remember being in the wings, feeling sick, I guess with nerves. But as soon as I walked on, with the light and the void, and the black hole of the audience and getting the heat from them, I felt completely at home. And I've always felt at home since then.

A silent screen movie star in Liverpool, which is where I'm from, encouraged me to go to LAMDA (London Academy of Music and Dramatic Art.) One of the judges offered me a job in the professional theater as an assistant stage manager, and playing small parts. The parts got better and better, and that's how I started acting professionally.

I was twenty years old, and everyone in London at the time believed the only real acting was on stage. But I thought the best actors were Hollywood actors, like James Cagney. Strangely enough, I always knew that my future lay before the camera, and it turned out that I am very much a cinema kind of actor.

By the way, years later, my character in GANGSTER NUMBER ONE – I loved him, he was such a son of a bitch – he was my homage to Jimmy Cagney. It was a silent, *Thank you, Jimmy*.

Anyhow, I got a few television parts and felt completely at home. Then I went to the Royal Shakespeare Company, and everything ground to a halt. It was prestigious, so of course I had to do it, but I hated it. I met some wonderful people there and I'm glad I did it. I just couldn't wait to get out.

Then I got myself an agent. I'd get close to a starring role, it would be between me and another guy, and they always went with the name. Ten times in a row, that's hard.

Building a Career

Luckily, the one movie I finally did get was with a genius director, Stanley Kubrick, in an absolute masterpiece: CLOCKWORK ORANGE.

My time at the Royal Shakespeare Company paid off, because the language the character of Alex uses is heightened, like Shakespeare. The book's author, Anthony Burgess, was extremely clever and created a new language Alex calls "Nadsat" – basically English with Russian mixed in.

Alex was such a nutty, crazed character, I felt like I was breaking new ground for myself as an actor, pushing the envelope as far as I could. Stanley wanted me to go even further, but I said, "No, you have to believe it. It's got to be real."

I was playing an immoral violent man, a rapist, a murderer – and the audience still had to like me. Alex does horrible things that are, of course, bad for the victims, but he loves life and does it all with such joie de vivre – which is an attractive quality – so that's one way to win over an audience.

Kubrick told me he had set the book aside because he couldn't cast it. I was flabbergasted because I thought a lot of actors could have done it. In retrospect, I'd say that I wasn't intimidated by Kubrick because I knew he had chosen me deliberately.

Early on, I said I wanted to talk about something and he said, "No, that's why I hired you," and just walked away.

I was a little pissed off. But driving home after the day's shoot, I realized, *Wait a minute, he just gave you a great gift.* He's saying, "Just do it. Show me." Now I understood why Peter Sellers loved working with him: Peter would try forty different voices and Stanley would pick one.

See, Kubrick hired the right actors, and they delivered for him. So whenever he asked what I thought, I'd say, "Let me show you."

Happily, he liked my instincts. He didn't know much about acting, he was more interested in the lights, angles, camera lenses, whatever, but he had good instincts himself, so I trusted him. I knew as long as I got my part right, he was going to make the movie look fantastic.

Of course, there are some directors you can't trust, because their instincts aren't that good, and sometimes you have to fight for what you believe in (see my other piece in this book: "Choosing Roles and Working with Directors.")

This past year I've gone from playing a grandfather in a sort of comedy series, *Critch*, which is a beautifully written show. I love it. We shoot in Newfoundland, a remarkable place. In the same year, I went from playing this granddad to the Devil to a serial killer.

I also recently did a Western, and I'd never done one before. When you get your heart set on playing this or that, you set yourself up for disappointment; sure enough, you'll never be asked. But when LAST TRAIN TO FORTUNE became a reality, I was thrilled because I've always had a hankering to do a Western, I just never said it out loud.

My character is a bit of a pompous schoolmaster who has two suitcases: one with his underwear, the other full of books. I was going to do it years ago with Bill Paxton, but Bill passed away. We got his son, James Paxton, and I think Bill would be delighted. It's very low budget, we did it for the love of it. I got my ex-wife Mary Steenbergen to do a very important scene at the end, and I also called in dear Bernadette Peters, whom I'd worked with before.

We did some takes around a campfire at night and started to improvise, and we were talking away. We came to the end and I said,

"That must have been a ten-minute take." No, it was twenty-two minutes!

Doing this great variety, I really enjoy it. When I work, I always have fun.

Acting Approaches

Honestly, I can make a case for both training and no training. I think training would help you get confidence, so when you first start you can go back to the technique you've been doing at school, whatever that technique is.

On the other hand, I'm coming to a part completely from left field, because I'm not approaching it as a trained actor, I'm an instinctive actor. An instinctive look at the material may give it a completely new viewpoint.

I personally would only trust my instinct and intuition because I've gotten this far with them, and I wouldn't know what to do without them. I very much work from the inside out.

Gary Oldman loves working outside in, putting putty on his nose, disappearing into a costume, and he's brilliant at it. Daniel Day Lewis is another one who loves doing that. I admire them immensely, and of course, there have been performances when I worked outside in. It's interesting and fun to do occasionally, but it's not the way I normally work.

For me, especially in front of a camera, you're working with the feelings, it goes straight to your soul. When you're acting, you know when it feels good, but you can't know what life you're giving a character – it's something from deep within you. I don't like to hide behind makeup or noses, I want it to be all me, and I want you to believe me anyway.

I used to like working in a studio better than on location, but now it's the other way around. It's weird because I'm not a Method actor. If I'm playing a boy scout, I don't go camping for the weekend. I don't have to do that and I don't want to, because I want something else to happen. I don't want to be bound by realism – I want to be real. I want to be real, but not realistic.

Lindsay Anderson, who directed O LUCKY MAN and a bunch of other films I'm in, once said, "Malcolm, you're very Brechtian."

I like Brecht and I'm happy to be a Brechtian actor, but what the hell does that mean?

He explained, "You let the audience know you're acting, but they believe you anyway."

Then I understood. I've never worked in naturalism. Plain naturalistic acting is boring for me. What interests me, is to do a performance in a style that makes it about something more. I don't want to get too pompous about this, and it doesn't always work out this way, but I like to find a style to work in that is heightened. I give it a certain attitude, or a certain life, which may not be in the dialogue or the script. Of course, in some performances that's not the case, but it certainly was with O, LUCKY MAN and CLOCKWORK ORANGE and CALIGULA.

When I walked onto those gigantic elaborate sets for CALIGULA, I knew instantly, instinctively, *I have to take advantage of what they created and not be intimidated by these sets.* I knew I would really have to move – the flowing costumes would only look great when you're moving at speed. It had to be bigger than life, otherwise I would have disappeared inside those sets.

Confidence

Lindsay Anderson used to say, "Malcolm, you certainly don't lack confidence."

I asked him, "Is that a compliment, or no?"

"Yes, yes, it's a compliment."

"Okay. It sounded like an arrow coming in, but I'll take it as a little of both."

Where did I get my confidence? I think it's something to do with the fact that I'm from the north of England, which is a no-nonsense kind of place. I didn't come from wealthy parents. Not that I cared about that, it wasn't an issue. But I had to stick up for myself, fight sometimes. Things did not come easily.

What I know is that if there's stress, anxiety or fear, you can't work. I know this because at times I've been stressed and I could not have given a really good performance.

It's irritating if you're in the wrong way, because you try every time. I don't care what it is, every time you go to bat, you want to do your best. Of course, that goes without saying.

As an actor, if you come to set with any fear or stress, worried about your lines, you can't be available and play and respond instinctively. It happens to the best, not just beginners.

Especially with comedy, there can't be any tension at all. It's just how it has to be.

PREPARATION

Pick Up Little Techniques

Lindsay Anderson had wonderful things to share. For example, he taught me how to do a screen kiss. It's a very technical thing:

When you go in for the kiss, you stop, bring your head back and look into the face of the woman you're about to kiss. Mark it, bring it into focus. Then you go, and it's a beautifully stylized kiss.

There's lots of little things like that. I've had to forget them, because they become tricks and I can't use them if I plan for them. A technique like that, you would just use once or twice and that's it.

You can pick up little ideas from watching other performances, not necessarily to copy, but for inspiration that can become part of your own instincts.

Enjoy Yourself

I think the most important piece of advice I could ever give is that you really have to enjoy it. That seems simplistic, but you'd be surprised how many actors, when I look in their eyes, I only see fear. I don't see relaxation or enjoyment.

To really be available and give of yourself, you have to be so relaxed and open to whatever hits you. That's why I never really plan much ahead of time. When I go onto the set, I want it to be the first time, so I can have a totally spontaneous response to everything.

Overcome Fear by Developing Confidence

Do whatever you can to cultivate confidence in yourself so, when you get to set, you can be present and have fun instead of worrying about making a mistake or what someone else thinks of you.

Do learn your lines, understand the character and the story, then when you get to set, let your instincts take over.

"Follow the wisdom of the great actor, James Cagney, you hit your mark, you look the other guy in the eye, and you tell the truth."

- LARRY MERCHANT

BUILD UP YOUR ACTING CHOPS

"Acting is standing up naked and turning around very slowly."

- ROSALIND RUSSELL

Chapter 5.

Develop a Character

"It's got to do with putting yourself in other people's shoes and seeing how far you can come to truly understand them. I like the empathy that comes from acting."

- CHRISTIAN BALE

KATHERINE WADDELL

Learn Your Character's Skills

Katherine Waddell is an actress, movie producer, and the co-owner of First Bloom Films, a female-focused, kindness-forward production company based in Los Angeles. She produced and starred in First Bloom Films' first feature, BALLOON ANIMAL, which earned twelve awards at national and international film festivals. She appeared in and was a co-executive producer for the acclaimed indie feature DINNER IN AMERICA, which premiered at Sundance Film Festival. She was an executive producer on the horror film WE NEED TO DO SOMETHING, a Tribeca Film Festival's 2021 selection, and on the animated adventure comedy, THE INVENTOR, starring Marion Cotillard, Daisy Ridley and Stephen Fry. Katherine is in development on four new projects under First Bloom Films.

My production company, First Bloom Films, did a feature film called BALLOON ANIMAL, about a girl named Poppy Valentine who grew up in a traveling circus making balloon animals. I executive produced, produced, and also happened to play the lead character, Poppy. For BALLOON ANIMAL, we had a balloon animal artist, much like a stunt double, because obviously that type of art would take years to learn, and at the time, I certainly did not have years before filming would start. But I didn't want to use that as a crutch in the sense of, *Because I have a stunt double, I don't have to learn how to make balloon animals.*

It's important to me to grab what I can about the character from beginning to end. In this case, it was to learn about a specific talent and how it informs my character, Poppy, as a person.

I'd never be able to do it well, but it's important to the character, so it should be important to me. It's her pride and joy. It's her expertise. So I wanted to know what it felt like physically, and I wanted to understand the difficulties and challenges for balloon animal artists, regardless of whether or not I would ever be able to master it.

So I started by looking at balloon animal artists on Instagram, searching "#balloonanimalart." The things people can create is astounding! I spent a lot of time enjoying it as myself. I saw an amazing one where it was a clam opening and there was a pearl on the inside, and it actually had movement. I was just appreciating how cool the art form is, almost from a museum perspective.

Then I started looking at ways for beginners to learn. I downloaded an app and ordered a balloon-making kit on Amazon. I would set timers for myself, thirty minutes a day, trying to make a balloon animal dog over and over and over again. And they were horrible! They were always popping and I couldn't figure out how to get my chubby little fingers around the twist tie. So there was a lot of research, practical research, where you're exploring something, and then you try it yourself.

I soaked in all that information and added it to my toolbox of who Poppy was, because you want to be able to do something your character is able to do, even if it's only half-assed. You want to know what it's like to tie the balloons and find out for yourself why it's so difficult. You want to be able to go to the director and say, "Let's get a shot of me tying them over and over again," because that's how the character practices her art. And we do have a scene in BALLOON ANIMAL where Poppy is in her room tying and retying to do a twist that she can't get.

As we got closer to production, we hired the balloon animal artist and her name is Theresa Harding. She and her husband Seth both make balloon animals professionally at MadCap Balloons in Los Angeles.

I came up with about fifty questions to ask them, like how they learned it, how long it took, and what were the challenges. What did they like about it, what didn't they like? What was difficult about doing a party for kids versus a party for adults?

I met with Theresa first, then Seth. Of course, their answers to my questions were different; they had two different perspectives, two different journeys. I was able to compare what they told me with what I had already experienced. I told them the twisty tying was hard for me. It's supposed to be the fastest, easiest part: blowing up the balloon

LEARN YOUR CHARACTER'S SKILLS

and tying it off so you can work with it. But it was hard for me and I was so slow at it. Theresa told me, "Oh, yeah, that was what we struggled with as well. When I got into it, I sat there four hours every day, just blowing up balloons and tying them. I wouldn't even try to make an animal, I was just trying to perfect the twisty tying."

It was fascinating to hear that what I struggled with, they had also struggled with, and that it took them four years to get their skills down and feel comfortable making balloon animals. I felt like kind of an idiot, thinking I could get a real understanding, or at least a semblance of one, two or three months before the movie started. As I said, it takes years.

Theresa and Seth still practice all the time. That's what they do in their free time. They go on YouTube and find something they don't know how to make yet. They sit there for hours on end, figuring it out.

Besides researching their respective journeys, I could also talk to them about technique. They sent me step-by-step, seven-minute how-to videos. I would send back photos, videos, comments about what I was able to accomplish, or not accomplish. They would let me know things like, "Your ears are a little disproportionate, here is a common solution for that."

I didn't expect to do balloon animals on camera, but I wanted to understand it and put it in my body. It was practicing a new skill so in case we did want to pick up a shot, I'd be able to provide that from the character's perspective, even if it's not perfect, even if you know it's mostly going to be done by a double.

It's the same as if you play someone who rides horses or has any special skill, especially at an indie filmmaking level. What can you learn about horse riding? If you're in a big budget studio movie, they can probably afford to send you to a horse-riding camp for two months, or have a balloon animal artist come to your house eight hours a day to teach you, so you will absolutely be able to make a koala balloon animal on camera, eventually. But when you're in the indie filmmaking industry, resources are limited and time is limited. Ask yourself, *What can I do to put the character's skill in my body?*

You do need to manage your expectations. Go easy on yourself and accept that you're not going to become a balloon animal artist or expert rider. As actors, we want to give a great performance, so there can be pressure to be able to get everything right every time, and there may be some disappointment when you can't. When I was in the process of learning and practicing with balloons, I thought, *I'm so bad at this, what am I doing? I'm going to ruin the movie because I can't even do the twisty tie.*

But that's not true. Sometimes you have to give yourself kindness and grace as a performer. The simple fact that you're trying to put it into your body is valid. And it helped me immensely to talk to Teresa and Seth and learn about their journeys.

When you're learning about a skill, you can go back in and do more discovery. When I had the lines sort of memorized and an overall understanding and interpretation of Poppy as a character, I explored what her balloon animal journey was like. *What was the first balloon animal she ever made? How many hours did she practice the twisty tie? Did it take her one month, two months? Is it something she still struggles with? How does she feel about that?*

PREPARATION

1. Approach a new skill from the direction that works for you. I like to start from the outside, as an audience member first; you may want to dive right in to trying the new skill, if you can do it safely on your own.

You can also research the advice and insights from experts in the field. Do they disagree with each other? What is your character's point of view on what the experts say?

2. Set realistic expectations for yourself. When it took experts three or four years to master a given skill, no matter how devoted you are, it's highly unlikely you're going to become an expert in three or four weeks or months.

3. Once you have some experience with the new skill, explore your character's experience with it. What was their journey like? How confident are they in their ability? Does it inform their choices in the story?

PRICE HALL

Subtext

Price Hall is founder of The Natural Act and one of the most popular acting coaches in the Houston, Texas area. He wrote and directed the movie MISSISSIPPI MURDER starring Malcolm McDowell. He has appeared in indie features and short films and, the TV series *Wildfire*.

Unfortunately, or not, my approach to the work of an actor flies in the face of most other approaches to the work. What I mean is that the title of this book is a bit off, a bit misleading, in relationship to my approach. *Now Act!* says to me, "Get ready to act: now go!"

This in fact, in my opinion, is the antithesis of true acting which is happening around us, all the time, in life.

In my opinion, acting is just like life. And it is birthed in the subtext, which is based on a choice an actor makes, and then they turn it loose, like a wild animal on the prowl, ready to wreak havoc, or to cozy up for a long winter's nap. And it shall be based on the choices we make.

The choices are many, such as:

Who we are (our history or past making us, justifiably, a good or an evil person.)

Who it is we are really speaking with? Not a brother like the script tells us, but which brother, or person – specifically, down to their name and the tiny scar above their left eye, the one that twitches just before they do something especially nasty – the actor needs to know this person intimately. The time and place (three pm on a sunny day in the park with your little niece feels very different from three am on a rainy, miserable October night, stuck in your old Pontiac LeMans, waiting for your cheating husband to sneak out of his lover's apartment.)

The reason for all of these choices, is to lead the actor to the most important choice of all: the choice of the "need to be satisfied" which, as subtext, is never spoken out loud, but drives every action the character takes.

It must be a NEED, not a WANT, one which grabs you by the throat and drives or pushes you forward in the conversation (scene) until it is satisfied, like air in a small room. When the air is sucked out of the room, what are you going to think about? Who's going to play in the world series this year? No-o-o-o. You've got one thought: *Air... I need air!!!* That's a NEED!

A want, or intention, if it does not get fulfilled, will most likely be replaced by another want or intention. It is not essential. A need is life-and-death, at least to the character.

Ideally the actor will choose a need to fit the overall piece. They must also justify for themselves why their character doesn't state their need out loud. The worst thing an actor can do is choose a need that is obviously apparent in the script, or worse, one which gets satisfied in the course of the conversation, because, once the need is satisfied, why should I pay attention to the other character? The conversation is essentially over, even if the scene, as it's written, is not. *Unless* it happens at the very end of the conversation – that supplies a nice surprise or a total turnaround for your character.

With this subtextual need (again, not a want) in place, which is a conscious choice by the actor for the character (both the same person, but never at the same time), which will likely never be satisfied in the scene (called the conversation), the longer the character goes without the subtextual need being satisfied, the more urgent it becomes, naturally building energy into the conversation, until, by the end of the conversation, either the need is satisfied, providing a huge sigh of natural relief to all concerned (including the audience), or, if unsatisfied, leads to a potential explosion.

For example, a wife <u>needs</u> to know if her husband is cheating – to her, it's life and death. She doesn't mention it until, at the end of the conversation, she finally confronts her husband – who either doesn't admit to his dirty deeds, or he does, with a big F.U. smile on his face (not knowing his distraught wife holds a loaded pistol behind her back.)

By the way, some of this can be gleaned from the script, like her loaded pistol, but much of it is a product of the actor's imagination. This is where I do the work, on the imagination. Because every actor, and every person, has a good imagination. But it's like a muscle, you've got to work it to build and strengthen it.

In every conversation you have as the character, you as the actor must choose a subtextual need for the character, a need that is not written into the conversation. This is where the actor gets to really play, because the subtextual need you choose will determine you and your character's experience in the conversation.

Even in a monologue, you must be speaking to someone specific, with a subtextual purpose, that is, a NEED, in mind. There's never really a time when the character is talking to no one about nothing.

For example: in *Hamlet*, when he is on the parapet screaming into the wind at his father's ghost, do you think his father is really there? Yes, for Hamlet, he is! And Hamlet has a very strong subtextual life-and-death NEED for something he believes only his father can give him, and this need <u>must</u> be satisfied. Guess what, Hamlet does not get his need met... and he dies.

The bottom line is to always operate from the subtext, and that only happens when you're living inside of your choice of a subtextual need that must be satisfied and makes sense within the overall story.

The following practice will help you build your imagination muscles. Make choices about time and place so you can close your eyes and describe both the person and surroundings in detail – so that you not only can see it, but more importantly, you can feel it and even smell it. Then do the same process with your eyes open, so you not only see it, feel it and smell it, but your audience will as well.

PREPARATION

1. Think of someone, a real person, who makes you feel a particular way. With your eyes closed, describe this person in detail, out loud, including how they make you feel.

With your eyes open, again, describe them out loud, and how they make you feel.

2. For a scene you're working on, think of a real person who feels or acts similar to the other character in the scene. Close your eyes and describe that person and how they make you feel. (If, in the scene, Jack is pissed at your character, describe a real person when they're angry at you, and how that makes you feel. Maybe it's your Mom the first time she got really upset with you. It's substitution, but not really!)

Do it again with your eyes open: describe out loud a real person who feels or acts like the other character in the scene, and how they make you feel.

3. Close your eyes and describe the real person again, then add a free-flowing conversation. *What did they say? How did that make you feel? How do you respond? What do they say next? How do you answer?* Again, do this out loud.

Open your eyes and describe aloud the real person and add the free-flowing conversation.

4. For the given scene, whether it's a monologue or dialogue:

Close your eyes and describe, silently or aloud, the character you're speaking with, and how they make you feel. Then speak your lines out loud. (You can do this with or without a scene partner present.)

Open your eyes and do the same thing again. If with a scene partner, they can do the same.

BRYAN CHESTERS

Acting Is Living Truthfully Under Imaginary Circumstances

Bryan Chesters' credits include FORERUNNER, for which he earned a "Best Actor" award at Los Angeles Movie Awards, and Amazon's A HAUNTING AT SILVER FALLS: THE RETURN. He has appeared in *Mad Men, Modern Family, Grey's Anatomy, Anger Management, Numb3rs,* and the TV movies *Wedding Daze* and *A Lesson in Romance*. Bryan's theater credits include *Sunset Blvd.* (first national tour, directed by Trevor Nunn), *Little Me* (George), *Singin' in the Rain* (Don), *The Secret Garden* (Major Shelley), *The Cherry Orchard* (Gaev), *The Clean House* (Charles), and *Hamlet* (Ghost/Grave Digger.) For Disney Magic's inaugural cruises, he originated the role of Hercules in *Hercules* and Captain Becker in *Voyage of The Ghostship*. Bryan is a member of the Musical Theatre Guild and Pacific Resident Theatre.

"Acting is living truthfully under imaginary circumstances," has not only become my mantra when preparing for a role, but has also saved me on more than one occasion when I've been performing on stage or set. Before I give some concrete examples of how this simple phrase has benefitted my own performances, let's look at where this concept originated and who should be given credit for my miracle elixir.

Often the phrase and concept have been attributed to the late great acting teacher, Sanford Meisner. However, Meisner was just one of the lucky members of the original Group Theatre, founded in the 1930s by Harold Clurman, Cheryl Crawford and Lee Strasberg, who embraced this concept or "method" taught by the guru of modern acting technique, the incredible Russian theatre director and actor, Konstantin Stanislavsky. Meisner and his contemporaries like Stella

Adler, and my own acting teacher, Bobby Lewis, were exposed to and influenced by the ideas and concepts of Stanislavsky, who insisted on performances that were grounded in reality and fully embraced the truth of a story's given circumstances, in a way that had never been seen before.

In Stanislavsky's book, *An Actor Prepares*, he goes into great detail about allowing yourself to investigate all the given circumstances of the story/scene, such as, *Where does it take place? When? What is happening? Why? How?*

Then, once you understand all your given circumstances, you must engage your imagination, fully commit, and honor the writer's intentions and dialogue truthfully. On page 47 he writes, "Sincerity of emotions, feelings that seem true in given circumstances – that is what we ask of a dramatist... and that is exactly what we ask of an actor."

Prior to Stanislavsky and the other artists of The Moscow Arts Theatre, including brilliant playwright Anton Chekhov, acting was very "over the top" and gesture-based – characters were portrayed completely externally, without a connection to an actor's internal life. In fact, French actress Sarah Bernhardt (1844-1923) is still remembered for this particular style of acting.

Even through the 1940s, the American movie studios insisted on gesture-based acting. My friend, actor William Chapman, told me that when he was under contract during this golden age of moviemaking, they gave him a book that literally had pictures representing the gestures. For example, on page 45 of a Warner Brothers acting technique book, there was a picture of "Anger" accompanied by a drawing of a person shaking their fist!

It wasn't until the 1950s that performances by the students of these Group Theatre alumni really made their mark on the modern American acting style. For example, James Dean and Marlon Brando, who both studied this approach, gave us riveting performances in films like EAST OF EDEN and A STREETCAR NAMED DESIRE that truly explored the internal lives of their characters and avoided antiquated, gesture-y acting.

Now I'm going to share three examples of how this little catchphrase helped me stay focused and committed to my performances under moments of extreme distress and uncertainty. The

ACTING IS LIVING TRUTHFULLY UNDER IMAGINARY CIRCUMSTANCES

first time was when I was in grad school at UCLA getting my MFA in acting. I was performing the coveted role of Gaev in Chekhov's *The Cherry Orchard*. (Which, ironically, Stanislavsky originated in the very first production.) I was overworked and exhausted, and during the opening scene I looked up and saw all the esteemed members of the acting faculty in the front row. I became so self-conscious that it was a total out-of-body experience; I had no idea where I was or what my next line was.

Then, I repeated my mantra, *Acting is living truthfully under imaginary circumstances* as I looked deep into the eyes of the actress playing my sister, Lyuba Ranevsky, and suddenly I was grounded in the world of the play and my self-consciousness was gone for the rest of the performance.

A few years later, I was producing and acting in a short film I had written called *Saving John Murphy*. It was our very first day of shooting and we were in downtown Los Angeles in front of a liquor store at a busy intersection. Mind you, I had done my due diligence and we had film permits and were legally entitled to shoot on the corner. However, the owner of the liquor store got very upset and attempted to stop our production. We had a large crew of camera and sound operators, extras, hair and makeup, wardrobe, etc., but she wouldn't budge.

We just had to make the best of it. As the cameras were about to roll, she was still inches away from my face, glaring and making snide remarks. I had to completely block her out, so I repeated my mantra, *Acting is living truthfully under imaginary circumstances.*

Lo and behold, I was transported into the given circumstances of the story and was able to give a truthful performance that some called "riveting"-! The film went on to play in many U.S. and international film festivals and was very well-received.

The third example I'd like to share occurred when I was playing a mentally deranged serial killer in a horror film called A HAUNTING AT SILVER FALLS: THE RETURN that was being shot in Oregon, not far from the mental hospital where they shot ONE FLEW OVER THE CUCKOO'S NEST. I was very grateful to be cast in this role because I often play "the nice guy" – typically those are the TV and film roles I get offered. However, this director saw my capabilities and believed I could play a killer.

On my day off from shooting, I toured the mental hospital and visited the museum they had on site. Suddenly it all became very real to me; I was able to convince myself that if pushed off the rails, anyone could be capable of despicable acts of violence and murder.

The shoot was challenging and one of my climactic scenes was being shot at two in the morning. Right before we shot the scene, the other actor, who was young and not well-trained, said, "I'm not scared of you – you seem like a nice guy."

Such an ignorant thing to say to a fellow actor. It's not an actor's job to judge the believability of another actor. What if I said, "I can't impose violence on you because you seem like a nice guy" - ?

If he isn't afraid of me, <u>that's not my problem</u>. If he isn't able to live truthfully under the imaginary circumstances that I'm a killer, he could have created a "substitution"– someone from his own life who posed a physical threat, or at least whom he found more threatening. But his comment really upset me.

Again, I focused on my mantra, *Acting is living truthfully under imaginary circumstances,* and I substituted someone from my past who I really wanted to impose physical force upon, a horrible teacher I had as an undergrad. I was able to conjure up all my internal dark feelings about this teacher and put it into my work. I ended up scaring the crap out of the crew as well as the inexperienced young actor.

I've taught acting technique for the last twenty years and I will say there is no magic pill or even the white feather that gave Dumbo the ability to fly through the air. However, if you're looking for a simple mantra to carry with you when situations become challenging, I highly suggest the phrase Stanislavsky gave us as the culmination of his many years of studying actors and artists: *Acting is living truthfully under imaginary circumstances.*

ACTING IS LIVING TRUTHFULLY UNDER IMAGINARY CIRCUMSTANCES

PREPARATION

1. Choose a character from a play or film or TV script that goes against your type, or how you are typically cast. Find an interesting scene to work on within the script or play – at least two to three pages in length.

2. Before you start the process of digging in and working on the character, do a cold self-tape of the scene on video. Find a friend to read the scene with you and tape the scene. <u>Don't</u> watch the playback.

3. Start the process of examining and investigating all the given circumstances in the scene, play, film or TV script. For example, get out a notebook and answer all of the following questions:
Who are you in the scene? Who are you speaking to? What is the relationship with the other person? Who has the power or status in the scene, and why?

What are you doing in the scene? What do you need from this person? What is your overall objective in the scene? The whole script? What is the conflict in the scene?

Where does the scene take place? Inside? Outside? Church? School? Office? Are you alone? Are there other people present?

When does the scene take place? Time of day? Morning? Night? Time of year? Winter? Summer? Fall? Is it light out? Dark?

Why are you in the scene? Why today? Why is this meeting taking place at this given moment in time? Why do you stay?

How are you going about getting what you need from this person? Are you begging? Are you demanding? Are you seducing? Find action words that make sense.

4. Now that you have investigated the given circumstances in the scene and the story, you need to make it your own. How can you relate to all of these things? Find things in your own life that make sense to you.

For example, you can use substitutions – if your character is talking to someone who intimidates them, ask yourself, *Who do I find intimidating in my own life?*

Pretend you are having the conversation in the scene with the intimidating person from your own life. How does it make you feel? Think of specific examples in which this person made you feel small or unworthy and put it into the scene.

On the other hand, if you have the status in the scene and you are in control, find yourself a substitution for someone who you think is beneath you in some way, and you feel more powerful when talking to them. Imagine specific examples from your past, a given situation when you were in control.

5. Now, try and memorize the scene as best as you can and have that same friend read and videotape you.

6. Watch both tapes and see which one seems more believable.

JAYCE BARTOK

How Could You Play <u>That</u> Part?!

Jayce Bartok is an actor, writer and director who has been in many television shows and movies, most notably Richard Linklater's SUBURBIA, Sam Rami's SPIDERMAN, Tom McCarthy's THE STATION AGENT, and Ava Duvernay's *When They See Us*. His first screenplay became the critically-acclaimed film THE CAKE EATERS, directed by Mary Stuart Masterson, starring Jayce alongside Kristen Stewart and Bruce Dern. He produced the award-winning documentary, *Larger Than Life: The Kevyn Aucoin Story*, and wrote, produced and directed the films THE PRINCE OF SOHO and FALL TO RISE. A contributor to the *Now Write! Screenwriting* anthology, Jace is also a columnist for *MovieMaker Magazine*, and an instructor at Neighborhood Playhouse.

Walking around my neighborhood in the summer of 2019, I couldn't take a few steps without engaging in incredibly meaningful conversations about a project I had just acted in called *When They See Us*, the award-winning Netflix mini-series directed by Ava DuVernay, that tells the story of five teens from Harlem who become trapped in a nightmare when they're falsely accused of a brutal attack in Central Park.

It's based on a painful true story I remember well, having grown up in New York City in the 1980s. These conversations with neighbors, friends, fellow parents, all revolved around the heart-wrenching brutality of the story:

"I cried my eyes out."

"I had to watch it over a few weeks because I couldn't handle it."

"It was so disturbing."

Then, "How could you play THAT part?!"

"Aren't you worried about your career?"

Long pause as I stared back at them. How do I explain that playing the bad guy is an essential part of telling a story about social justice that you want to see told? Let's rewind...

I was meeting Ava DuVernay for the part of Detective Hildebrandt, a real-life detective who interrogates Antron McCray (played powerfully by Caleel Harris,) and has a pivotal scene with Antron's dad, Bobby McCray (played by the extraordinarily talented Michael K. Williams.)

As many of you know, Michael K. Williams tragically passed away in 2021, leaving a hole in many of our hearts. I was privileged to work with him, and I've been thinking about this experience a lot recently.

In preparing for the callback, I remember thinking to myself, *How can I do this terrible thing? How can I play this part?*

I knew I had to try, as I felt a strong desire to be a part of this project no matter what the role; I knew it could be important for people to see it. I thought, *I coach little league on my son's team. He's not much younger than Antron was at fifteen years old. How would I talk to kids on my team?*

I adopted a hushed, gentle tone when auditioning for the role of Hildebrandt. Ava was taken with my approach. "You could talk anyone into anything," she smiled and nodded.

At the time, I was thrilled that I satisfied the director, but I didn't yet piece together how chilling that statement was in regard to the character. Weeks later, my agents emailed me that I got the part.

Cut to a set somewhere in Staten Island that summer – a faithful recreation of a gritty 1980's police station. A bare bones interrogation room where we had already begun to shoot our gut-wrenching interrogations of Antron. I was shooting my scene with Bobby McCray (Michael K. Williams.)

Now, we had rehearsed (which is a luxury,) and Michael and I had an easy rapport. I was naïve in thinking it had something to do with me. Michael was just an incredibly warm, giving person and performer. In rehearsals, we got into a dance of sorts, ad-libbed, there was a spark that boded for something incredible when we started shooting. Ava was happy.

HOW COULD YOU PLAY THAT PART?!

However, on set, everything was about to change. Specifically, my blocking, some of my lines…. and most importantly, my inner voice suddenly asking, *Why are you doing this?*

The scene between Hildebrandt and Bobby McCray is devastating. In a matter of just a few pages of dialogue, Hildebrandt befriends Bobby, only to convince him to make his son, Antron, confess to a crime he didn't commit.

You might be asking yourself, *Why would a father make their own son confess to a crime they didn't commit, and who would make him do that?*

Well, I had to do this. The project required it.

In *When They See Us,* Ava DuVernay powerfully shines a mega spotlight on what it means to be black in America, terrified of a police force run by systemic racism, intimidated by the fear of imprisonment, and feelings of shame and being completely invisible.

In the scene, Bobby appears to connect with Hildebrandt, and he thinks, (as does the audience), that he has found someone who may actually listen to him... listen to him explain that his son, Antron, couldn't have done this horrible crime, and is too young to even understand the crime.

Then the tables turn, and a hideous cat-and-mouse game begins in which Hildebrandt instills fear and shame into Bobby – fear he will lose his job, fear his son will follow in his footsteps.

Finally, Hildebrandt physically forces Bobby to go in the room to "talk sense" into Antron, "Help him, so he can go home tonight."

Of course, we as the audience get what a horrendous act this is.

Okay, I am a father in real life, I generally try to do the right thing. Here I am on set, in this moment, a moment I have been dreaming about my whole life – getting to act in a meaningful project with a great director and amazing actors, in a scene that is challenging, to say the least.

As the close-ups were being set-up, Ava wanted to rehearse a new scene beat she had just added in which I force Bobby to get up, I dominate him. I knew how important this scene was for the piece, for Bobby's character who is haunted by his actions in this moment.

Ava sat where Michael's character had been sitting in rehearsal. "Make me get up," she said. I tried once, twice, three times. She wouldn't move. I wasn't able to force or intimidate her.

I raised my voice, I yelled. It came across as just empty threats.

Then I tried again. Something dark and quiet in my voice.

Her eyes lit up. "What was that?"

I thought for a second, trying to work it out. "Disgust?" I said.

"That's it." She walked away as the Assistant Director told me we had a few minutes while they were lighting. I walked off, in a haze. What was I doing? How could I portray these horrible emotions?

I stumbled toward craft service where they keep all the snacks on a movie set. I certainly wasn't hungry, and was just trying to move, to search for some reason WHY I would do this. Playing generally "evil" never works, I knew that, and I knew I could fail miserably in a few short moments. I started to sweat. I needed to find a reason why Hildebrandt did this. How could someone, anyone do this?!

I had invented a backstory for my character that he coached baseball, lived in Long Island, and longed to get off work, to get home and throw the ball with his son. How could someone like that do this horrible act? Suddenly, it hit me. I (as the character) think Bobby is a 'bad' father, he let his son get into this mess, and he needs to go help him get out of it by confessing. Of course, none of this makes sense outside of the dynamics of the scene. My character's motivation seems ridiculous, in the context of the story, but we as actors know that to portray anything, even something so horrible as what happens in this scene, we need to have a "want" and a reason "why." It's our job.

Soon, "Action" would be called, and I would walk up that hallway, and go to another place and time. I forgot what was happening and found myself engaged in a dance with Michael K. Williams resulting in one of the most gut-wrenching depictions of police brutality – a father making another father send his son to prison.

Ava called "Cut," and peered around the corner. "That was it!"

My knees were shaking. I looked at Michael. We both knew, and we kept going.

Fast forward to that night on my block when my friend asked, "How could you play THAT part?"

Well, these stories need to be told. And it takes a lot of committed performers to do it. Netflix had let all the cast know about emotional support hotlines that had been set-up for anyone experiencing trauma as a result of working on this set. I know that at the premiere of the film at The Apollo Theater, when that scene between Michael and myself played, there was a literal gasp from the audience.

Now, I'm not sure that is exactly why I became an actor, but being a part of telling a story that makes an audience feel something, realize something, react viscerally to injustice, that is really the most important reason for becoming an actor.

Sometimes, playing that part is of vital importance. If you believe in something, playing a character who is hated because of their own hatred can be well worth it – to be a part of change. For the few people who asked me, "How could you?" so many more told me how important it was to play THAT part.

PREPARATION

Evaluate if the part you are auditioning for tells a larger story or is merely exploitative for shock value. A lot of times, evil characters, for lack of a better word, are indiscriminatingly violent or horrible in two-dimensional portrayals.

Approach your process with sensitivity, mindful that your actions in the scene are hurtful, yet important to raise awareness. Work with the director to approach the material as honestly as possible.

Always endeavor to answer the "why?" of your character. And *why* is an extension of the age-old actor question, *What do I want in this scene?*

This isn't an easy task when you're playing a flawed or downright evil character, but it will make the impact of the piece even stronger. Again, it's your job to portray life truthfully, with an unflinching human eye.

No matter what conversations or social media jabs you might experience, know that you are being brave in portraying all facets of the human experience. That's one of the challenges, and privileges, of an actor's job.

"I look for the thing I really don't want to find. I keep asking questions about the character and about myself back and forth pertaining to the story to get at some kind of truth I feel is the center of the person's engine. It's like getting at something that will catapult whoever you're playing into action."

- PHILLIP SEYMOUR HOFFMAN

Chapter 6.

Practice Tools and Techniques

"The gratification comes in the doing, not in the results."

- JAMES DEAN

KIMMY ROBERTSON

The Little Brain in Your Heart

Kimmy Robertson is a screen and voice actress with 73 movie, TV and short film credits. She began her career as a ballet dancer, performing with San Diego Ballet Company, Pilot Ballet Company and American Folk Ballet. Known for her distinctive sense of humor and quirky style, Kimmy appeared in movies that include THE LAST AMERICAN VIRGIN, HONEY I SHRUNK THE KIDS, SPEED II, DON'T TELL MOM THE BABYSITTERS' DEAD and David Lynch's THE MISSING PIECES. She was the voice of Ariel's little sister Alana in the animated feature THE LITTLE MERMAID, and Fifi the Featherduster in the animated feature BEAUTY AND THE BEAST. She has also voiced numerous characters in animated series including *Ollie & Scoops, The Tick, The Simpsons, Batman Beyond,* and *The Little Mermaid.* Live action TV series include *Becker, Psych, Tales from the Crypt, Ellen, The Louie Show* and the ongoing role of Lucy on *Twin Peaks.*

For me, the most important part of comedy, if you're with other people in the scene, is listening. That's where you get all your material from: the other person, when they are talking or saying their line. If you're listening instead of waiting to say your line, it's really easy to respond naturally. And if you're listening, you can improvise, unless of course your director says, "Absolutely not."

With comedy, there usually is a lot of leeway to improvise. I've rarely done anything where I'm using the lines that were written, except for *Twin Peaks.*

When I got to the set of the first film I did, THE LAST AMERICAN VIRGIN, the director said, "I want you to come to work every day, even if you're not in a scene, and stay by me." He had his script supervisor write down whatever I would say, and that ended up being my lines. I was just talking and responding to whatever was going on. He'd ask me questions about the weather, anything – no matter what I said, he found it funny.

When you're in a dysfunctional family, comedy is your defense. My sister was very quiet, so I was the opposite. I'd do a tap dance or imitations to pick up the slack of her not doing anything. She would be reading or having a serious conversation with our father about science. Then it was my turn to do something, and that's what I did instead. I loved science too, but I certainly would not let them know that. I did not want them to know what I knew.

I recently remembered that I cheated on an I.Q. test. The room was quiet, the fluorescent lights were off, the teacher was doing some work, everyone was at lunch, and I sat down and did the test. I thought it was a joke because it seemed so easy. It sounds odd, but it just happened that I knew all the answers somehow. I stood up and the teacher said, "Are you finished already?" And I heard in my head, *Change some answers*.

I'm not a good liar and I couldn't make anything up, so I just said, "No," and sat back down. I knew I had to change some answers because I'd been watching my sister, who's brilliant, and the pressure that was put on her was otherworldly. I didn't want that, I wanted to be left alone, so I became an "average" student. That's what they called me.

Ever since I was a kid, I'd get excited when it was time for bed. I'd go to bed early and think of something I wanted to do. When I was little, I'd see a whole scene, in a cartoon form. It would slowly go into my heart and that would take over and make the most amazing little cartoon movie that I would watch with this grin on my face and then fall asleep. I'd try not to, but I would fall asleep anyway.

Sometimes it would continue as a dream, sometimes not. Later, in eighth grade, I decided for sure I was going to be a famous ballet dancer. So I would picture myself taking the bows after a perfect performance, and that would start a whole little movie. I didn't put the movie together in my head, I would just decide on a subject. *Okay, I'm going to think about this tonight. I'm going to dream about this tonight.* Then my heart would take over.

I did become a ballet dancer. I was in a modern ballet company. When it closed, everyone went to the American Folk Ballet, but I didn't want to do that. American Folk is about the ethnic dances that immigrants brought here, and how they changed and evolved once they were here for a while. I only wanted traditional ballet and I wasn't ready to give up on that career.

I needed money so I did eventually join American Folk Ballet. Then I went to New York for a vacation and met the band Devo while I was there. When we were all back in L.A., Devo was making two music videos, one for "Whip It" and one for "The Girl You Want," and they asked me if I could help them cast "The Girl You Want." They needed lots of girls with long hair, so I brought all the members of American Folk Ballet.

For "Whip It" they needed some Western sets, so I brought a bunch of stuff from American Folk Ballet: a split rail fence, a barrel, bales of hay, even the whip. After the shoots, the producer, John Thompson, said, "Okay, I officially owe you a favor."

Around this time, Devo went on a long European tour, and I went with them, as a girlfriend. As soon as we got back, American Folk Ballet was gearing up for a tour of their own. I didn't want to go, so I ended up working as a receptionist in their agent's building, which was crawling with agents. This giant phone had a billion buttons and I didn't know how to work it, so I hung up on people a lot. An agent in the next room, Helen Barkin, kept laughing at me. She told me, "You have to be an actor. You're so funny."

I was like, "I don't want to be an actor. I can't stand actors."

She asked me why not, and I told her, "I don't want to wear black nail polish and patchouli oil, and say, 'Allo, Love, 'ow are ya?' all the time, in a Cockney accent."

She didn't know what I was talking about, but that's what all the actors did at my college.

Anyhow, Helen, made me take a picture and she helped me create a resume. Years later I was questioned about what role I played in Sweeney Todd, and I said, "I wasn't in Sweeney Todd." He asked why it was on my resume and I told him I saw it in college, along with all the other plays that were listed on my resume by Helen. Like I said, I'm not a good liar.

So Helen called me into her office one night and had a big stack of manila envelopes on her desk. She asked if I was related to anyone or knew anyone in the movie business. I answered, "No," to all of her questions.

She thought for a moment, and then she asked, "Does anyone in the business owe you a favor?"

I told her about the producer John Thompson. She picked up the envelope on top of the pile and it read, "J. Thompson, c/o Cannon Films." A week later Helen told me I had an appointment at Cannon.

When I got off the elevator, John Thompson was waiting for me. "Kimmy, this is your favor," he said. "You're here to meet a movie director. Everything else, you're on your own, okay? I can't get you a part or anything."

So I talked to this director, Boaz Davidson, for forty-five minutes, and for some reason he was laughing the whole time. Then he said, "You're hired."

"For what?"

"To be in my movie."

The first time I ever acted was the first scene we filmed on his set. I was ready to go and the A.D. said, "When the director calls 'Action,' run out, hit your mark and say your line."

I said, "Okay." He walked away and I thought, *I wonder what a mark is?* But I figured it out, because it was there on the floor.

All of a sudden, I was in a movie, THE LAST AMERICAN VIRGIN. I had taken no acting classes, I didn't know any techniques. I just somehow knew what I was supposed to do and what I was supposed to say. My heart was so happy.

Boaz Davidson always let the camera run, so things would go on a bit. What I learned was, it was pretend. It was just pretend. You pretend like all this stuff is true, and it's really fun, and all this creativity starts happening, this whole other world happens, and there you are, you're in it.

I've since figured out that, at least for me, my imagination for acting is in my heart. I found out why: there's 40,000 brain neurons in your heart, that are not connected to your brain. It's called the "little brain" inside your heart, that is part of an imagination function of our body. That's how you manifest, how you bring things into your life – by imagining with those heart brain cells, and since they're in your heart, you feel it. When you've felt it, the job is done. Whatever you've imagined, like a new yellow dress or becoming a ballet dancer, it comes to you somehow. It always comes. It's actually science – a function of the heart. That's what I was doing going to bed as a child.

When I was acting, I would shut off my brain: *Okay, you're not needed, thank you.* What was going on behind the camera didn't bother me, because my brain was taking a vacation and the little brain in my heart was doing the work.

David Lynch used that part of my brain, a lot. He would be ready to shoot, and he'd say, "Everyone have their lines. Lucy, do you know your lines?"

And I'd go, "What lines?"

He'd smile and say, "Somebody get Lucy a script."

I'd look at the script and know it. Sometimes he'd write long speeches, and I'd just read through it once and know it. That brain came from dancing from a young age – picking up steps. It's called a video optic memory. I was recording the lines temporarily, and I could see them in my head, and I'd just say them. Frankly, I think it's something to do with being a little on the spectrum.

From that first movie, it was all very natural. It felt easy. I was instantly in love. It was the feeling I was looking for that I could never find in ballet, because I wasn't connecting. With acting, I felt a connection to the infinite field and all this imagination started pouring in, and it was a very comfortable feeling. I knew that was what I wanted to do.

It takes all kinds of people to be actors, and as long as you get the job done, it doesn't really matter how you get there. It's just a lot more fun when you use your imagination, because then you don't really have to do anything. The character does it. My exercises below are about waking up your imagination and the heart brain.

The main thing for an actor is to commit. Completely commit. Like the Goethe quote I'm always telling people about, which was elaborated on by the Scottish explorer, W.H. Murray:

"Concerning all acts of initiative (and creation), there is one elementary truth, the ignorance of which kills countless ideas and splendid plans: that the moment one definitely commits oneself, then providence moves too. A whole stream of events issues from the decision, raising in one's favor all manner of unforeseen incidents, meetings and material assistance, which no man could have dreamt would have come his way. I learned a deep respect for one of Goethe's couplets:

"Whatever you can do or dream you can, begin it. Boldness has genius, power and magic in it!"

That's very important. It applies to a role and to your career. Don't be wishy washy.

Just do it. Commit.

PREPARATION

1. Start any imagination work with three deep breaths. It doesn't have to be in through your nose, out the mouth. It doesn't have to have any kind of count. There's no right or wrong way. Just take three deep breaths. The human brain automatically connects to the field, and the field is where all creativity is.

If you do those three deep breaths first and then do imagination exercises, you'll get an endless stream of stuff coming down into your head from the infinite field, or the Akashic record, or whatever you want to call it.

2. An exercise I absolutely recommend is taking a walk with no cell phone. If you have a dog, take your dog, and no phone. Listen to your dog. Look at where your dog is looking, what they're sniffing. Step into the walking mode, where anything is possible. There's sparkles, there's rainbows and dew drops. Those are the things you're supposed to be noticing.

You're slowing down time and making it serve you instead of you serving it. That exercise – walking once around the block, or going somewhere pretty and green – that starts waking up the subconscious and unconscious. I think that's where imagination comes from. I recommend doing this as a first step.

3. If you're a person who has trouble imagining or visualizing, or just wants to wake up more of your imagination, sit down without having any agenda, close your eyes, and listen for twenty minutes. Listen to the birds, listen to the gardener noises, or airplanes going over, or parrots flying by. Just listen. Anytime your brain starts to think, go immediately back to focusing on your ears and listen. This is a huge big deal, this exercise, and most people never do it. They never just listen.

4. Here is a sort of backwards, inside out way of getting the background of a character. You live though a scene and see what comes up.

Sit in a comfortable chair and give yourself twenty minutes – set it on a timer or alarm. Say you're preparing for a scene where you go in to a coffee shop, you're looking for somebody. You know you're going to find them, because it's written in the script. You know you're going to sit down and have a conversation with them, because it's in the script.

During that twenty minutes, make up what the coffee shop looks like, as much as you can in your head.

Then let your heart take the reins, let your imagination take over and take you through the scene. Let the other character say whatever they want – they might talk about stuff that's not written in the script. Let them go on, and let yourself go on with whatever you want to say.

Maybe you finish a sentence that's in the script – allow yourself to go on with the thoughts that come after that sentence, because our brains don't shut off after we say a sentence. We're still thinking stuff. And whatever your character is still thinking, that's the key to who they are.

You can do this once and have your character right there accessible all the time until you're done with whatever you're shooting. Then let it go, completely. For actors, we're using a video optic memory, so it doesn't get put into our psyche.

5. You can do imagination work in bed before you go to sleep. Pick something you want to experience. Imagine sitting in a pile of money, living in a treehouse, working with your favorite actor, being on a TV

series, being in a movie that shoots in Switzerland. That's a good example – picture the flight to Switzerland and all the stuff around that as nicely as you can. Then just let it sink into your chest and let your imagination take over. It does take a little practice, so keep trying it with different topics on different nights. Enjoy yourself.

DIANA ELIZABETH JORDAN

Emotional Personal Touchstones

Diana Elizabeth Jordan is an award-winning actor, director and producer who works in theater, film and television. She has appeared in numerous short films, and TV shows that include *7th Heaven, S.W.A.T.* and *Heartbeats*. She is also in the feature film LA GRIT, directed by Ryan Curtis. Diana earned an MFA in Acting from California State University Long Beach and has over 35 years' experience working as an artist educator and acting coach. She is the founder of the production company Dreaming Big on a Swing Entertainment, and the content creation and consulting company, The Rainbow Butterfly Café. She is a consultant and advocate for equity and inclusion for performers with disabilities in the entertainment industry.

I remember being in an acting class my sophomore year in college. I was working with my scene partner John and noticed he had a masculine-looking wedding ring which he wore on a chain around his neck. When I asked him about it, he shared that it belonged to his dad who had been killed in a car accident the year before, right after John had started college. It was very obvious to me by the way John spoke about the ring that it had a deep and personal meaning to him. It was what I like to call an Emotional Personal Touchstone.

Before I continue to share about Emotional Personal Touchstones, I will introduce myself. I'm an award-winning actor, filmmaker and disability inclusion artivist. I have been in over sixty theater productions, worked in film and television, and produced and created my own solo projects. I was also the first actor with a disability (cerebral palsy which mildly affects my speech and gait) to obtain a Masters of Fine Arts in Acting from California State University Long Beach in 2001. I am a member of SAG-AFTRA and The Actors Equity

Association. I'm also a teaching artist and acting coach. I love teaching and sharing with fellow actors and artists about the craft of acting, and I am happy to share my thoughts on the value of Emotional Personal Touchstones for this book.

I freely admit I don't think I'm sharing anything new. Uta Hagen speaks of the value of personalization techniques in her book *Respect for Acting*, as have countless other acting craft books. I'm just sharing that in my thirty-plus years of working as an actor, and nearly twenty-five years of teaching and coaching, I want to underline the value and need for personalization and creating what I call an Emotional Personal Touchstone. I also want to emphasize that this is just a phrase I use because I don't like the word "trigger." So feel free to replace it with a word or phrase that works for you. It really doesn't matter, but for the purposes of this essay, I will be using "EPT" as an abbreviation for Emotional Personal Touchstone.

We experience many EPTs in our everyday real lives, whether we're thinking about it or not. Whenever I hear the song "September" by Earth Wind & Fire, I'm immediately transported back to my youth. I feel so much joy and I just need to dance. I am sure there are many parents, aunts, uncles, grandparents and godparents who have an art project made for them by a child they love that they have held on to for years because of the sweet memories it brings.

An EPT can be an object (a picture, a piece of clothing, a book) or something non-tangible, like a song. It is anything that elicits a specific memory or feeling. While hearing "September" and countless other songs from my childhood always makes me smile, seeing pictures of my friend D.C., who took his life two years ago, brings with it a mixed bag of emotions because I miss him so much.

My point is that an EPT (whether joyful or painful) elicits a specific memory of a real-life experience. EPTs occur on the regular: that song that comes on the radio, an old toy found in a junk drawer, a picture of a sibling or a first love, but as actors we need to <u>create</u> EPTs. I believe when we do that, we strengthen and deepen the emotional lives of the characters we play.

For example, in 2008, I had the honor of playing Ruth in Cornerstone Theater's World premiere of Julie Marie Myatt's play *Someday*. The play was very personal for me in many ways: Ruth and

I were both single women confronting the reality that our dream to become a mother may not manifest. Unlike me, who grew up in a very loving home, the character of Ruth grew up in the foster care system and aged out without being adopted. In the play, Ruth finds an abandoned baby whom she wants to adopt so she can keep the baby out of "the system." It was important for me to create a rich and emotional backstory that embodied Ruth's painful history of feeling rejected and unloved, giving her a strong reason to want to adopt the baby she had found. I also wanted to give Ruth a powerful EPT.

So I decided that Ruth met her birthmother only once when she was twelve and her mother gave her a gold locket. I imagined every detail of the meeting, including Ruth receiving the locket. (For clarification, although I am referring to Ruth in the third person, when I do my personal work, I always do it from a first-person point of view.)

The locket became an EPT for me. I endowed the locket with so much value and found moments to touch it throughout the play. I do believe having the locket as an EPT supported my emotional embodiment of Ruth.

Our real-life EPTs are very individual and personal (the song "September" may do nothing for someone else) and so are the ones we create for our characters. I also believe EPTs are best when they come from our imaginations rather something from our own personal histories, especially when it comes to tangible, touchable objects. I have many pieces of jewelry that have special memories for me, but I don't use them for my characters. When I shared my locket idea with the costume designer, she was kind enough to find me the locket I used in the play.

It's not necessary, however, to share your EPT ideas with anyone. They're meant to be very personal and private and support you as you develop and live your character's backstory and history.

When I was cast in the film EDGE OF ISOLATION (written, directed, produced by Jeff Houkal), as Ella, a woman who lost her child when he was a little boy, I created a little memory box in which I placed a baby jacket and a pacifier. I had the memory box on set with me and would look at it and think about the "son" I lost before I would go on set to film. Again, I found this technique very beneficial for my preparation.

I love acting and in my thirty plus years of working and pursuing it professionally, I've read numerous books and taken lots of classes with a variety of teachers. Some teachers and coaches taught me tools that have changed and impacted the way I approach and create with my craft. Other techniques and tools didn't click with me, but I still learned a valuable lesson. I think it is just as important to learn what doesn't work for you in developing your characters as what does.

One of the techniques or tools that has always worked for me is gifting my character with an EPT.

PREPARATION

I like to create a new EPT for each new role and don't like to repurpose an object. In other words, I have never used the memory box I created for EDGE OF ISOLATION as something else for another project. This is just my personal preference but I do recommend it.

I do *not* recommend, nor have I ever spent a lot of money on an EPT. Thrift and dollar stores are a wonderful go-to resource for EPTs.

Additionally, while I think having a fully-developed backstory with your character memories is important, I don't believe an actor needs tons of EPTs. For example, I don't think you need a different EPT for every scene your character is in. Rather, I recommend selecting one EPT as a type of emotional through-line during the film or play, especially if the writer hasn't provided one.

Again, I want to emphasis the importance of EPTs being very personal. I rarely share what my EPTs are, except as in the case of the play, when I felt obligated to share my EPT with our costume designer because the locket would have been considered a part of the costume design. In the case of EDGE OF ISOLATION, I never really shared anything about my memory box or why I had it with me.

I hope you will find this technique supports your work as much as it has mine. I wish you much success and happiness as you continue your artistic journey.

LEIGH MCCLOSKEY

The Art of Getting Out of Your Own Way

Leigh McCloskey is an actor, artist, author, and philosopher. He was classically trained at Juilliard and began his professional acting career in the miniseries *Rich Man, Poor Man,* starring Nick Nolte and Peter Strauss. He went on to lead roles in three nighttime television series: *Executive Suite, Married: The First Year* and as Lucy Ewing's husband Mitch Cooper on the original *Dallas*. Leigh guest starred on many series, played villains on four sci-fi series, appeared in a number of daytime soap operas including *General Hospital,* and starred in numerous made-for-television movies and miniseries. He also appeared in movies such as JUST ONE OF THE GUYS, and in the cult classic INFERNO, directed by Dario Argento.

As a painter, McCloskey has produced a number of works focused on occult and esoteric themes, including his own Tarot deck ("Tarot ReVisioned") and a mixed-media art installation on the walls of his home library called "The Hieroglyph of the Human Soul" or THOTHS Library. His artwork toured with the Rolling Stones (A Bigger Bang Tour-05-7) and his *Codex Tor* illuminated books formed the album art work for "Cosmogramma" by Flying Lotus.

    Any actor knows: I am only as good as I am in relation to another. We depend on one another's generosity to perform well, which is why we do not appreciate the actor who is not generous. It's a bit strange when you run into that, because the nature of creative beings is to be collaborative. For the most part, any competitiveness is not with one another, unless it's a psychological problem. Rather, it's about the "fight" to bring out one another's excellence. We pull it out of each other.

That's what I loved about certain actors I've worked with – they were so dynamic that, to fly with them, in a sense, you had to be willing to soar. You had to let go. And in doing so, you realized you weren't controlling anything, you were simply allowing the energy of rapport, of relationship, to become a type of shared quantum field that amplified both of you. A very different experience from someone being "in charge" or controlling the outcome of the scene.

Acting is why I've been able to do the artwork I've done. Acting teaches you to get out of the way of the energy that is coming through you. To be both yourself, and also willingly to become 'possessed' by the psychological dynamics of someone else, who can be the complete opposite of your own character.

That's why actors were not buried in holy ground. They were considered possessed. They were willing to let others speak through them, let the devil speak through them, and that's a type of giving up one's soul. At least it can look like that from the outside.

I would argue that was a myopic view, to think of the soul as so limited. I view it as the soul is expressing itself through an actor and can make them fit to play any role, no matter how challenging, by providing whatever energies the actor needs to become that character, temporarily.

We can channel energy to shift from one identity to another, without ever losing our own humanity and individuality. That's what I've experienced. I've played murderers and felt their energy, and at the same time, I realized I wasn't going to become them, I was not going to lose myself. I could open up to devil-like energies and express them in a theatrical way.

On *General Hospital,* I had a great opportunity in playing a character named Damien Smith, because I was able to play my opposite. As I went into his mind, I realized that he would look at everything I personally value as weak and silly and unprofitable. He actually helped me learn the difference between being "nice" and being "good." I also became aware of how if you're nice or good, you have a tendency to distrust and not understand power.

So there was this conversation literally playing out inside myself, and I could see the reflection of this other being. I was able to understand him, even though he was opposite of me.

To me, life is a study of how do we overcome our inhibitions to life. Not just getting drunk to drop your inhibitions, because there's going to be a negative chaotic result, but I do think the desire to overcome those inhibitions – inner limitations – comes from the same place of a desire for a feeling of inner freedom and creative flow.

I think the root and nature of theatre itself was to express the reality that when creative energies don't have a healthy outlet, they get backed up and can become negative and destructive. That can lead to what we call dark or criminal acts, because the great energies of creation are so powerful that if they don't find expression, they can become devouring and destructive.

So I want to break down all of these right angles in my psyche, I want to stop having these edges in my mind. How do I find flow? How do I let my energy out?

All of this has led me to the realization that a key to the healthy psyche is, to a great degree, what the actor knows inherently, which is that although we live in one psychic territory that we think of as ourselves, all human beings are based upon assumptions like, I am this and I am not that.

The actor finds the key to other terrain. *What am I? What are my assumptions about myself, and about the character? How do I know what I am? What is it that I am not?*

We're talking about the creative questioning process and not the repetitive thought processes of the psyche. By repetitive thought processes, I mean instinctively trying to deny or get away from something you don't like about yourself, or focusing on what you do like about yourself, or what you think you ought to be or do – basically living by an unconscious self-definition, like, *I'm this and not that. Therefore, I cannot do that.*

We can engage in a creative thought process that starts with questioning automatic repetitive thoughts and beliefs. In addition, that repetitive process is a lens through which to view a character: what does the character unconsciously believe about themselves and what is possible for their life?

For example, that dark character I talked about has an armored psyche, where they are in fury about what they believe to be true, and what is owed to them. And that blinds them to any other point of view.

So in the process of being an actor, we find a way to deeply understand people, not just from the outside – people's actions, but through the inside – people's beliefs and motivations.

The more empathic and sympathetic the actor feels toward the character they're playing, regardless of its so-called darkness, the better the actor, I think. If you give yourself to a dark character, oftentimes you're able to experience more of your own humanity – through hurt, through pain, through sorrow, through separation.

I feel that, even in the educational system, the more we could teach role-playing, the more we would allow people to step out of the limiting assumptions they have about themselves, the more individuals would be able to understand and manage their own impulses, and have more empathy, both for themselves and for others. When we stretch our view of ourselves, we start to see that what we think and believe about ourselves may not be who we inherently are. From there we expand our very psyches.

Let's say you're playing a king. You're not a king in real life, but you can experience "kingly-ness." You can feel a sense of power, a sense of place, a sense of responsibility – with your imagination, how you carry yourself, physical behaviors and actions.

What that does, I realized, is expand your psyche as well. Because that experience of 'playing' a king, of 'being' a king temporarily, makes it so that your psyche becomes more open to greater possibilities, like what a king may take for granted. These are greater expressions that most people don't explore, because they're told not to – so greater possibilities are not what they assume for themselves.

When young people, especially creative people, start to understand and listen to the world around them, the danger of blocking up their creative energy arises as they start feeling apprehensive, not connected to themselves, inhibited, not spontaneous – but that's not the real problem.

It's the innate challenge of being human. Being human is difficult. There is a heroic nature to the difficult journey of being human. I know that's not what we're taught. We're taught some people have it easy and other people don't. Guess what, nobody has it easy. It's hard to be human.

Part of the reason it's so hard is feeling repressed by what is demanded of us at different ages. We feel bound by others' expectations, even if we don't realize it.

I have all sorts of regard for psychology in certain things, in certain ways. To me, psychology in the therapeutic sense would ideally be to help an individual explore their own psyche and how to live up to their own creative energies, rather than to figure out "what's wrong" and how to become more "normal."

There are those who give up. They think, *My ideas are nothing, it doesn't matter, society is unfair, the world is crap,* and that becomes a justification for not honoring and exploring their own psyche and their own creativity, and that can become destructive to that individual.

There are others who understand that no matter how dark the morass of your inner journey, through all the difficulty, you are learning what your capacity actually is. If you think of someone being thrown into a rushing river to learn how to swim, that's the nature of being a human with a psyche. There are those who will drown, and there are those who become damn good swimmers.

If I have to say anything about my life, it's that I might have drowned, but I think I've become a damn good swimmer. I somehow figured out that I needed to find the tools that would allow me to synthesize and assimilate the different parts of myself.

It was also acting that taught me to trust a type of inward mentoring. The process of inwardly considering, *Maybe I'll try this.*

And I realized that's basically the job of the performer. Nobody stands there and tells you what to believe or what you need to study. They look at you and think, *Are you embodied? Do I believe you? What is your role in this scenario?*

So that inner voice, the inner mentor as I call it, I came to recognize as my creative spirit. I believe that as human beings, we are the art form. Not what we do. What we do is the outcome of that art form that is a human being. We are each essentially living as a unique art form.

What I realized on my own journey, is that the art form I've been living is a type of natural creative and imaginative interaction with the environment. All of the years, going from nightmares to lucid dreaming, from my work as an actor to work on the tarot to painting murals on my walls, to creating a series of illuminated books – all of these different works, all these different directions – they're like spokes of a wheel that ended up creating a type of psychic resilience: the actor in me. The one who acts.

PREPARATION

For the most part, you're alone, even when you're acting. Many great directors sort of leave you alone, so you're in a place of, *How do I find the truth of this character? How do I find the feeling nature, the feeling tone of this character?*

As with any creative challenge, we always learn something useful when we embrace big questions like that.

Try starting with your body. See if you can experience the energy of the character – *how does it feel in my body? How does it awaken in the body?* I would get paint on my hands and see what the character does with that.

I think an actor must become syn-aesthetic, meaning able to taste the color of sound, to smell intentionality. In other words, to not be so divided within our own psyches, rather to understand that an exploration of energy allows us to experiment.

Question your assumptions and give yourself a lot of permission to explore and play, and make so-called "mistakes." Your own willingness to <u>not</u> make assumptions – especially about the character – can alleviate a lot of resistance.

One way to side-step your own resistance is by thinking of it as a wave of energy. This is like a martial art; I call it the Aikido of Consciousness. It's a practice of, *I don't have to identify with everything that comes to my mind, I can let the energy flow in and ebb out like a wave.*

This can help you side-step a self-critique, rather than letting it slap you right in the face.

When you hit a place of resistance and, for whatever reason, you can't just let it flow away because you're feeling nervous, unsure, uncomfortable, *I don't want to* – stop, take a breath, and say to yourself, out loud, if possible, "I give you permission to explore these territories."

See, the scared part of your psyche thinks somebody's going to show up and say, "You're right," or, "You're wrong."

That won't happen, it's just that you need to give yourself more permission to do the work without judging it.

Yes, there's goals. You want to deeply understand and embody the character, and learn the lines. At the same time, you want to explore all that without worrying about the outcome. So let go of the idea that there is one "right" way to get where you want to go.

"Most of the characters I'd played were so different from me, so far from me, that I had to transform."

– LANCE REDDICK

DEVORAH CUTLER

Dueling Animal Opposites... Creating the Electric Moment on Stage or Screen

Devorah (aka Devo) Cutler has dedicated her life to creating art and helping artists negotiate their dreams. Having worked with Stella Adler, gained insight as a writer/producer/director, improv performer and former studio executive, Devo helps actors launch their careers, and coaches at Acting International in Paris. She has a Masters in writing from USC and teaches in their summer program. Her short film for Showtime Entertainment, *Peacock Blues*, won First Place at MIFF. Her documentary *Not Afraid to Laugh*, about using humor to heal herself of breast cancer, was nominated for a Peabody and is archived in the Museum of Broadcasting for "Social Relevance and Historical Significance."

Devo co-authored *Dating Your Character... A Sexy Guide to Screenwriting,* and was a contributor to both *Now Write! Screenwriting* and *Now Write! Science Fiction, Fantasy, and Horror.* Her poems, short stories, cartoons and nonfiction have been featured in many publications. Devo is happily living in Ojai, CA helping out with its mission as "City of Peace."

There is nothing better on stage than an electric performance. This kind of memorable occurrence could seem to be a fluke; even an actor might not trace the dynamics that led to the audience getting so quiet you can hear a pin drop, or conversely, the audience so riled up that they spontaneously jump to their feet, cheer, stomp, or clap from sheer exhilaration.

DUELING ANIMAL OPPOSITES... CREATING THE ELECTRIC MOMENT ON STAGE OR SCREEN

From a lifetime of theatrical observation, I can confirm, that this "electric moment" is usually NOT a fluke, but a destination an actor arrives at through their preparation preceding the performance. There are many ways to accomplish this, and what I am about to share is one tried and true approach.

Whatever side of the page, stage, or camera you find yourself on, knowing how to trigger glorious, luminescent acting is what we all strive for. During the process of building a scene with a scene partner – or working solo preparing a monologue – actors can lose the initial spark they found during the audition. Also, that root connection to a role can be forsaken during the prep and rehearsal process. A final performance can lose its initial "dynamic life," and a role can become predictable, stale and void of its original juice that was there at the beginning of rehearsals.

While it is important to honor the intention of the playwright and the theme of the play, an actor has to transcend the obvious and the mundane – isn't that what we came to the show for? To get hired over and over again, an actor cannot just merely hit their marks... they must be the bearers of a transformative experience for any movie or theatre-goer.

It is an actor's duty to avoid sleepwalking through their part in a director's vision. Take note as even well-meaning directors (or writers) working with actors can contribute to this disconnection, if care is not taken to keep the actor's authentic connection to a role alive.

As a director, coach, and actor, I myself have marveled at how one exercise in particular has helped me consistently generate electric performances.

Keep in mind, the audience often does not know what the actor is working on to bring about a memorable performance. Audience members are the recipients of the journey; they look on, mystified by the discoveries and choices that an actor makes, choices that often precede a performance, or evolve on the spot during a live performance, or filming.

As a director, I have introduced this exercise all over the world, from Edinburgh to Paris to Auckland. It works in private coaching sessions with a solo actor, helps in dramatic acting classes, and often illuminates choices for an actor within comedy formats, even in "act-outs" during a stand-up routine.

This acting exercise can be utilized as well during rehearsals for plays and films – always with benefits. During the exploration and repetition of using the chosen animal opposites, an actor finds depth, actor's business, and stage movement that all serve a more resonant and connective presentation of a role.

Keep in mind, as with any new technique, some actors may be resistant initially, but if they jump into this "game" they will be energized! They will reap the reactions from their fellow players on stage and hear the applause, even during performance, for their bold choices found through this exercise.

Another result is that actors often experience more energy and focus; a character's core values can surface and, aside from the obvious development of the physicality of a character, as mentioned already, there seems to be an enhanced connectivity to self, one's partners and the audience. Whether the approach is solo, group work, or as a performance appearance, even spoken word, the work becomes more relatable and dimensional.

Working solo, an actor can also take cues from this exploration; for instance, I recall working with one actor whose homework was to go home and experiment with different animals. He came back the next day and told me, "I feel that my character might growl his complaint to his wife…"

So, I asked him, "What kind of a growl? Is it more like a lion, a domesticated dog, or a wild chimpanzee?"

When it came time to perform the monologue from the scene for the class, the audience leapt up and cheered when he crawled across the couch, very much like a possessive gorilla, and growled for his dinner. It was perhaps the most memorable and surprising moment in the scene. The actor surprised himself and the audience followed suit. In the end, the exercise cracked open the character's need to take ownership of his turf, as he was losing it to his wife. (The scene was from the movie *American Beauty*, where the husband character was feeling powerless.)

I once worked with an actor whose voice was very soft. It was a stage play, and it would have been difficult for her dialogue to be heard by the audience, especially in the back row of the mid-sized theater.

I had her laugh, prance, and chortle like a hyena through the entire scene. I had her do the dishes and pretend to fold the laundry like a hyena. I suggested she look for other places or actions she could experiment with as this unusual, high-spirited, and loud animal.

Then she was asked to do the scene again – this time as her human character; however, she needed to allow herself to spontaneously incorporate some of the movements, sounds and hyena's laugh we had found during the exercise. This helped her immensely in overcoming her vocal shyness. It also helped her to open up vocally and embrace her physicality. She was able to discover (authentically "find") some moments for her hyena voice that resulted in a compelling, louder, voice for her character.

Until we opened it up for her to inhabit the animal, she was stuck in an idea of what was "right and wrong" for her character. Now she said, "I feel as if I'm truly living my character. Before I was not 'living' it."

PREPARATION

Whether working solo, with a fellow player, or in a group rehearsal setting, the process is almost the same. If you do not have the luxury of a class setting, you can experiment with several different animals, and also imagine the animal's closest opposite. For instance, would an opposite to a parrot be a cobra? A speedy, delicate hummingbird might be the opposite of a slow-moving sloth.

I suggest you, as the actor, or coach or director, choose an animal that surprises – but also one that most seems to have the rhythms of the character.

Working with a Group in a Class Setting

Most of the time, as a director, teacher, or actor, you will be working in a group setting. As such, if you are leading the exercise, have the actors who are doing the scene stand in front of the group.

Have people from the class call out loud the names of animals that an actor standing in front of them reminds them of, for instance: cat, dog, pig, giraffe, snake, shark, lion, monkey – these are a few that often come up.

Have the actor select one of the choices that feels most like themselves, not necessarily appropriate for the scene, but that can help if the dynamics reveal certain animal characteristics to the actors, or other players present.

Do this for each actor involved in a scene.

Have the actors perform the scene as they normally would.

Then back up to the beginning of the scene. Have each actor redo the scene with only the noises and movements of their chosen animal. So, if it's a lion, they can growl, toss their mane, stalk, lick their paws, languish on the couch – like a lion on the Savannah.

Obviously, the actions of a monkey would be different from those of a lion. How would a monkey get what they want versus a tiger… or a snake versus a blue jay?

After they have marked the scene as the animals… have the actors discuss what they learned or gained from their animal choice and interpretation of the scene. Remind them of the difference between a visceral experience and a mental one, and ask what are the take-aways. For example, are there any animal moments they could bring to the scene as a person?

If yes, make note of those.

If working in a buddy system, one scene partner can take notes and keep a diary of the work. We all need reminders from the trenches of our journey.

The note-taker can ask their partner about specifics that seemed to come alive. After a brief dissection (no more than a few minutes, to keep it fresh), have the actors run the scene again, including any details that felt good from the animal version.

Again, this may only be felt on an almost pre-conscious cellular or physical level. However they experience it, the actors will now have a

DUELING ANIMAL OPPOSITES... CREATING THE ELECTRIC MOMENT ON STAGE OR SCREEN

potentially deeper connection to the desires of their characters, and how those desires could be played out in any scene.

Working With a Scene Partner or Coach

In tandem with a coach or a fellow actor, the work is the same, and perhaps even more challenging. With a coach, you might ask for a suggestion for an animal or two. The coach would watch you do perhaps the first part of your monologue or scene as that animal, sans words, only voicing as if the animal were speaking. This will undoubtedly feel awkward, as you are not making any logical sense with the sounds. But your mind as an actor is tracking the animalistic gibberish, the animal rhythms and kinetic movements that the "animal" is making as if they were the character.

In redoing the scene, now with the words from the monologue or scene, the body and vocal memory of just having been an animal shakes loose the imposed ideas you may have had, and then opens up your imagination to bring in new choices; in essence, the exercise has enlivened the scene with details from the animal opposite exercise.

With a scene partner you would take turns being the coach... but perhaps play out the animals in the scene, only bringing words after the animals have fully landed on the stage to make the scene electric.

Upping the Stakes

Discuss with the class, coach, or scene partner how each animal fighting for survival can be viewed as a mask – acting as an animal dueling with another animal to get what they want can be a rich source of subtext for a character's inner emotional struggle.

If one animal does not seem to resonate with an actor, have them start again. If a cat doesn't work, suggest an alligator or a lion. Each choice brings a different flavor. You may choose to emphasize that there is no right or wrong, and the actor can usually tell when the behavior of an animal is opening up the world of the play and impacting the bottom line of a successful performance. The possibilities for fun, the surprise and renewed energy are endless.

Now Reader, your turn: what would you choose to be as an animal opposite for Romeo, or Juliet? Would you bark, howl, slither, or coo like a dove? Find an animal "spiritual skin" that fits, and open your mind to expand your imagination!

"An actor is never so great as when he reminds you of an animal – falling like a cat, lying like a dog, moving like a fox."

- FRANÇOIS TRUFFAUT

Chapter 7.

Learn Your Lines

"I hate seeing in my eyes, or the other actor's: 'I think he's searching for his next line'.*"*

- HUGH GRANT

SARAH RUSH

Memorization and Stage Direction

Sarah is best known for originating the role of Flight Corporal Rigel in the BATTLESTAR GALACTICA movie and TV series, and appearing as the secretary in the movie CATCH ME IF YOU CAN. She has appeared in many other TV series, from *Happy Days* to *Tales from the Darkside* to *Friends* and *Monk*. She has also performed in numerous plays and commercials. Sarah both narrated and starred in the 2005 documentary, THE BITUMINOUS COAL QUEENS OF PENNSYLVANIA, produced by Patricia Heaton and directed by David Hunt, which won the 2006 Heartland Film Festival Award. Rush was herself crowned Coal Queen in 1972.

I want to share a few thoughts about working on a script, whether it's a play or a film. I was cast in a filmed pilot for TV, and the actors were told to memorize the script before the first table read. I followed the instruction and was completely off book at the first rehearsal. It was surprising to me that the other, more seasoned, actors had not memorized their lines and were still reading from the script.

Nevertheless, knowing my lines completely freed me during the shooting of the film. Because the lines were already ingrained in my memory, I had the freedom to find fun and spontaneous moments in the acting.

I learned from that experience to always memorize my lines thoroughly, so that I can relax and be in the moment of the scene, not worrying about the text. By now I do learn lines quickly, and I don't think it's because of a quick mind. It's just because I learned that habit.

I know a young movie star who works very differently. He's very successful and a wonderful actor, and he barely learns his lines. He likes to "find them" on set. I could never do that in a million years because I'd feel too unprepared, and that would be terrifying to me. But his approach works for him.

One of the most challenging roles I've ever played is Emily in *The Belle of Amherst*, which is a one-woman show about the life of the poet Emily Dickinson. It's literally two hours of Emily talking to the audience, reciting her poems, and in scenes with other characters who aren't present on stage. Memorizing that script, and actually playing Emily every night, was really difficult. I still can't believe I did it.

I had a day job as a personal assistant when I was preparing for the role, and kept my script in my overall blue jeans so that I could work on it at every possible moment.

This reminded me of one of my university professors who was a brilliant and well-known actress, and also a mother. She shared with us that life can be filled with tasks and responsibilities, and finding time to study and work on our craft isn't always easy, like me studying my play surreptitiously, hiding it in my overalls!

I also recorded myself reading the script, so that I could listen to the text over and over until it marinated within me. That helped me memorize the huge text.

One of my favorite books about acting is *Julie Harris Talks to Young Actors*. Julie Harris originated the role of Emily in *The Belle of Amherst* which is why I was so inspired to do the play. Ms. Harris advises actors to always memorize new pieces of literature, poetry, and Shakespearean sonnets and monologues.

As a young actor in college, I memorized at least a dozen age-appropriate and distinctly different monologues. I had the opportunity to audition for Eleanor Kilgallen to become a Universal Contract Player a few months after graduation. After one monologue, I asked if she would like to see another, and proceeded to do several. She placed me under contract.

I've worked as an actor for many years in theatre, TV, and films, and many commercials.

Capturing a character or a moment in a thirty-second or one-minute spot is also a challenge, and can be a lot of fun. Even for a commercial, I will go over the script multiple, multiple times.

However, everything can change quickly, and they don't always let you know until you arrive on set. I recommend calling the night before a shoot and asking if there are any script changes, but you still have to be ready for anything once you get to set.

I remember working on a commercial for eleven hours with one half-hour lunch break. They text was changed considerably during each and every take. It was so helpful that I had learned to memorize quickly, and to work moment to moment.

Another time I arrived for a commercial at six am and the Assistant Director handed me a new script. I took one look and oh my goodness, it was a huge monologue – brand new.

I was in my dressing room in a fetal position trying to memorize it. I called one of my great gal friends who works a lot as an actress, and she helped me calm down. Of course, they always say, "Don't worry, it doesn't have to be perfect."

But when you start shooting, it really does. I mean, knowing your lines is a big part of the job.

Stage Direction

When working on a play, don't be too faithful to the stage direction notes that are included in parentheses throughout the script. One of my teachers at the HB Studio was the wonderful actor, Austin Pendleton. Austin had originated the role of Jonathan Rosepettle in the 1962 off-Broadway production of *Oh Dad, Poor Dad, Mama's Hung You in the Closet and I'm Feelin' So Sad* by Arthur Kopit. Austin's character begins to cry at one point in a scene, and since he originated the role, "crying" was written into the script's stage directions.

Later, when Austin reprised the role, he found himself stumped, because he was having trouble crying at the moment the stage directions told him to. And that had been Austin himself!

He decided to forget the stage directions, and found that he actually began crying a few beats later, when the emotion began to move in on him.

Another acting note is to not despair when something goes awry on stage or even when you're shooting a film piece. So often, experiences bring moments that we can use as actors that serve a scene beautifully.

I remember Uta Hagen talking about doing *The Country Girl* on Broadway. In a rehearsal where she's having an argument with her alcoholic husband, she grabs her coat from the coat rack and threatens to walk out. The stage manager had inadvertently left one of the sleeves inside out, so when Uta tried to put on the coat, she had to struggle with the sleeve.

I'm certain that the stage manager must have been horrified, as Uta was a strong presence who could intimidate anyone. Instead, Uta insisted that the coat sleeve be inside out for every performance, as it fed her and enhanced the action of the scene.

PREPARATION

Memorize something new at least once a month if not once a week, especially if it's a down time. This will help you build the habit, and stay in the habit of memorization, and it will get easier over time. As Julie Harris says, it keeps our minds agile, and is good practice for memorizing lines as we age.

For inspiration, read her book, *Julie Harris Talks to Young Actors.*

For a very long role or one-person script, try recording yourself reading the whole script and listen to it as often as you can to marinate in the lines.

When working on a play, ignore the stage directions and see what emotion and physical activity moves in on you in the moment. You may even find a happy accident, like Uta Hagen's inside-out sleeve.

CRYSTAL CARSON

Learning Lines by Heart

Crystal devotes herself to deepening the authenticity of actors. She is highly recommended by major managers, agents, directors, producers, casting directors, and professional actors, including Oscar-nominee Russell Crowe.

As an elite acting coach in Los Angeles for over 30 years, Crystal is especially skillful at accommodating an individual's methods and personality. She has traveled the world teaching her advanced yet accessible process to generate a character's life, known as the Carson Method, which emphasizes creating personalized histories that allow an actor to easily come from truth. She offers retreats for actors who are differently abled and works with the Professional Actors Theatre of The Handicapped, sponsored by CBS-TV.

A former actor herself, Crystal studied with Uta Hagen, Sanford Meisner, Howard Fine and Eric Morris. She performed in over 25 plays and had a career in film and television, including a five-year run as Julia Barrett on *General Hospital*. After studying human psychology, she developed The Carson Method to humanize the technical aspects of the actors' auditioning process. Crystal's companion piece, "No Schm-acting Please!", is in Chapter 9.

Rather than memorizing your lines, learn them by heart. The difference being, if you memorize them, you're only using your head. You may play all kinds of tricks to remember the words, but that is only engaging the mind.

Our egos hate for us to make a mistake, so when we're practicing lines on our own, we tend to quickly bail out and check the script.

My advice is: don't do that.

Even if you know you're wrong on the line, do your very best to just speak. Say something. *If I were in this situation, what would I say?* Even if you know what you're saying is not in the script at all, say something – out loud.

I know if you say the wrong thing out loud, your ego hates that even more. If you look down and check what the writer wrote, you may get mad at yourself if you said the wrong thing.

In my other essay for this book about reading and preparing a scene for an audition, I use this line as an example: "Let's wait, he'll be here soon."

If you couldn't remember that line, and instead you said, out loud, "I thought he'd be here," you were imagining and feeling the situation from your character's point of view, and that generated the words, "I thought he'd be here."

It came from a way of thinking about the scene and the character before, "I thought he'd be here," came out of your mouth. It's not the correct line, but it's not all that far off.

Now you can consider the context that the actual line implies – that it isn't just about what your character expected, it's about telling the other guy in the scene something, perhaps to calm him down, and making a suggestion that we wait.

If I had read the scene and imagined this person might kill me if the other guy doesn't show up (as explored in my other essay), I may have generated the words, "Don't kill me, he'll be here."

You didn't remember the line, but you did put yourself inside the story and you read the other character's lines out loud, as if you were listening to them.

Then you said aloud what this moment made you think or sense or feel. In doing so, you discovered where your thoughts went, and when you uncover the actual line, instead of focusing on what words were right or wrong, you discover what your character's thoughts were that generated the words you spoke. What an insight!

Okay, now I know how the character is feeling, I just haven't learned what words they're saying. My imagination generated an idea of making a panicked excuse in my own defense for the sake of self-preservation and, I say, "I thought he'd be here," as opposed to a rather calmer idea of: *I expected he wouldn't be here, but I'll lie and gain some time until I can figure out how to save myself*, which makes me say, "Let's wait, he'll be here soon."

Instead of focusing on the <u>product</u> of the thinking, which is the line, I'm focusing on the thinking <u>process</u> that produced that particular line.

Working this way gives me a real sense of how my character is thinking and feeling and reacting to the other person, in a much shorter time than if I had simply tried to memorize the lines.

Why? Because when I memorize a line, I also accidentally memorize how I said that line, without much clarity about what's causing me to say those words. This can lead to misconceptions about the character and how they think, feel, and what they want. Once I've memorized my lines, I may just fall back on saying what I know the lines are, without ever discovering what the character was thinking.

If you simply memorize saying the lines, you'll be speaking them without deeply thinking about the context of the scene. You're not exploring them as your character. You're just saying lines and trying to sound natural.

By focusing instead on the thought process that produced that line, I'm naturally getting more curious about the character's backstory and can invent more of that for myself. This happens automatically, simply because you put yourself in the situation.

You start by just considering what the other character says, and responding with something, anything, that you feel in the moment. You let yourself be the writer in a way, and generate a line. It probably isn't the right line, but it will be in the same universe, and the difference between what you said, and what was on the page, can give you a lot of insight into how you think about the character, what they are thinking, what they want in the situation, and the stakes. With that, you can make conscious decisions and adjustments.

So if you don't know the lines yet, don't memorize them. Approach them instead from inside of your understanding of the situation, the people in the scene, the history that got you here, and what you want. If that's not all provided in the scene or the script, make it up. Then when you get the line right, you will know you're on the right path to becoming the character, because you are <u>thinking like the character</u>. You'll understand their concerns, considerations, and values in each moment. And you're going to be more human.

At an audition, they don't expect you to have the scene perfectly memorized and they're not going to care that much if you get a line wrong. They just want to see that you can create a character who is listening, thinking, and responding truthfully. I often hear, "We're not hiring somebody who says the line perfectly. We're looking for the character."

But this isn't just about auditioning. You can use the same approach to learning lines for a play, a TV show, a movie, even a commercial. It'll move you into the character so much faster than just memorizing the lines.

At first, it's hard to make yourself <u>not</u> memorize the line, and it's so hard to make yourself say something out loud, when you know you've got it wrong.

But once you do this for a while, you'll be like, *Oh my gosh, I know the lines!* You will have read it five times and not only do you know the lines by heart, you have a grounded-ness in your listening, and in the character you're being, because <u>you've generated the thoughts that create those lines.</u>

You'll be amazed – you can move so much faster.

If you already have the part, you have more leeway, but if you have an audition, it might be tomorrow and this is your best option for getting prepared. If you just memorize lines, chances are you're going to say them the way you <u>think</u> the character would say them, instead of <u>being</u> the character.

When you explore the lines in this more engaged way, even if you get some of them wrong, it's going to come across way better than just reciting memorized lines.

PREPARATION

As recommended in "No Shm-acting Please," first read the scene or the script as an audience. You just want to understand the story and what is going on.

If it's only a scene, and you have no idea what's going on, engage your imagination to come up with some logical explanation for this scene, and how this situation came about.

Now read the other characters' lines out loud. It will be easier to generate lines as your character if you've read and "been" the other character/s first.

Cover your line, read their line out loud, and then say something in response to what they just said. You don't know the line yet, so all you can do is listen to what the other person said and think of how to respond. Say something out loud.

You generated an idea, and you said it, and it was probably wrong (and the sky didn't fall.)

What happened was, you were thinking about the situation or what the other person said and something came out. Now, look at the actual line. In an instant you will have a better idea of what your character is thinking.

The thing you're going to fix automatically, without even having to worry about it, is memorizing the words wrong. As you explore the lines this way, you're going to correct the words easily, because they're going to take on genuine meaning for you, naturally and organically.

I encourage you to incorporate, "No Shm-acting Please" with "Learn Your Lines by Heart" – they work together!

CINDY MARINANGEL

Eleven Memorizing Tricks and Tips

Cindy Marinangel is a lifetime member of The Actors Studio. She appeared in BEVERLY HILLS CHRISTMAS and has performed lead roles on stage since kindergarten, when she played her first queen. Cindy originated many new roles to rave reviews, including Misti in *Fractured* at New Circle Theatre's NYC workshop production. Cindy acquired the rights to the solo show *Dietrich* which she mounted in New York City and continues to perform in Los Angeles. She also sings as Marlene Dietrich in a cabaret show.

Cindy narrated Beyonce's E! Entertainment special, and voiced two characters in BRUTAL LEGENDS, the popular video game featuring Jack Black and Ozzy Osbourne. With an international creative team (including Laurie Lamson), her company Angel Baker Productions produced the multi-award-winning metaphysical romance short film *Eternal Waltz* for which Cindy also played the lead role. She is a competitive ballroom dancer with a passion for Latin dancing.

First of all, congrats on either booking an audition, a role to memorize, or picking up a piece to work on in class or for personal growth. It's exciting, yet daunting at the same time, but once you have the lines in your head you will be able to fly, on set or on stage.

Each actor has their own process and way of working. Some are of the school of thought that you have to be completely "off book" in order to begin to delve into the character. I personally don't work that way. I prefer to use rehearsals to explore and actually save some of the memorizing for after I deeply understand what is going on with the character in a particular moment. Respect your path within your craft

ELEVEN MEMORIZING TRICKS AND TIPS

as an actor, but also be willing to adjust if you find yourself with a director or production team who feel otherwise about a particular scene or line of dialogue.

A little about me: I played my first leading role in kindergarten – a queen. My mother rehearsed me so well that I knew everyone else's lines and mouthed them as the other actors spoke. (Why didn't the director stop me?)

At that time, simple repetition worked. My mother went over the lines with me constantly whenever we had a few spare minutes.

Most recently, I have been starring in a 70-minute, one-woman play, written by Willard Manus, about the legendary actress Marlene Dietrich, called simply *Dietrich*.

Set in May, 1960, the play takes place when the actress returned to the Berlin stage for the first time since fleeing the Hitler regime in the 1930s. Inside her dressing room at the Tatiana Palast Theater, Dietrich weighs whether to go through with the live performance despite threats on her life by Nazi sympathizers who resented her for having spent much of World War II entertaining American soldiers on the front lines. To them, Dietrich is a turncoat, a traitor who deserves to be shot and killed on stage.

After each of these performances, one of the most commonly asked questions is, "How did you memorize all of those lines?!"

Well, it wasn't as easy as having my mother rehearse me incessantly as a six-year-old, but I am happy to share some of the tricks and tips I've collected over the years that have helped me immensely.

Memorizing a 70-minute show is a separate challenge from memorizing dialogue in a play. Dialogue is easier since you have the other actors' lines to prompt you. Once my fellow actor forgot his line during a fight scene. He just shouted, "I don't know!" and stared at me.

I knew he had blanked, but, to his credit, he let me know within the energy of the scene. His forgotten line was accusing me of kissing another man, so I threw back an improv, saying, "Oh, I suppose you think I kissed that guy."

I then went on with my own next line. It's great to know you have each other's backs onstage.

The bonus to doing a solo show is that if you mess up, you won't affect another person on stage. The kicker though is that if you blank during a solo show, you have only yourself to save you. Or not. (Tips on getting out of this nightmare below.)

So here we go! Give the techniques below a try and see which memorizing tricks work best for you.

PREPARATION

1. Become One with Your Script

Carry the current pages of the script you are working on with you everywhere. You never know when a few free minutes may pop up and you can load more lines into your brain. I personally am not good at just sitting and memorizing, so I sometimes find it best to wander through stores as I go over a section of the script.

Honor how you work best. Time at the hairdresser or nail salon is like study hall to me. Public transportation is a gift, as is any type of mindless cardio exercise. Alas, simply putting the script under your pillow will not help your brain to absorb the material – I've tried it, to no avail.

2. Memorize Sober

This would seem obvious, but I have a friend who would complain she couldn't retain her stand-up comedy set when memorizing – only to find out she would wake and bake. Weed (legal or not in your neck of the woods) prevents memorizing. And, whereas alcohol may provide some liquid insight into a line or a character, trust me, you will not retain much of it unless you record or write it down immediately. Many of the subtleties and tricks that help memorizing disappear after a glass of Prosecco or a shot of Limoncello.

3. Read the Lines Backwards

The best trick I have for getting stubborn paragraphs of dialogue loaded into my brain is one I heard on an episode of *Inside the Actors Studio*.

Just before you're ready to go to sleep, take the section that you want to memorize (length doesn't matter,) and read it BACKWARDS from the end to the beginning.

Why? The brain actually imports data faster reading right to left!

So, for example, if I wanted to memorize the last sentence written above, before bed I would silently read from the end: *Left to right reading faster data imports actually brain the.*

Now close your eyes and go to sleep. Do not look at your phone or read anything else. Focus only on your breath until you wake up.

Upon rising and before you pick up a phone, turn on a TV, or read anything else, review the material you read backwards the night before: now reading it normally: FORWARDS.

Next, mentally run through the lines and see if you can remember them from the beginning. You'll be amazed at how much you've actually retained! And you will save so much time. It's my favorite go-to exercise.

4. Repetition – An Hour a Day

The next way to memorize lines is the old tried and true "repetition method" of my kindergarten days. If you have a show coming up, or a large amount of lines to memorize, you must spend an hour or more a day going over and over what you're memorizing.

Twice a day doesn't hurt. I could never seem to find time in my crazy schedule to devote to this, until my brilliant actress friend Louise Davis told me her trick of mentally running lines at night when she couldn't sleep. This also works in the post office line.

When meeting a friend, ask them to run your lines with you, before you consume the entire first cocktail. (See #2 above.) Friends LOVE to dip into this process and go over your part with you! So, don't be shy about asking. You can also just email them the script and have them run lines with you over the phone or a Zoom call. Ask them to mark where you go up on lines and go over these errors at the end, rather than having them interrupt you each time – unless you're stuck and call "line."

5. Link Words and Ideas

Let's say you're having trouble with a dropped line, or simply what comes next in the piece. Another trick I utilize is to link words or ideas from one sentence to the next. (This works great with dialogue.) Here's an example from *Dietrich* for a turn I had trouble making/remembering:

"Of course, you were too young to have been in the war. Would you like to have a glass of champagne?"

These two lines aren't in the same vein of thought. So, after stumbling over this spot a few times, I consciously built in the thought that the tragedies of the war made me drink champagne.

War = champagne.

"Of course, you were too young to have been in the war. Would you like to have a glass of champagne?"

Voila! I never had trouble with those lines again.

6. Link Physical Gestures

Pick something you have trouble remembering and assign it to a physical gesture. (Thanks to Anzu Lawson for this one.) For example, "The tree is blooming."

Sweep your arm every time you say "tree."

Try it. You will be amazed at how well this one works.

7. Hearing, Seeing and Saying

Doing these three things increases retention. Read your lines into a recording app or device and then play it back while you read along out loud. He utilized this method while studying for the Fire Chief Captain's test and scored the highest of anyone.

8. Examine Every Word, Even the Little Ones

Think about each word and why it was chosen. I thought I had a line correct until my dialect coach, Glenda Morgan Brown, pointed out a single word I had unknowingly substituted. I thought the line was, "He told me what kind of car to buy, what kind of pictures to hang on my walls."

She pointed out that the word was "paintings" not "pictures." Paintings are more expensive... higher end. That changed it forever for me. I got the meaning of why that word was chosen.

"He told me what kind of car to buy, what kind of paintings to hang on my walls." Done and done!

9. Write Down What You Remember

Handwrite (on paper with a pen or pencil, not on a phone or computer, as the brain works better this way) what you think the lines are. Then go back and check the script to see what you forgot. Note that, as an actor, forgetting something typically also means that you don't fully understand what the writer was conveying in that moment. Sometimes lines or thoughts at first seem similar, but the author put them in there to further the plot or character arc.

Rediscover the line and which word is key to the idea. You won't skip over that part again. (Murphy's Law: it will happen somewhere else next time!)

10. Break It Down

Actor/teacher Gary Swanson also helped me greatly. He pointed out that I had been tackling Dietrich's 70 minutes as one giant piece. He instructed me to break it down into not only a beginning, middle and end, but also into chunks of thoughts and topics. Then to list these topics into a skeleton frame and memorize that framework. It made it all much less daunting and easier to go confidently from section to section.

11. Build in a Hail Mary

During the *Dietrich* rehearsals, I told the technical director and my pianist that if I ever said the word "Shnapps" that it meant I was completely lost. Here's where you have to rely on your amazing team! "Schnapps" meant I need them to jump to the next technical cue to save me.

So, I actually marked and tagged each of their cues in both of their scripts with different colored sticky notes. This way, the appropriate person would know to take action.

I have now and then not had the luxury of a proper dress rehearsal due to time constraints, and the first performance night became the dress. A phone ring was missing once in a show, and, as I hadn't memorized this cue (mistake,) I panicked, thinking I had dropped a line. The scrambling in my blank brain finally blurted, "I wish I had a shot of Schnapps right now."

The next thing I knew, my pianist Russell Daisy played a tinkling on the piano like a phone ring. I covered with, "Could that be the phone? Odd..." and I picked up the receiver. Show saved!

We later learned that this phone cue had not been loaded properly on my thumb drive. Had the pianist not realized that the tech guy hadn't come in with the expected phone cue, it could have been a disaster. Go team!

Months later I realized I could have also initiated the call myself, but in that moment it was nothing but panic, then "Schnapps" came to mind.

So, don't forget to memorize your cues along with your line. Don't just assume they will always be there to prompt you. Mistakes happen on that end also. Ah, the joys of live theatre!

Finally, once all of the memorizing is done and it's showtime...

Bonus tip: Keep Going!

For a super long script, monologue, or stand-up comedy special, just know that if you suddenly realize when performing that you forgot a line, DON'T go back mentally to try to find what you missed while you were performing. Keep your mental train flowing forward with what you do recall. Just flag it in your mind that something felt off there. The missing line may come to you later and you can weave it back in, or decide to skip it altogether.

Remember that the audience has no idea what the order of lines is supposed to be and won't know you missed it. Of course, the writer and technical director will know... but they can also be helpful after the show in figuring out where you went up. Then you can try to implement an association, gesture or other tip listed here to ensure it doesn't happen again... at least not on that line!

So go forth, memorize, absorb each brilliant word of the author. And then let it all go once those lights come on... it's now time to enjoy the storytelling and connection with the audience. After all, isn't that what it's all about?

"I do mental exercises. I don't have any trouble memorizing lines because of the crossword puzzles I do every day to keep my mind a little limber."

- BETTY WHITE

ALLISON BERGMAN

Methods and Strategies for Learning Your Lines

Allison Bergman is a prolific stage and screen director with two films and over 40 stage productions to her credit, featuring actors such as Phylicia Rashad, Leslie Uggams, Tamara Tunie, Leslie Odom Jr. and Josh Gad. She co-authored the acclaimed training text, *Acting the Song,* and is recognized for her broad knowledge of acting techniques and insightful coaching skills. Ms. Bergman empathetically inspires actors to tap profound depth and consistently deliver vulnerable, layered, courageous performances. The first West Coast Musical Theatre Conference was launched under her guidance with numerous new musicals shepherded toward production. Ms. Bergman is lauded as an *Outstanding Woman in Theatre in Los Angeles* by Women in Theatre, and her directorial talents have been acknowledged with a *Drama-Logue Critics Award.*

Over time, every actor develops their own way of tackling line memorization. Some start as soon as they are cast, with a goal of "line security" before they even begin exploring the script and character.

Some resist it completely and never achieve full memorization, still grasping for approximations and paraphrases up to and including in performance.

Most actors fall somewhere between these extremes.

There are as many ways of getting "off book" as there are acting methods – and with good reason. How and when the text is imprinted is directly connected to the way you approach your character, relationships, actions, intentions, and physical movement. Ultimately,

METHODS AND STRATEGIES FOR LEARNING YOUR LINES

whichever way keeps your performance relaxed and responsive is the one you should choose.

It's important to remember that most characters you'll play are intentionally flawed and are written as humans. Humans struggle to find words when they are formulating and building thoughts. The more complex the thought, the more work they must do to find the right words to match. It's the natural way we think.

Know what your character is trying to achieve with their thoughts and their words, and what means they have to communicate their needs to others. If you do this, the words you study will stay with you much more easily, and when it's time to deliver them, they will come.

Here are some behaviors I've observed, as a director and an acting coach, that indicate it's time for an actor to rethink their memorization strategy. Below are exercises to try if you recognize similar patterns in your own preparation.

Eyes Inward

If you aren't spending enough time reading your lines out loud, it's likely you will rely on the sight of the printed words as part of your muscle memory. Trying to recall your lines in rehearsal, your eyes may close or you'll look away from your scene partner, sometimes up and to one side, attempting to visualize the page.

This is especially true for lines that initiate beat shifts. Beat shifts are critical moments of transition, transformation and momentum in the action. This is exactly when turning your focus outward to your scene partner is most crucial.

If these disconnected moments of turning your eyes inward go unchecked too long, you will start to normalize them as if they are a natural state for your character. It's important to recognize that appearing to listen while you are internally visualizing words, and actively participating in a scene are not the same. Doing so unintentionally creates a vacuum in the action instead of an acceleration.

Habitual Movement

In an effort to cover up patches of a scene where you cannot remember what line comes next, you might come to depend on some non-specific habitual activities that you insert into your performance, such as quick exhales, or rocking from one foot to the other. Maybe you cough, clear your throat, shrug your shoulders, or purse your lips and shake your head. They don't seem significant by themselves, and might help diffuse any actual panic that would derail your performance entirely.

But if you regularly depend on them to stall the action while you search your mind for the words, these movements will cloud your communication, halt the rhythm of the scene, and create confusion about your character's intention and state of mind. Over a career, they might also be misconstrued as your choice to use the same set of generic mannerisms in every role.

When I see an actor defaulting to one of these mannerisms, especially if I'm familiar with their work, I know it's a spot we'll need to address.

The Sing-along

If you've ever had to memorize large sections of dialogue quickly, there's a trick for that, but it comes at a price. Some actors make fixed choices about the melody of the words – the highs and lows, the pauses, the tempo, etc. Then they learn it like a song.

If you've ever tried to get off book before you were ready, you've likely employed some of this yourself. Your ear remembers that the section where you speak fast and high comes right after the quiet, reflective-sounding phrases. That's followed by the list of questions which all rise at the end, as most questions do. And, so on.

This is a quick way to gain some confidence that you can get through it, and it's very consistent from take to take, or performance to performance.

Unfortunately, it's also filled with sand traps because you're literally creating a mechanism that encourages an auto-pilot delivery. If you later discover better thought processes, want to play other actions, or the director wants an entirely different approach, it's extremely difficult to unlearn the sing-song patterns you created. Worse, you leave no room for authentic response or interaction with another actor.

METHODS AND STRATEGIES FOR LEARNING YOUR LINES

PREPARATION

1. Antidote to "Eyes Inward"

I suggest you memorize by reading your lines out loud every time. Look at the phrase and make some choices about what it means, and why you are saying it.

Then look up from the page, choose a focus point, and say the phrase out loud. With this method, you will be marrying your words to your thoughts, and delivering them to an imaginary person outside of yourself. Turning your eyes outward will free you to say the line a million different ways – whatever is necessary to get your point across and reach your scene partner with your words.

It's also incredibly valuable to read the entire script out loud, including all the stage directions, before you start to memorize. You'll absorb the story in a visceral way, experiencing the varying rhythm, language and tone for each of the characters, and unlocking powerful information about your character's relationship to all of it.

2. Antidote to "Habitual Movement"

Once you identify where you're pausing the action with mannerisms, you can begin to explore the question, "Which dots have I neglected to connect?"

There is a bridge, a reasoning, a cue that propels your character to move from one thought and line to the next, and if there's a gap in your thinking, then it's yet to be discovered.

If it doesn't become apparent from revisiting the text, or reinvesting in what your scene partner is up to, then you may have to invent something from your own imagination.

I encourage you to think of these markers as a gift. Any opportunity you have to get more specific, exacting, and honest in your process will exponentially improve the quality of your performance by making it more engaging and unique.

3. Antidote to "The Sing-along"

If you're faced with a dense amount of dialogue, I encourage you to identify the structure of it, much like you do when you analyze the script as a whole.

What is the story of the text? What's the journey? What is the form?

Look at the overall framework, and how each part is related to the others. Is it a series of questions followed by a discovery? Or, maybe it's in three sections: an emotional rant, an apology, and a decision.

Break up the dialogue into sections you can label, then highlight the singular most important idea or phrase they each contain. These are the peaks of each mountain. All the other lines are part of the trek up to that peak, or the trip down the other side.

Melodies will naturally still occur, but they'll be more responsive to the changing circumstances, keeping the scene alive and fluid. With this technique, you can concentrate your efforts, focusing on only one piece at a time, knowing it will lead you to the next piece, because you've figured out how they're related.

Chapter 8.

Prepare a Scene or Performance

"Like a duck on the pond... on the surface everything looks calm, but beneath the water those little feet are churning a mile a minute."

- GENE HACKMAN

LEANDRO TAUB

Mind, Body, Emotion & Spirit

Leandro Taub is an actor, author and lecturer. He wrote, starred in and co-directed the feature film EXTERNO with his brother Jonathan. EXTERNO earned multiple awards and nominations at film festivals around the world. He also played leading roles in the feature films ENDLESS POETRY by Alejandro Jodorowsky, WOODWIND by Fin Manjoo, and AN INNOCENT MIND HAS NO FEAR by Ralf Schmerberg. Leandro has written five books and 25 audiobooks, including *The Hidden Mind, Homemade Wisdom* and *The Anarchist*. He has given more than 300 conference lectures to thousands of people from Latin America, Asia and Europe. As an entrepreneur and economist, he co-founded an investment advisory company, a film production company, a multimedia agency and a publishing company.

I've been doing solo shows in theaters for the past twelve years. During this time, I discovered something ephemeral and tangible that happens when performing on a stage. When I truly feel what I am saying, I see the audience paying attention and engaged with my performance. But if I disconnect from what I am saying, just for a moment, the audience stops paying attention. And if I do it without feeling, I completely lose the audience. There is a special hypnotic event happening, every time, on every stage.

So, how? How can I make myself be effective in this flow and relationship with the audience? The solution I came up with has four stages.

Stage one: the mind. I have to learn very well what I will say. Understand so well that I can explain the concept and the message in different ways. It is about reading, reading, reading, reading, and reading. And it is also about writing, making a character resume, breaking down the concepts, until the ideas and my mind become one.

Stage two: the body. I have to feel what I am saying. Sometimes the concept expects my body to be still, to lay down, or to be sitting. Sometimes the concept pushes my body to be walking, running, jumping, and stretching. Sometimes the concept needs my body to be open, and sometimes it needs my body to be closed. The more I work with the first stage (the mind), the closer I get to stage two (the body.) The more I understand the script and the character, the better my body reacts with it. I walk practicing the lines, I run practicing the lines, I ride a bicycle practicing the lines, and many times I listen to music and dance practicing the lines. I test different body movements to have big flexibility. And the emotional experience follows.

Stage three: the emotion. Emotion is what happens when we are in touch with our heart and we feel what is happening. The more I practice with the mind and body, the more I feel related to the text I am practicing. And here we are getting into an area that is not so easy to manage, because we can choose what to think-say-do, but we can't directly control our emotions. But we can affect our emotions indirectly. The more we live, the more we experience, the more we feel: all these memories stay with us and they are reflected in our performance. If we truly connect with what we are saying, we will be able to connect emotionally with it.

Stage four: the spirit. From difficult we are moving forward to more difficult. The spirit is not something we can control easily, but it is there and it is a key part of the performance. Also, with respect to what should not be said, I prefer not to put too many words here. What I want to share with you is that the spirit is there and once you get it, the attention of everyone follows it.

PREPARATION

Grab something to eat, and instead of eating it directly: look at it, smell it, listen to it, and very slowly, eat a small piece of it.

Once it gets inside your mouth, close your eyes and focus your attention on what you are eating. Do it slowly. Very slowly.

Now, try the same with a line of the script.

ALI CHEFF

Click In, Click Out

Ali Cheff is an actor, documentary filmmaker, and humanitarian clown who works and plays in different areas of storytelling, including stage, screen and voice over. They have appeared in short films, the feature comedy A LOOK IN THE REAR VIEW, the series *Hellbound* and *Deadly Affairs* and will be voicing Ionah in Netflix's animated series *Maid Chronicles*. Ali has performed as a Humanitarian Clown with Patch Adams for over fourteen years. They also spent three years documenting the ratification of the Equal Rights Amendment in Virginia. Ali believes in compassion, love and authentic choices on camera, on stage, in the booth, and in life. Their other piece in this book is "Mantras for Actors" in Chapter 13.

Sets and theaters have so many moving parts, so much skill and talent in one place, so much distraction! We need to show up prepared, engaged, and ready to do our job. If we accomplish that, then we did our part toward being caring and supportive to the production. We are helping to get the day completed so everyone can go home.

What I like to call "click in, click out" is knowing how to easily get into a character, and how to quickly come back to yourself – to step out of your character and take a break. The more comfortable it is to be in both spaces, the healthier it can be for your mental state.

Some use ritual, some work out specific movements. I used to use yoga, now I do Myofascial Release and say mantras after leaving the set or the theater or the recording booth, and after meeting with my acting coach. (See also "Mantras for Actors.")

There is 'being in the moment,' and there is moving past the previous moment and into the current moment. Kind of like when a seatbelt clicks on and off, we can click into our character and scene, and then un-click afterwards, without any lasting imprints, we hope.

Vulnerability is the gig, it's the job. If I know I can "click out" and move from the character back to me, with all my walls up, I feel safe to be vulnerable while I'm acting. I can hop in and hop out of the character, even with everything happening on set, and even when Imposter Syndrome rears its head.

Click In and Out for Voiceover

Clicking in and out is useful when jumping between styles of voiceover. Perhaps you start the day narrating an audiobook, and then you have an active animation or video game. The energies and approaches are very different. I also love <u>feeling</u>, so I need to get rid of the previous performance's emotional residue.

I do vocal warm-up like trills, and gargle water. I say some tongue twisters with my tongue positioned on my teeth, outside my mouth, all around the place.

Then I bend over and touch my feet and roll up to standing, raise my hands above my head and shake them out. or at least do a head roll or stretch my fingers. Anything to get some kind of energy flow, and get me moving out of what "was." Sounds like theater warmups...well, yea!

To prepare for the next performance, I put my hand on my heart and visualize who I'm talking to and what they need from me, or why they should listen to me. (With narration, "they" is the audience.) Then I begin.

I even added a physical clicker to this routine – the kind used to train dogs. I click when I enter the booth, and the scene, and I click when I wrap. For example, a commercial audition. I click right before I start playing and performing. When I finish my last take and decide to move on to the next audition, I click again – it helps me mentally and emotionally click out of the previous audition.

When I'm recording myself at home, I also click whenever I stumble or make an error – makes it easier to edit the recording.

In Person

Prior to getting to set, I make a short history for each scene. I visit the different needs and inner conflict of the character. Even if my only line is "Sign Here", with the objective "I have ten more deliveries to go before lunch," I know who I am, and where I am, when I click in.

For me this helps a lot in film, with its many stops and starts. You may not have an hour to get into character and maybe only a couple of minutes between takes. Knowing when and how to quickly click in and click out helps.

When I hear "Sound speed, rolling, settle," I think of my "pinch," that is, the moment before that makes my character feel like they want to take a breath. So instead of using a clicker, it's the calls before "Action!" that I use to click in.

I was working on a film once that was full of trauma scenes. My character was being abused throughout the film, so every day on set I was getting into a state of pain and confusion, with a deep sickening feeling. (I did not yet have my "click in, click out" system.)

The character who assaults me causes most of the trauma. The actor was wonderful: sweet, considerate, and very aware of checking in with me through all our scenes.

Years pass and I see him on the street. I don't remember why I recognize him, I just feel sick, and anger overwhelms me.

It was the emotional residue of those scenes. He was associated and linked to "living" those unpleasant moments and feelings. All the chemical reactions in my body were triggered by the unprocessed experience.

It happened with love scenes in long-running theater shows; those feelings you start stuffing down when you see your co-star. Our bodies chemically react the same way they do when we have emotional experiences in our real lives.

So I decided I needed a method for clicking in and clicking out. I need to know that when they call "Cut!" and they say, "We're moving on," that I *can* move on.

If, amazingly, they're shooting a sequence linearly, (I have never experienced this, but say it is), I may want that build-up of emotions, so I might wait for "It's a wrap," to click out.

But, thinking about this now, I would still click out and back in for each new take, because for me it strengthens my ability to be ready, to keep myself emotionally safe, and to be able to be immediately vulnerable.

My approach is an elaborate system created by Martin Blank, mixed with my own physical movement observations. I have learned that I track my eyes differently when I'm having different feelings – I can use an eye movement to <u>trigger</u> a feeling, and it shows up authentically as different expressions on my face. I also pick specific gestures or specific pacing.

After all that, I improvise. I visit my lines, I improvise, I re-visit my lines, then I improvise again. I am fast with memorization, so often the improvisation is movements, feelings and actions to go with the lines.

Now I press record if it's for an audition or audio work I'm doing at home. I may snap my fingers or click the dog clicker between takes of a scene.

When I do my last take or finish a recording, I give myself a moment to feel the reverb. I settle. I snap or click, and then I celebrate. I dance, I stretch, I throw my hands in the air, I smile real big, I laugh, sometimes I cry. Then I drink some water and move on. This is how I train it into my system.

I might attach a snap or a small gesture that I can use discreetly on set. Between scenes I do my small gestures discreetly – that allows me to be present with the crew and my surroundings, without feeling like I will lose my character and where they are – I'm just snapping out temporarily.

The celebration is to create new feelings. The elaborate dancing and stretching and celebration I do after a project wraps, is intended to punctuate that the project is indeed finished and that I can break completely from the character back into me.

I do all this so I can be super vulnerable and also know how to swim back to safety. After the scene ends, I can use that little gesture and settle back into being me. Sometimes, I'll need to weep and weep and weep to release the scene and go back to being me.

As actors, we are doing something most people don't wish to do – feel the spectrum of pain, joy, anger, sorrow, delight, ecstasy, terror – to heightened realities, and then we're supposed to act like it was nothing. As if just because it is "made up", the recovery should be quick and easy.

It isn't. We are experiencing traumas, tragedy, great joys, intense love. But without a mourning period or sick leave.

We are playing in the sandbox of humanity. It is fabulous and we love it, but no one is going to protect us. It is our responsibility to care for our own emotional well-being, and we have to create ways to do that. I click in and click out. I want to be 100% in each scene, *and* walk away from set knowing no one is afraid of me, *and* know that I will sleep well and wake up feeling healthy, free of my character's emotional residue.

PREPARATION

Find a process for clicking in and out of a scene and a character that works for you, whether it's some kind of physical release, snapping, taking a very deep breath, saying a specific word or phrase to yourself... whatever you want to practice to signal your mind and body that now you are going into a character, and now you are stepping out of the character to be in the present as yourself.

Practice clicking in and out at home. Practice with scenes, self-tapes, monologues. As you're doing your prep for a role, whether it's research, journaling, learning lines, practicing physical movements, even figuring out a costume – include clicking in and out each time you work on the role.

And right before a big scene, try this: put your hand on your heart and visualize who you'll be talking to, what they need from you, what you want from them, and why they need to listen to you.

JENNIFER ALLEN

Preparing a Character for the Stage

Jennifer Allen's Broadway credits include *Kimberly Akimbo* (stand by for Kimberly), *Sister Act* (Mother Superior), *Cats* (Grizabella), *Guys and Dolls* (Miss Adelaide), *The Bridges of Madison County, Memphis, A Catered Affair, Little Me*, and *City of Angels*. Off-Broadway and national tours include Disney's national tour of *The Little Mermaid* (Ursula), *Jerry Springer: The Opera* (Irene/Mary), *Ragtime* (Emma Goldman), Jerome Robbins' *Broadway* (Ma and Tessie Tura), *Cabaret* (Sally Bowles), *Brigadoon, Funny Girl* and *Jesus Christ Superstar*. TV appearances include *Late Night with Jimmy Fallon, The View, Good Morning America, Dancing with the Stars* and the comedy series *The Other Two*.

I'm an actor, mainly in musical theatre. I've been involved in nine Broadway shows, as well as national tours in leading roles as well as ensemble, and understudy gigs. I often wonder what kind of career I'd have had if singing and movement were not in my skillset.

Preparation is constant throughout the day, involving life balance, research for the role, working with fellow company members, history of the piece, historical period of the play/dramaturgy – which is so easy and fun to do online and integral to the craft.

My approach to character is layered among the emotional tone of the music and the lyrics that the composer has mapped out. I try to serve the writing and the storytelling motion.

I connect to the character at first on a personal basis, that is, what we have in common. If we don't have anything in common, I will try to inhabit a person I have known, or know currently, who is similar to that character. Sometimes it is a mix of both, myself and others.

PREPARING A CHARACTER FOR THE STAGE

I will start first with physical character traits and then let that organically marinate an emotional life, from the outside in. I like to work inwardly and outwardly simultaneously, to transform into the character.

The goal for me is to inhabit the character so completely that it feels like I'm channeling them at a séance, which is exciting and scary.

However, on stage there is a self-awareness that must exist in multiple delicious tantalizing layers. These complex flavors present themselves to serve the story, enriched by the depth of listening, feeling, seeing, reveling in the ever-changing textures and shades of colors that your fellow actors are "painting." These will inform your storytelling differently in every performance.

I like to use Method on and off ramps, and the moment before the character enters, or reenters. I suppose for a shoot that has an end date, one can go Method and live in a character 24/7, like Daniel Day Lewis, who doesn't do theatre. (He did once, and that's a famous story.) However, that's impractical for eight shows a week for long runs, where burnout is always around the corner.

Even if you've been doing the same role in a play, eight shows a week, for many years, it can stay mostly fresh within the confines of the direction, and the original intention of that direction stays intact. (That is always a tricky one for me, and I get notes for trying different choices that don't serve the original direction, which I've learned to take with grace.)

Many actors are like me; our strategies change for each role.

Perhaps I'll need to warm up my voice or body more before getting on stage, or go to a darker place, or a lighter place, depending on the demands of the character. A lot of people I know say a personal or group prayer or meditation before each show, in a circle or by themselves.

Most actors do create preparations depending on the environment and type of role. A certain actor I know said his preparation for *Taming of the Shrew* was drinking a stout beer before every performance and that was it.

Sometimes a director will have the cast do some improvisation in character to build community, with or without words being used. This usually happens at the beginning of the rehearsal process and not after. As professionals, we are trusted to be ready out of the gate.

PREPARATION

I'm always working on something to better my craft. To keep things fresh, I like to challenge myself with a new focus or word, or physical characteristic of my fellow actor to focus on.

Recently the word I use in my head before a performance is "generosity," and it has helped immensely to relax and ground my work, listening with all the "in the moment' integrity I have to offer.

KIM KRIZAN

Save It for the Camera

Kim Krizan is a writer and actor who appeared in Richard Linklater's DAZED AND CONFUSED, SLACKER, and as herself in WAKING LIFE. She originated the story and characters for the "Before" movie series, co-wrote the Oscar-nominated BEFORE SUNRISE screenplay with Linklater, and co-wrote the story for the sequel, BEFORE SUNSET. Kim is the author of the graphic novella *Zombie Tales 2061* and a contributor to the *Now Write! Screenwriting* anthology.

The problem with acting is that you know exactly what you're going to say in advance – and that's not how life works. In real life, we react. In real life, we listen and we respond. So how to do this – this mental trick – when we've exhaustively memorized and rehearsed lines?

Let me tell you the story of how I delivered my lines when I played the high school teacher who gives the Bicentennial spiel in DAZED AND CONFUSED.

I had done very little acting when I landed the part of Ginny Stroud in DAZED. I had taken no acting classes and had never been on a real Hollywood film set. But I got the part and went to work learning my two scenes, one at the door of my classroom with a student named Don, and the other a monologue about the origin of the United States of America: "Just a bunch of slave-owning aristocratic white males who didn't want to pay their taxes."

I distinctly remember pacing around my little rented 1930's house in Austin, with the script in hand, imagining I was the history teacher, imagining my situation as the leader of a bunch of rowdy teenagers, imagining how I'd feel.

I knew that I'd have a much richer secret life than they knew, that I had a past. As a young high school teacher in 1976, my character was probably about twenty when political controversy over the Vietnam War exploded in the U.S. – and perhaps she'd been a protestor or held slightly radical views. Perhaps she'd studied history and become a teacher because of what she witnessed and felt. Perhaps she was a bit of a hippie, or a secret yippie, or a bit of a lightweight Bolshevik.

I did not develop these ideas in great detail. I certainly didn't create an elaborate biography or backstory. Instead, I had an impressionistic feeling: Ms. Stroud (definitely Ms. – for gods sakes, not "Miss" or "Mrs.") was going to enjoy laying it on the kids in her last act. But first she had to deal with Don Dawson.

It always helps me to walk around as I'm ruminating on an idea, so as I reviewed my lines, I paced around my bedroom imagining the conversation at the classroom doorway with "Mr. Dawson," the randy, testosterone-filled football player who comes to my class and graphically propositions not only my student Vicky, but also me (in the form of Ginny Stroud), and I realized very clearly that... I'd want to pat his head. I'd want to pat his head as in, "You couldn't handle me, little boy."

This gesture was not written in the script, but I knew it had to happen.

Unfortunately, when I was finally on the set and rehearsing with director Richard Linklater and Sasha (the actor who played Don), I *did* pat his head – which made him genuinely angry. Sasha asked Linklater if I was really going to pat his head. I instantly realized my mistake. Sasha's real-life response was priceless, but I'd ruined it by giving him a big heads-up. Sure enough, when we did the scene for the camera, "Don's" face did not register the indignation of the high school stud thwarted and humiliated in his effort to proposition his teacher.

I knew then never to reveal the surprising little twists that are not written into the script, so the other actors can respond authentically. I've learned since then that actors have gotten permission from their directors to do things such as smash glasses, punch walls, and destroy bathroom sinks without the forehand knowledge of their fellow actors – who then react with fear, tears, and all the "acting" required to make the scenes powerful.

But I do have to hand it to myself when it comes to my next scene in DAZED, which is now played every July Fourth. I'm the one who does the famous Bicentennial spiel. As I sat with the actors and the crew was setting up the scene, the actors were bratty. I tried making small talk, but they were not amenable. Perhaps they were in character. So I got in character.

Now, on the rare occasion when I watch that classroom scene, I see that the gestures of Ginny Stroud, the teacher I played, are not my real gestures as Kim. Instead, that character is Ginny Stroud, who was quite swaggering in her effort to slip some truth to the kids (today we would say "drop knowledge on") in one last effort to educate them. All I can say is that I learned the lines pacing in my bedroom, but when I was on the set and filming, I was responding to the students, intent on Ginny Stroud's desire to impart her truth to those students before they slipped out of her clutches.

PREPARATION

My advice to you is this:
As you first review your lines and feel your way into your character, lightly and impressionistically imagine their life and what they've come from.

Then get into the physicality of your character. Are they standing? Sitting? Lying on a bed? Imagine their natural responses.

When you've created twists and angles that are not in the script, hold on to these. Tell no one. Save it for the camera.

When the camera is finally rolling, bust out your head pats, eye rolls, laughter – whatever you've prepared – and allow your fellow actors to react authentically. Then, listen and react and respond with whatever emotion you are feeling in the moment.

You've got the lines in your head, but every gesture, every flicker is not mapped out. Perhaps the feelings are a surprise to you. Let the emotions inspire cadence and tone that unspools organically. If you genuinely listen, you'll feel the feeling and react with authenticity. And that will be visible. Save it for the camera.

JOSH MARGULIES

Let's Get Physical

Josh Margulies is a comedic and romantic actor who was born under a full moon in Nepal and raised in Hawai'i. He earned recognition for his quirky lead role in the comedy TV pilot *Surreal Estates,* which was featured at Cannes. Other TV work includes playing a champion sex-alete in the TV comedy *Coitus of the Week,* which won "Best Pilot" award at Sunset Film Festival, and performing alongside Dylan McDermott in Fox's *LA to Vegas.* He also earned a "Best Actor in a Comedy" award at the Hollywood Fringe Festival. Josh has appeared in numerous short and feature films, including SAND ANGELS for which he earned a "Best Supporting Actor" award, Paul Thomas Anderson's Oscar-nominated THE MASTER and "Best Picture" Oscar-winner, THE ARTIST.

The fire within me that fuels my performances comes from many different sources. This is why the secret to my performance comes from a variety and diversity of tools.

A little context… when I think back on what seeded my desire to be on the big screen, it came from watching action heroes. I had a physical and visceral connection to characters like Rambo and Rocky Balboa (maybe because my middle name is Raphael!) who were fighting against all odds.

For example, in ROCKY IV, the personal drive to achieve fitness as a boxer is what I saw as the major challenge of the film. The character of Rocky had a flesh and blood Russian demon of an opponent, but the truest struggle was within himself, and it stemmed from power and love.

With that being said, allowing my performances to "just be" while getting out of the way of my own fears has been my biggest struggle.

When I first landed in Los Angeles from Hawaii to pursue my acting career, I was starry-eyed over the possibility of becoming the new "king actor" of Hollywood. I came with the idea that show business had been waiting to discover me and I was finally doing the entertainment industry the honor of giving it my time and attention.

My bravado didn't automatically open any doors, so I took all sorts of acting classes. I enrolled in classes in audition, booking, scene study, script analysis, technique, tricks, you name it.

All this theory left me a little overwhelmed and full of static. Where I actually found myself and my "voice" (as they say in the acting world) was in improv class. I learned that it had a strong structure and it challenged my fears, but there was always such freedom within that structure. This was just what I needed to bring my scenes and auditions to life.

Improv formed the foundation of how I would build out my acting technique. It brings the lifeblood to a black-and-white page, because it allows me to relax within the structure of the writing.

It is, however, still only one tool, and to be a well-formed actor, one must use a variety of tools. These tools are a little different for everyone because we are all different.

Since I already mentioned ROCKY, I'll use boxing as a metaphor. Improv is my jab in the ring of acting, but like any good fighter knows, there are multiple combinations we use to win a match. We need to find what tools and what combinations of those tools work best for us and help us bring out our truth. I believe there is no better way to find this than through experience.

I treasure those early days when I saturated myself in all the methods of acting. It formed me to be a "brawler" in the ring of acting as I come out swinging. Each individual has their own way of training to bring out the truth on camera and stage. For me it was experiencing and feeling many methods, and going with my instinct.

To be honest, many of the classes I took were the teacher's agenda and did little for me except to bring confusion. Much wasted time and money, until I eventually found a specific acting technique that stood out and allowed me to bring out my truth in acting.

Meisner, and specifically the exercise of repetition, allowed me to focus on the moment at hand, and <u>become</u> the character. Whether it was for a scene or an audition, the simple act of eye contact gave me a sense of grounding with the other character in the scene. (Shout out to the Ruskin Theatre!)

Another secret to my technique came from the same class and it's writing out dialogue and repeating it. To work on a scene, or even a few lines freely, is to first know the dialogue back to front and inside out. The fastest and most efficient way for me to get there is through repetition.

Once the lines are like a monologue in your head, then, within the moment of the dialogue, you can freely play with or improvise how you would behave while saying the lines.

These are a few combos from Acting 101 that work for me.

Acting is a personal endeavor that requires the experience of life. I think babies do it perfectly because they can just "be." They are simply there. When a certain age is reached, however, we humans become more complex, and there are all sorts of thoughts and correlations involved with making decisions. This can create static that paralyzes our decisions if we don't find the tools and technique to get out of our own way.

For me it has to be physical. Preferably related to surfing or boxing. We already spoke of boxing but surfing brings me closer to Nature and reminds me to enjoy the moment. Not that surfing has helped me as an actor directly, but it has reminded me of what is true and real.

We cannot be actors without first being full, life-living people. Riding the waves of life and experiencing the ups and downs in all types of weather has given me a fulfillment that I hope all of you who pursue this endeavor of acting can experience. Aloha.

PREPARATION

An exercise I will do before a performance is breathing and stretching, and of course surfing, boxing or other exercise, if time allows.

If you're short on time, this breath and stretch can be done anywhere to aid you to get into the physical, which will help you feel more grounded and present in a scene.

The signature "Margulies warm up" is as follows: stand on comfortable ground. I prefer being outdoors under a tree with my shoes off, but any comfortable area will do.

Remember to breathe the whole time. Start with rolling your head in circles to stretch out the neck. Then go into shrugging the shoulders first forward, then backward.

Follow this with large circles with your arms going backwards, then make forward arm circles.

Now place your hands on your belly and twist the torso side to side.

Place hands on hips and do hula hoop hip circles, making sure the lower back stretches.

Now, with legs spread out, lean over to one side to stretch the thigh, then alternate.

Lastly, bring your feet together, interlace your fingers and raise your hands up to the sky. Breathe in and breathe out as you bend or stretch over to one side. As you raise your hands back up high, inhale, and exhale as you bend to the other side.

Last time, inhale as you bring your hands back up high, and finally, exhale.

Fold over and touch your toes.

This routine will take five minutes or less, and afterwards you will feel relaxed and ready to take on the world!

PUT YOURSELF OUT THERE

"In the performing arts, you have to have thick, thick, thick skin, because of all the rejection you face on a daily basis, and the fact that work never lasts for very long. But you need thin, thin, thin skin in order to access all of your emotions and your creativity so that you can express it."

- AUDRA MCDONALD

Chapter 9.

Audition

"I don't think actors should ever expect to get a role, because the disappointment is too great. You've got to think of things as an opportunity. An audition's an opportunity to have an audience."

- AL PACINO

HOLLY POWELL

The Six Audition Tools Method

(Edited Version of Chapter 2 from *The Audition Bible: Secrets Every Actor Needs to Know*)

Holly Powell is an Emmy Award-winning former casting director and recipient of the Casting Society of America's Artios Award. She served as CBS Network's Director of Casting, both East and West coasts, and as Senior Vice President of Casting for the Greenblatt Janollari Studio. She was also an independent casting director for many years with Holly Powell Casting, Stone Powell Casting, and Powell Melcher Casting. Through Holly Powell Studios, she teaches workshops at drama schools and universities around the country. She won the Backstage Readers' Choice Award, 'Favorite Audition Technique Teacher,' two years running.

Holly is the author of *The Audition Bible: Secrets Every Actor Needs to Know* and released a second edition to stay current after the COVID19 pandemic changed much about audition protocol. She recorded the Audible version of both editions of *The Audition Bible* and co-authored her mother's cookbook *Mavis' Kitchen: A Southern Cooking Lifestyle*.

Holly is a founding member of She Angels Foundation, co-founder of Beyond Ranch Foundation, and a supporter of SANGO-Kenya.

I always liken the actor to the athlete. Athletes must have mental discipline in order to accomplish the task at hand. "The tyranny of the scattered mind, can be the downfall of the pitcher," writes sports psychologist, H. A. Dorfman in *The Mental ABC's of Pitching*.

"The pitcher should only be thinking about three things: pitch selection, pitch location, and his target, the catcher's glove. If the pitcher focuses on these three simple tasks, he will be able to control his scattered thoughts and achieve mental discipline."

In my audition workshops at Holly Powell Studios, I teach The 6 Audition Tools Method. They are Sense of Place, Relationship, Intention, Pre-Beat, Listen, Respond in The Listening. When these six tools are used together, they help an actor master the audition process and produce real results.

Actors benefit by thinking of themselves as pitchers on the mound. If the pitcher, as Dorfman advises, should only be thinking of three things to achieve focus before he steps on the mound, then the actor should only be thinking of the first four tools – Sense of Place, Relationship, Intention, Pre-Beat – to achieve focus before an audition.

Once the scene begins, the ability to *Listen* grounds you, and being able to *Respond in the Listening* will make you present in the moment.

Tool #1: SENSE OF PLACE

Where are you in the scene?

A prepared actor needs to convey a more compelling visual for viewers than just, *I'm in my office,* or *I'm in a grocery store,* or *I'm in my car*. You must get a specific visualization of the place the scene is set. For instance, if the scene occurs in the character's office, you need a specific mental image of where the phone, desk, window, and door are.

The physical location of the scene will often determine whether the actor stands or sits in the audition. Is your character walking down the street? Or drinking in a bar? If the scene describes the character driving a car while talking with friends, the better choice would be to sit. Let the viewer know that you understand where the scene takes place, and visualize specifically what the car looks like.

One of the most confusing things an actor struggles with in preparing for an audition is how to deal with all those stage directions. Remember that you can't audition a scene the way it will be filmed, so be sensible about portraying a sense of place. It's in the actor's best interest to stick as closely to the writer's intent as much as possible, but the stage directions do not necessarily need to be taken literally. If they state that the character is sitting on a couch but the dialogue has

THE SIX AUDITION TOOLS METHOD

no reference to sitting on a couch, it's the actor's choice whether to stand or sit, based on the character's intention in the scene.

In the five seconds before the audition starts, as you survey the audition room (or your own room if the audition is remote,) visualize specifically where you are in the scene. If you imagine the place through your mind's eye, viewers will start to see it too, before you even speak your first line. If you're not specific as to place, the viewer may think you don't understand the scene, are not prepared, or worse yet, are not talented enough to create a compelling sense of place.

Tool #2: RELATIONSHIP

Who is your character talking to? Who are they talking about?

It's a lot of fun for me when I recognize that an actor is visualizing a specific person to match a character being addressed. It makes the audition very personalized.

A wonderful actress, Susan Parks, came to coach with me for an audition. In the sides, her character wanted her boyfriend to do something for her. Susan had taken my audition workshop before and knew all about my Six Audition Tools. As we ran through the scene, I couldn't quite put my finger on what was missing. I asked if she had a boyfriend in real life.

Her body and face tilted slightly to the side in a coy, sexy way. "Yeessss ...," she said, practically purring.

"Do the scene again, and put your boyfriend's image on my face." Bingo.

Susan had understood through doing her homework that the scene was with her boyfriend, and intellectually understood how her character felt about him. But working on the scene initially, she hadn't been specific in visualizing someone in her personal life. When she thought of her current boyfriend, I could almost see his image in her mind's eye.

Relationship is not only who you're talking to in the scene, but who you're talking about. An entire scene can be about discussing someone who is never present. So, if you don't have a clear understanding of what your relationship is with that third person, plus a clear visual image, your audition will lack specificity.

If I mention to you that my ninety-two-year-old mother called me from Dallas last night, I am visualizing my mother in my head as I'm telling you this story. And the tone in my voice when I mention my mother will speak volumes about how I feel about her.

Your character need only mention another character's name once, and viewers should be able to imagine that person, and know how you feel about them. Let's say your character is hanging out in a bar with friends and your dad walks in the bar. Just by how your character says, "Dad," viewers should be able to visualize him and know how you feel about him.

<u>Visualization and being specific are key.</u> Even if you have the sides for only a short period of time, it's imperative to get specific about what your relationship is to the person or people in the scene. This will save you when the casting director is reading multiple parts.

Tool #3: INTENTION

What does your character want?

Often an actor doesn't have a clear handle on what their character's intention is (what they want) in a scene. When I ask actors in my audition workshops what the intention is, the answer is sometimes, "I don't know," "I'm confused," "I haven't decided," or it could be a long, convoluted explanation.

My advice is to keep the intention simple: I want to change his mind, or I want to convince him I'm right, or I want to make her like me.

Often actors make the mistake of lacking a clear intention, or they play only one intention throughout the scene. When working on an audition scene, it's your job to identify what the character's initial intention is, and exactly where the intention changes. The scene will then have a beginning, middle, and end, and help you steer clear of making your audition a one-note scene.

<u>Whatever the character's initial intention, it almost always changes during the scene.</u> That's what makes it interesting. It's also likely why the casting director has chosen this scene for the audition, because something shifts – the character changes their tactic or their intention – and the casting director wants to see how you handle that.

Intention changes in a scene are based on circumstances and/or what another character says. The writer has written these changes into the dialogue and actions to further the story and/or create a surprise for both the characters and the audience.

Let's say your character goes into a grocery store to get some milk. Tool #1: Sense of Place is the grocery store. Tool #3: Intention is that your character wants to buy a carton of milk. But as your character walks briskly down the aisle, she bumps into her ex-husband, and Tool #2: Relationship comes into play. What is her new intention? It might be to confront him, physically assault him, or get past him to leave the store. The character's intention has changed.

One of the essential goals of an audition is to demonstrate your range. Writers often use the scene description or stage directions to give the actor a roadmap, for example, Joan talks a mile a minute as she rushes to get ready for work. By all means, use this description as a guideline, but don't take it to mean you should literally talk fast throughout the entire scene.

Maybe you've decided your intention at the top of the scene is to punish your boyfriend for breaking up with you, and you've made the choice that your character is openly angry. The writer may even have described the character as "yelling." But if you yell throughout the scene, it becomes tiring for an audience; it devolves into a one-note performance, and you've missed the opportunity to explore a variety of emotions, nuanced manipulations, and different tactics.

In my audition workshops, I discuss one of the Seven Universal Laws: The Principle of Polarity, which states that everything has an opposite, and opposites are identical in nature. Therefore, emotions rise in dualities: happy/sad, love/hate, angry/calm, meaning we wouldn't be able to fully understand "anger" if we had never experienced "calm."

As an actor, it's your job to find the duality of emotion in the scene and make sure you understand not only that your character feels angry, but recognize that calm is the flip side of anger, and also needs to be explored. Once you hook into your intention in the scene, exploring these dualities of emotion will not only infuse your audition with depth and range, it will help you facilitate a smooth transition when the intention changes.

Tool #4: PRE-BEAT OR THE MOMENT BEFORE

What just happened?

Right before the audition begins, when an actor stands in front of a casting director, it's a "make it or break it" moment. Just like a pitcher stepping onto the mound, if your thoughts aren't focused, odds are the audition will get off to a rocky start.

When asked, "Are you ready to start?" an actor's instinct is often to please the casting director. So, instead of taking a few seconds to get mentally focused, they'll dive right in and start the audition. Don't want to keep the casting director waiting!

The comment I've heard too-often from producers and directors after an actor left the audition room was, "That actor was okay about halfway through the scene."

That's because they did not focus on the moment before the scene. Rather, they started too quickly. By not being in the middle of something before the first line, it took the actor a bit to warm up, by which time the viewers lost interest.

One of the simple tools to control mental focus in an audition is Tool #4: Pre-Beat or The Moment Before. Be specific. If you can't figure out from the sides exactly what happened before the scene started, make something up. Mining the sides for as much information as you can get, as well as reading through any crossed-out sections of dialogue, can help you piece together a pre-beat.

When I was working with Bob Greenblatt and David Janollari as their Senior Vice President of Casting, they were developing *Six Feet Under* with Alan Ball. Alan had recently finished AMERICAN BEAUTY (for which he later won the Academy Award for Best Original Screenplay.) He told me a story about Annette Benning, who plays Jessica in the film.

Jessica had to drive up in her car, get out, then walk through the front door of her house, where she encountered some kind of situation.

The director, Sam Mendes, turned to Annette and asked, "What was happening right before you opened the front door and entered the house?"

Without missing a beat, she answered something like, "I was looking at my blouse that I just got from the dry cleaners, and there's a spot on it!"

THE SIX AUDITION TOOLS METHOD

Annette gave her character a specific thought as she entered the house, one which was not spelled out in the script. So, there was no anticipation of what awaited her on the other side of her front door. She didn't just start a scene, she was in the middle of something.

Before you say the first line of your audition scene, touch base with the first four tools: Sense of Place, Relationship, Intention, and Pre-Beat. By taking five seconds to ask yourself, *Where am I? Who am I talking to? What do I want? and What just happened?* – you'll begin the scene prepared and in the middle of something. Make eye contact with the reader, and go!

Tool #5: LISTEN

What is the other character saying?

Listening at an audition can be challenging. A casting director, or their assistant, is usually just feeding the actor lines, or worse, attempting to act the role.

In response, actors expect to get nothing back and tend to put up a wall. This leads to merely waiting for the reader to finish speaking and thinking about how they're going to say their next line. The actor shifts into a technical performance instead of being in the moment and genuinely listening.

My former mother-in-law, the wonderful Tony Award–winning actress Frances Sternhagen, was doing a play in New York with a TV star who had done very little theater. He was so used to acting in front of a camera, he would barely look at her onstage. She was frustrated that she wasn't getting anything back from her fellow actor.

Frances had studied with Lee Strasberg, and to get through each performance she applied his "as if" concept: to find a specific visualization of someone in her own personal life to apply to her fellow actor. In this case, Frances visualized her co-star "as if" he was her current husband whom she loved, to bring up the emotions necessary for the onstage relationship.

Frances had also studied with Sanford Meisner and remembered his words: "When you aren't getting back from another actor what you need, you have to let the words be enough."

So instead of listening to "how" her co-star was speaking every night, she listened only to the words he was speaking. The "what," not the "how." Using these two teachers' techniques saved her every night onstage.

I was just starting to cast in New York theater, and when she told me about how she dealt with the situation, I thought, *That's exactly what an audition is like!* Actors don't get back what they need when reading with a casting director or reader.

The concept of "as if" had its roots in the Group Theatre in New York City in the 1930s, and derived from Constantin Stanislavski's The System. Lee Strasberg advanced this technique in the 1940s and 1950s, and named it The Method.

He asked actors to use substitution to recall emotions from their own personal lives, and replace the circumstances in the script with their own similar experience.

Members of the Group Theatre included Sanford Meisner and Stella Adler. Meisner broke from Strasberg to develop the Meisner Technique, best described as living truthfully under imaginary circumstances. He asked actors to remain in the moment, to concentrate on their scene partners. And when the partner was not present or "there," he instructed actors to focus on the words themselves.

That's what an actor has to do in an audition: to listen to the words being read to remain present in the moment. Don't listen to how the lines are read but rather what is being said.

Stella Adler believed that drawing on personal experience was too limiting, so she also went her own way to create an approach that didn't rely on the actor's own personal memories to summon emotions, but instead used a scene's given circumstances.

The point to describing these different iconic acting teachers' techniques is that Frances Sternhagen had studied with both Strasberg and Meisner, and these amazing teachers both had an influence on her own acting technique. To save herself onstage every night in that play, she called on both mentors' teaching.

Listening to the reader's words grounds the actor in the present moment. Comparing notes with fellow casting directors over the years, we all agree, the biggest compliment we can relate is, "That actor was so present."

THE SIX AUDITION TOOLS METHOD

It's easy to spot an actor who is listening, compared with an actor who's just waiting for the next line. The most interesting audition for a casting director is seeing an actor truly listen.

Tool #6: RESPOND IN THE LISTENING

Many TV and film auditions these days are recorded on-camera for the producers and director. It's important to remember that when your audition is on-camera, you are usually framed just below your shoulders. The reader is reading off-camera, and all viewers can see is you and your responses. So, fifty percent of a recorded audition is watching you listen.

You must visualize the reader as the character you're talking to in the sides. This is where Tool #2: Relationship comes into play, and if it's used correctly, viewers watching the recorded audition will believe you're talking to the character in the script, not the reader.

If you listen to the reader, responding silently to what is being said, the viewers will see a person who is present in the scene. The viewers should see the thoughts running through your mind as you listen to the other character(s) in the scene. There is action in reaction.

Trust me when I tell you that if the viewers of the recorded audition see a blank face as you wait for your cue, they'll skip to the next actor. They can see when you're merely waiting for the next line rather than actively listening. After about fifteen seconds, they'll lose interest. "Next!"

I love telling the story of a role I was casting for the pilot of *Beck and Call*. It was for a coffee barista to answer another character's question, "Where's Oscar?"

The barista's single line was, "He works at the 57th Street store now."

That's it. One line. What was unique about this barista role was that the actor had to listen for a full page of dialogue, while miming making coffee. For each audition, I read the entire page of dialogue so my producers could see the actors respond in the listening.

Remember that Tool #5: Listen and Tool #6: Respond in the Listening go hand in hand in making the audition successful. Silently responding to what another character says is fifty percent of an actor's audition. For the casting director, seeing the thoughts go through an actor's head as they form a response is often the most powerful part of the audition.

PREPARATION

The Audition Bible Checklist: The 6 Audition Tools Method

Tool #1: SENSE OF PLACE

Where are you? Use visualization to imagine the physical location of the scene. Looking around the audition room, place exactly where objects are in this particular environment.

Tool #2: RELATIONSHIP

Who are you talking to? Who are you talking about? Decide how you emotionally feel about the other character(s). Use a specific person from your life to bring up the right emotions.

Tool #3: INTENTION

What do you want? Figure out a simple clear goal for your character in the scene, based on what they say and do, or fail to say and do.

Based on the circumstances and what the other character says, figure out how, when, and why your character's intention changes as the scene unfolds.

If there's not enough information in the sides, make up a simple clear intention for your character. Also find a place to shift your tactic and/or change your intention.

Tool #4: PRE-BEAT OR THE MOMENT BEFORE

What happened just before? Make a decision about what happened, or was just said prior to the actual first line of the scene. Remember, you are always in the middle of something.

Tool #5: LISTEN

What dialogue do you hear? Listening grounds you in the present moment. Don't just wait for your next cue, actively listen to the words being read by the reader.

THE SIX AUDITION TOOLS METHOD

Tool #6: RESPOND IN THE LISTENING

How does your character respond to the words being said? How do you feel? What is a natural nonverbal response? What new intention or tactic arises in your mind?

I read somewhere that during the taping of *Friends*, the producers always cut to Lisa Kudrow for reaction shots because she was so brilliant at Responding in the Listening. I recommend you watch a few episodes of *Friends* to see how Lisa used this vital tool to hilarious perfection. Consider it homework.

"Strong reasons make strong actions."

- WILLIAM SHAKESPEARE

CRYSTAL CARSON

No Schm-Acting, Please

Crystal devotes herself to deepening the authenticity of actors. She is highly recommended by major managers, agents, directors, producers, casting directors, and professional actors, including Oscar-nominee Russell Crowe.

As an elite acting coach in Los Angeles for over 30 years, Crystal is especially skillful at accommodating an individual's methods and personality. She has traveled the world teaching her advanced yet accessible process to generate a character's life, known as the Carson Method, which emphasizes creating personalized histories that allow an actor to easily come from truth. She offers retreats for actors who are differently abled and works with the Professional Actors Theatre of The Handicapped, sponsored by CBS-TV.

A former actor herself, Crystal studied with Uta Hagen, Sanford Meisner, Howard Fine and Eric Morris. She performed in over 25 plays and had a career in film and television, including a five-year run as Julia Barrett on *General Hospital*. After studying human psychology, she developed The Carson Method to humanize the technical aspects of the actors' auditioning process. Crystal's other piece in this book is "Learn Your Lines by Heart" in Chapter 7.

In an attempt to get actors to be "real" during their auditions, some acting teachers advise: "Memorize your lines and then just be yourself, and listen and react." On its own, this advice often leads actors to become self-conscious, because of the way our brains work.

Human brains tend to overgeneralize, meaning the better an actor listens and reacts in the scene, the more their brain can't tell the difference between acting and real life. This sounds like a good thing, and it is, <u>unless</u> the brain tries to find memories of what's being discussed, and they're missing. If the actor doesn't create them, images of these memories can't be found and the brain starts to race. This extra energy is often called the fight-or-flight response, anxiety, panic, or what we in our industry might label as, "stage fright."

See, your brain is measuring what you're saying against your own past experience. When there's no 'lived' history and no images to recall, the brain decides that what is being said is a lie, and a subconscious network kicks in, which is the autonomic nervous system reacting with an 'alarm' response.

The brain wasn't made to lie, so when you say what it knows to be untrue, it strains the frontal lobe, which is responsible for reasoning, motor control, emotions, and language. Glands secrete adrenaline causing sweat. Hands and feet go cold and clammy as blood flows away from the extremities toward the struggling brain. Core muscles, like the stomach and bladder, tighten up, causing shallow breathing and a need to pee. The heart pumps faster; the gastrointestinal system slows down, excreting acid, gas, sometimes even diarrhea. The actor valiantly attempts to ignore all this and say the lines appropriately.

However, it's impossible not to be conscious of the self (mind and body) when it's manifesting such internal chaos. There's a reason 'self-conscious' and 'nervous' are synonymous.

And that's just what's going on inside. Externally, the auditioning actor attempting to respond 'naturally' to their off-camera reader, who is only supposed to read lines quickly, quietly, and without emotion, puts the actor into turmoil as the scene goes flat.

Scripts aren't about boring circumstances, but the actor who prepares by memorizing alone might wonder, *How dynamic or 'big' can I be if I need to react honestly to a reader who's not going to give me anything?* The temptation can be to ignore how the reader says the lines and work out how to deliver your own lines in advance, an effort I call "Schm-acting."

There is nothing more insulting – to the craft or to an audience – than an actor who has pre-shaped lines to sound 'natural' or 'real', or predetermined how 'big' they should be, or which words to punch. The problem is, real people don't <u>try</u> to be real, they <u>are</u> real.

While it's true that for an audition you're not given much time, information, or the whole script, it's still your job to use your imagination to invent what you don't know about the relationships, history, and what you need from the other person... complete with images. If done right, your brain will interpret these inventions as actual memories.

When you prepare this way, it's incredible how easily your attention focuses on the other person. Not only does self-consciousness drop away, but the emotional truth of your character's life comes out. Suddenly you know your lines without trying, and you're the 'right' size, while reacting honestly to even the most stilted reader. (See also "Learning Lines by Heart" in Chapter 7.)

For example, the reader says, "Where is he?" and your line in response is, "Let's wait. He'll be here soon."

If it's not provided in the scene/s, (also known as "sides"), you need to invent context for yourself, or you won't have enough to hang your hat on, and it won't be interesting to you.

Imagined history calms your brain and supports your focus, so you can stay inside the story and generate your character's thoughts, which will produce real feelings inside you.

On the other hand, when you say lines without any backstory, you're 'schm-acting': <u>trying</u> to sound like you're thinking and feeling. No matter how natural you sound, the line will ring false to your brain if you're speaking about something you haven't invented for yourself.

If you schm-act, the viewer may not think you're a bad actor. If they're into the story, they'll likely give you the benefit of the doubt, but think, *This character doesn't mean it, they're pretending to be a certain way, this character is full of crap.* They'll watch you, but they won't step inside the scene and experience the character through you.

If the next actor has something real at stake, feels the potential consequences of failing, has personalized the relationships, and created specific moments of backstory, it's a whole different experience for everyone.

When you first read the piece, don't approach it like, *I'm going to audition for this,* but rather, *Ooh, this is an interesting little slice of a story.* Pay attention to any description of the location and the stage directions. Imagine the sounds and temperature and smells – the things outside of yourself. We react differently if we're on top of a mountain

NO SCHM-ACTING, PLEASE

than we do if we're at a doctor appointment, so the environment matters, a lot.

After you've read the scene once, figure out if you understand what's going on.

Okay, my character is going to be in trouble with this heroin dealer if someone else doesn't show up with ten thousand dollars in the next five minutes. Besides how it feels to be in this environment, that's all I know. That's all the scene is so far.

On the second read, imagine yourself in those circumstances, and feel the environment you created. Put your focus on the other characters' lines. You will automatically pay attention to your own lines, so what you want to do is get your attention where it would naturally be if this was happening in real life; which is focused on everything *outside* of yourself.

After the second read, ask yourself, *Why do I know this heroin dealer, and for how long? When did we meet? What were our other interactions like?* Picture a little backstory of moments between you and the heroin dealer.

What if the sides don't tell you your relationship with the character who isn't here yet? Ask yourself, *Who is this person? Why do I think they'll give me $10,000? Why aren't they here?* Again, picture small scenarios around your answers.

You could imagine the missing person is your Dad, who you hope will bring the $10,000 you owe the heroin dealer. Ask yourself, *What will the dealer do if Dad doesn't show up?*

You could decide your character has been using heroin for the last nine months. Your parents already loaned you a lot of money. Your sister told them you stole the cash meant to pay for her dorm room. Every time they turn around, they catch you lying or stealing. They say you've been looking ragged and have dark circles under your eyes. You finally confessed you've been shooting up. Your parents are retired and have gotten into trouble borrowing money to help you for things they now realize were complete lies. They're fed up and no longer believe you.

Still, you called and begged, "I need you to bring ten thousand dollars or this guy's going to kill me. This is the address. Please be there, Dad."

You cried on the phone, because you know he doesn't trust you and he doesn't have that kind of money, but you hope he'll bring it anyway.

Now that you've prepared a history like this, during your third read, when you hear the dealer say, "Where is he?" your breath will catch, your heart will skip a beat, and you're really going to listen, because it's a matter of life and death to you. You may try to hide these feelings from the dealer, but they're still there inside you as you respond with, "He's not here."

As actors, particularly auditioning actors, we often forget to <u>feel</u> the character's fight, meaning what the other character/s want from you and what your character wants from them.

In this scenario, maybe you decide you want to get out alive and the dealer wants the debt paid, with money or your life. Next, personalize what losing the fight will mean for you. Together, these thoughts will produce a feeling of pressure from the other character when you say, "He's not here."

During this third read, maybe you're looking around the room and out the window, allowing character thoughts to bubble up, like, *Can I see my dad pulling up outside? How fast can I get out of here if he doesn't show up? Is that a dead body in the other room?*

You push down the fear and say, "Let's wait. He'll be here soon." Perhaps you try to sound casual to cover up your doubt that your dad will actually show up.

An actor who has created a real situation like this doesn't choose to sound casual because it's a clever way of acting, they do it to <u>keep the other person from killing them.</u>

Given this kind of preparation, it doesn't matter how the reader in the audition says, "Where is he?"

Since you created context for all the characters, you've imbued their lines with subtext that puts pressure on you. No matter their line delivery, your prep will allow you to respond truthfully, with real thoughts and feelings. It's just amazing.

Your made-up context and details may or may not be accurate to the script. As long as you extracted them logically from the givens, don't worry about that. It's not what matters for a compelling audition. Directors have told me, "I'd rather hire somebody who is wrong about the way I saw the character, but I can see that they have great instincts. They're a really good actor."

The best you can do with limited information is show that you have the intelligence and imagination to make strong backstory choices, commit to them, and express genuine emotion. The people hiring you want to feel that you aren't pretending to be scared, but that you actually are scared. If you imagine being in a specific threatening situation, like we created above, they'll see your face flush, your eyes water, and they'll feel your feelings along with you!

Those physical responses can't really be faked because they only happen when you have the actual feelings, and we can tell instinctively if they're not authentic.

If you take the time to understand what's going on in the scene and make your own strong choices, they will get why you went in that direction, even if it wasn't accurate to the script.

They're going to 1) give you re-direction, as they're considering you for the role. Or if you don't have the right look for it, they may 2) consider you for a different role on the same project, or, at the very least, 3) they're going to remember you as somebody who did a good job on your audition and whom they would like to see again. Maybe they will bring you in to audition for the next project. One of those three things will happen, and that's how you get a career.

PREPARATION

To begin your preparation, it can be helpful to look up previous productions the writer, director and company have done to gain a sense of the possible tone. People tend to work in the same genres. That, added to the breakdown, storyline and any other information is a great place to start, even before reading the scene.

Now prepare for an audition without 'schm-acting.'

<u>First Read of the Scene</u>
Read it as a piece of a story. Read it as if it were a couple of pages in a novel, without reading any lines out loud. Imagine, in as much detail as you can, what is and what is not on the page. Do you understand what's going on? Where is this scene happening?

Read the stage directions out loud so you don't miss anything. When you're finished, ask yourself: *Is it indoors or outdoors? What time of day is it? How big is the space?*

Do you think it's cold? Is it warm and cozy? Too hot? Is it starkly furnished? Is it quiet or noisy? What kind of noises? How does it smell? Is it familiar – have you been here before? How does this space make you feel? Take a moment to breathe and picture that place, and what it feels like to be there.

Second Read of the Scene

Sit or stand in the space you imagined, based on the givens in the script. Commit to that space, feel what it's like to be there. Feel the boat moving, or hear the air conditioner come on, or someone paging a doctor; smell the cookies or the gunpowder. Now, from this place, read everybody else's lines out loud. Put your attention on the other character/s.

If you want, you can read the stage directions and your lines silently in your mind. Feel how your character moves. Does the scene say they try to exit to the next room, but are stopped? What does that feel like?

When you finish reading everyone else's lines, ask yourself, for your character:

- Who is the main person I'm dealing with?
- How long have I known them?
- What do they look like? Are they tall, short, gruff, sexy, strong, intimidating?

Third Read of the Scene

By now you sort of have an idea of the arc of the scene, and you're getting what the scene is about, how it feels to be where you are, and who the other people are. It's time to discover what it is that you want from them, and the consequences of failing.

- What is the "fight" between you and the other character? (Your objective.)
- What kind of pressure are they putting on you?
- What kind of pressure are you putting on them?
- Given the situation, what is at stake? What are the most serious consequences possible for you, if you don't get what you want? Is

it literal life or death? Or an emotional life or death, like losing someone's love?
- What is the backstory, meaning your history with this character? What led up to this fight?

As you explore these questions in your imagination, in the context of what is given in the scene, thoughts and feelings will bubble up, and you may just surprise yourself at how quickly you can deeply inhabit "your new life."

I encourage you to also explore and incorporate my other preparation in this book: "Learning Lines by Heart" – they work together!

PAUL GUAY

Audition Notes

Paul Guay is a writer/actor/director whose movies have grossed over half a billion dollars. He conceived and co-wrote LIAR, LIAR, at the time of its release the sixth-highest-grossing comedy in history. The screenplay received an Honorable Mention in *Scr(i)pt* magazine's list of the Best Scripts of the Past 10 Years. He co-wrote THE LITTLE RASCALS, Universal's second-highest-grossing film of the year, and co-wrote HEARTBREAKERS, starring Sigourney Weaver, Jennifer Love Hewitt, Gene Hackman and Jason Lee, which opened #1 at the box office. After directing the most successful comedy (or for that matter, drama) in the 75-year history of Santa Monica's Morgan-Wixson Theatre, Paul made his movie-directing debut with the three short comedy films discussed herein. He has a bunch of cool shit coming up. In his spare time, he acts.

So I'm auditioning an actress to play a sultry and uber-confident femme fatale in my short film *The Godfather*, and I'm not getting the confidence I need.

I suggest to the actress that if her character encountered Lauren Bacall in a nightclub, her character would laugh dismissively, because she was everything Bacall *wanted* to be.

"Lauren Bacall?" the actress inquires. "I'm not good with names."

* * *

Through Breakdown Express, I list thirty roles I'm casting in three short films I wrote and am directing. I attach the full script for each film. I make it clear that these are comedies, and that for two of the films I'm looking for classic leading-man types.

I receive over five thousand submissions.

I look at maybe a thousand reels. I see tons of angsty, violent, dark, shouty, quirky character work, some of it very good.

I see almost no leading men.

And I see almost no comedy of any kind.

* * *

An actor tapes a wonderful audition for the role of Caesar in my short, *Who Guardeth the Guards?*

At the callbacks I give him an adjustment. He's done an operatic rendition of the silly song I wrote for Caesar, and now I ask if he'll try a rock rendition.

I'm asking for two reasons:

One, I want to see which I like better, so I'll know which to shoot.

Two, and more importantly, I give an adjustment to every actor I audition for every role, because I want to see how creative and how flexible they are.

He bristles.

"I studied <u>opera</u>," he informs me. "I wouldn't know where to <u>begin</u> with rock."

* * *

If the above is <u>not</u> what I'm looking for at an audition, what <u>am</u> I looking for?

One of the actors auditioning for Van Helsing in my short *The Vampyre* shoots himself from several camera angles while playing the scenes and cuts them together.

This isn't why I cast him. I cast him because:

a) I need a leading man for Van Helsing, and he is an actual leading man;

b) he understands comedy; and

c) he is absolutely excellent.

But the professionalism with which he shoots the tape, the effort he goes to in putting together his audition, and the desire for the role that effort implies, stand out from the other five thousand submissions.

One of the actors auditioning for the Living Statue of Mercury in *Who Guardeth the Guards?* submits a tape that is just okay. I invite him to callbacks. There he is so creative and offers me so many choices that... well, here's the recommendation I write for him after we wrap:

"Seventy actors submitted for the Living Statue of Mercury; R. was my only choice. His audition was so inventive, it suggested comedic possibilities that I subsequently used in the film. When we were in production, R. was a pro. Shooting on a tight schedule in a cold wind while wearing skimpy robes and body paint, R. remained focused, hardworking, and collaborative, offering me both physical and attitudinal options for every scene. I'd work with him again in a heartbeat, even without a cold wind."

What else do I care about as a director – and as a writer and actor and audience member?

I care about actors who are <u>alive</u> onstage or onscreen. Actors who have a spark, a sense of fun, of spontaneity and danger and unpredictability. Actors who are <u>interesting</u>.

The purpose of acting is to bring a written character to three-dimensional life. But there are many ways to do that. I'm looking for the most electric, intense, responsive, immediate, playful, specific, committed, alive version of the character.

Sometimes less is more. But sometimes more is more.

When it comes to acting – when it comes to any of the arts – I want to be moved. I want to be excited. I want to be entertained. I want to believe.

And most of all, I want to care.

PREPARATION

1. Know your art. Know your craft. Know the field you've entered into – which includes not only today's stars and character actors, but also the luminaries of the past. You are part of a continuum; acting didn't begin when you were born, and it won't die when you leave us. Enjoy, marvel at, learn from the work, not only of your contemporaries, but also of the best of those who preceded you.

2. Pay attention to the genre of the piece you're submitting for. For example, if a film is described as a comedy, submit something that shows your comedy chops. If a script is attached, read it. Submit something similar in tone to the script.

3. A lot of actors are submitting angsty, violent, dark, shouty, quirky character work. Stand out by offering something they're not. For

example, if the director is looking for a classic leading-man or -woman type, offer something that shows you fit the bill.

4. Welcome adjustments. They are an opportunity to show your creativity, your flexibility, your range. Your way may be the best way – but it may not be. And maybe the director is looking for something other than, or in addition to, the "best" way; maybe he's looking to see how you take direction.

5. If you really want the role, go the extra mile in your audition video.

6. Offer choices. Working with an actor who brings invention and options to the table is a director's dream.

7. Be bold. Be memorable. Better a fascinating, specific, committed "wrong" approach than a boring, bland, generic "right" one... especially if you're flexible and directable.

DANIELLE ESKINAZI

Casting Directors Do Care

With over two decades in film, television, theater, and commercials, Danielle Eskinazi is a respected casting director with the ability to draw out audition-nailing performances. She has cast David Bowie, Rosanna Arquette, and Woody Harrelson, and launched the careers of now-successful actors including Hank Azaria and Milla Jovovich. Danielle Eskinazi Casting has cast over three thousand national and regional spots, and is known for finding edgy and talented actors to suit her directors' and clients' needs. She was nominated for the Talent Managers' Association's prestigious Seymour Heller Award for "Best Commercial Casting Director" of 2009, and was a two-time runner up for "Favorite Commercial Casting Director" in *Backstage West*.

Danielle speaks on industry panels and teaches workshops. She is affiliated with the AFI Women's Program, helping first-time directors cast their shorts. She is the creator of the DE Casting App for actors.

I'm definitely not an actor. I was in the retail business for many years, as a buyer, and I wanted to get out of it. I was so bored that I went to a friend of mine who was one of the big agents at Triad. There was CAA, Triad, ICM and William Morris. I told her, "I want to get into something in the entertainment business. What do you think I should do?"

She said, "I think you'd be really good at casting." Three days later, she said, "I got you a new job."

It was with Risa Bramon and Billy Hopkins, who were huge, but I had no idea who they were. They were doing a couple of movies on the East Coast and needed a West Coast casting assistant to read actors for a film called AT CLOSE RANGE.

I asked my friend, "Do they know I've never done this before?"

They just needed someone to schedule and read actors and I thought, *I can do that.* I was very naive, which I think got me through it, because I asked tons of questions. I didn't fake it. They said, "Okay, great, you're hired."

They gave me an office on Sunset Boulevard with the most incredible view and I was like, *Yeah, this feels good so far.* I got to my office and there was a guy sitting on the floor. It was Sean Penn and he was on the phone with Madonna — they were married at the time. He said, "Oh, is this your office?"

I said, "Yeah, but it's fine, you can sit there."

He said, "That's okay. It's a private conversation," and stepped out of the office.

Ever since then, I went gleefully every day to my job and loved everything about it. It was awesome and I thought, *This is my niche.* I still thank my friend all the time.

I went on to work with Victoria Thomas, and Amanda Mackey, and Ronnie Yeskel, who did all the Quentin Tarantino films. My biggest mentor was Lee Daniels. He was a manager at the time, and I would call him and ask, "What do I do now?"

He'd say, "Calm down. You got this. This is what you need to do."

I did film for ten years and helped some directors at American Film Institute. Then a production company was looking for someone to cast their commercials with a theatrical eye. I thought, *Yeah, let me try it.* I loved it and never went back. So now I do commercials.

This is the process: I send all the agents a description of what we're looking for – the character, the ethnicity, the age, maybe the height range. But I want to say that one of my favorite things is to pepper in a few people who don't match the description, whom I think might still be good for the part. Sometimes the director and the ad agency say, "Wow, we never thought of that. That's kind of cool. Let's bring them back and see what they can do." That's when I kind of pat myself on the back.

After I send out the description, agents start submitting, and I go through everything. Basically, we do all the dirty work before we present a short list to a director.

I build an audition schedule, and make sure the dialogue is up, so there's no excuses.

Today, everything's basically online, so an audition is obviously a lot different from what it used to be. When you're on Zoom you're worrying about camera angles and WIFI signals, and I want all that eliminated as much as possible. Ideally, when the actor is in the room, we can just work with them without any distractions.

I was a movie buff before I got into casting and had my ideas of what was a good performance. But seeing someone on the big screen or in a commercial is different from being in the same room with an actor doing an audition. With experience, you learn what to look for.

Sometimes with nonunion actors, you can tell they're thinking they might want to be an actor, do some commercials and then maybe some theatrical work, all <u>without taking any classes</u>.

They imagine it's that easy, but it's not. Acting is an art and a discipline – you can't fake it.

If someone is green and they just don't get it, you can tell right off. They're not centered. There's no foundation. It's empty. You know you can't get them there, because you're not their teacher. They're not here for a class, they're here to work.

I can see immediately when someone doesn't understand how to develop a character. When you read the script, you have to read between the lines. You can't just read it; you have to feel it. Even if it's a commercial, you have to feel it.

For example, some of the pharmaceutical ads are many paragraphs long. If you just read it without knowing what you're saying, it won't work. We want to hear you talk about the product like you've experienced it.

So my advice is to get some training before going to your first audition. I also think improv really helps with auditions, as well as working with a director. If a director switches something up on you, you better bring it. You can't say, "I don't know what you mean. I'm confused." A director wants to work with an actor who says, "Got it."

I want the actor coming to audition to feel as comfortable and confident as possible. If they're in a bad mood, I say, "Why don't you go outside (or outside the Zoom room), get yourself together, and then come back in?"

Sometimes they're just not prepared. Then we have to go through the whole thing with them, see if they can understand the character, and then show us their essence.

But the most common mistake I see is that a lot of actors come in overly-confident or cocky, and we have to kind of strip that away, because that's not their core personality and essence. It seems like they prepared a scene so much they can't undo it, they're not flexible enough for us to redirect them. They're stuck in a certain approach.

If the actor has something in their mind, we let them do it, we want them to do that. We want you to prepare for an audition and make specific choices. I want you to bring in what you think the character is.

I want you to be able to portray the character we're looking for as well. If it's not what we're looking for, I'll say, "Wow, that's an interesting way to do it. I like what you did. Now let me tell you more about what we're looking for and see if you can adjust to that."

This is where improv comes in – it can help you think on your feet.

If I ask an actor to try it another way, it's because I've had many conversations with the director and the ad agency, so I know what they're looking for. I'm trying to help the actor with their audition. What I would call cockiness is if they are certain their way of doing the scene is the best way and don't want to listen.

Here's a tip for a commercial audition. Look at the brand. Get a feel for their voice and style because that can inform your preparation. Consider dressing in a way that shows you know who they are – if you're going in for a Target commercial you might want to wear red, or blue for Best Buy.

I also teach classes once a month. Something I've noticed is that when some actors, actresses mostly, get really nervous, their voices go very high, like everything is a question. I always tell them, "That's great. But in order for us to believe you, bring your voice down a little."

You want to communicate with your audience. As an audience, we don't want to feel like you're questioning everything. That questioning sound of the voice going up at the end of sentence makes it sound like the actor is doing the questioning, not just the character. It comes across as if they're not really sure what's in the script.

In an audition, one of the main things we're looking to see is your essence, your own believing in yourself as an actor, and your confident questions. A lot of actors come in and they're really stiff, they come across as unsure of what to do. If you're not sure about something, if you have a question, don't just do it and see what happens. Ask first, because our answer might change your mind a bit.

We are <u>on your side</u>. We want you to book. We don't want to make you feel like we're above you. We're not. Without actors, we don't have jobs. Neither do directors, nor do production companies. So agents, managers, casting directors, we all have one goal, and that's for you to book a job.

If you don't get the job, it does not mean you were "bad." You're in a position of having to depend on other people's opinions and them getting exactly what they want. Their choice has nothing to do with your look or anything else, so don't take it so personally. Just let it go and move on to the next one. The minute you leave the audition, let it go. The last thing you want to do is bring any insecurity about your last audition into your next audition.

Even if you didn't get the last job, there's always another chance. It's called tomorrow. So let it go and keep on moving forward.

I often tell actors, you're in the toughest business you could possibly pick. But the one thing keeping you going is that you're passionate about it. So keep on being passionate about it. Don't let anything discourage you. Every single callback, every decline is a potential lesson learned. See if you can bring something new to the table next time.

It's important to me to help actors feel good about themselves. I give them a lot of encouragement, because they generally don't hear it from anybody else. Nobody tells an actor, "You didn't get it, but you still did great."

I always say that one phone call will change your life. One positive phone call will change the whole trajectory of your career. However, I want you to look for the little miracles, not the big ones. Look for the small, tiny miracles – those are what will enhance your progress and keep you moving forward.

PREPARATION

Don't Give Up Your Day Job

You can't just act. It doesn't work like that. Build your own foundation. It's really important to have a structure for your life, and to also have people in your life that believe in you and support you emotionally.

Hopefully you can support yourself financially, because the last thing you want going into an audition is to feel desperate: *I have to book this or I won't be able to pay my rent.*

When you feel confident you can put food on the table and a roof over your head, you can do the classes, and go into an audition, to do the work without anything attached to the outcome. I guarantee that will be a better audition.

Don't Be Daunted by a Character Description

If you get the character and can be that character, it is worth submitting for the role.

Be Confident, Not Cocky

Do come into an audition prepared with a character and a point of view on the scene you will be reading. Do ask thoughtful questions.

Do listen to the casting director and be ready, willing and able to try something different from what you prepared.

Keep in mind the casting director is on your side. When they ask you to make adjustments, they are helping you with your audition.

Keep Taking Classes

This is really important because you can learn something new from different teachers. And as I said, improv training helps a lot with auditioning.

Put Periods at The End of The Sentences, Not Question Marks

In real life, we ask questions all the time without going up in that questioning voice. Even if there's a question mark in the script, try delivering the line without your voice going up. This one thing can impact a performance a lot – in a good way.

Take In the Positive

If a casting director says, "That was great. Exactly what we're looking for. But we need to just shift it a little bit," all an actor usually hears is, "You did something wrong. We need to shift it a little bit."

Make the adjustment without taking it personally. They are treating you as a professional capable of doing the job. What I want you to also hear is, "That was great. Exactly what we're looking for."

Stop a moment to take that in. Take that positive comment home with you.

Acknowledge and Celebrate the Small Miracles

Applaud when you get a callback. A callback is just as great as a booking. It means they noticed you and liked you. Recognize and take in all the small miracles.

As I mentioned in #6, if a casting director tells you one tiny helpful or encouraging thing, keep it in your brain. Those positive little notes, those are the ones that are really important, because they will help get you there eventually.

JOY OSMANSKI

Let It Go

Joy Osmanski was adopted from Seoul, South Korea and grew up in Olympia, Washington. After receiving an MFA from the University of California, San Diego, she moved north to Los Angeles and has worked steadily ever since in film, TV, theater and as a voiceover artist for video games, podcasts and audiobooks. She has appeared in live action and animated TV shows including *1923, Stargirl, Santa Clarita Diet, The Good Doctor, Shameless, Monsterland, It's Always Sunny in Philadelphia, Duncanville, Family Guy* and *American Dad*. Besides acting and teaching actors, Joy loves playing monster with her kids, exploring new locales, and eating pretty much anything.

Acting takes courage.

It's nearly impossible to truly explain what life is like as an actor – trying to convey the constant insecurity, both emotional and financial, unzipping your heart in front of a room of strangers, the ups and downs of a business that often makes absolutely no sense. People who aren't in the business make sympathetic sounds, or shake their heads. Baffled, they say, "I don't know how you do it."

But we do. We get our butts out of bed and take the steps necessary to keep moving forward. It's not that exciting; it's rarely glamorous. It often gives out giant punches in the gut. For free!

I've been lucky to work with so many actors whose passion for what they do means they live full rich lives, apart from acting. They've unlocked a simple key to staying healthy and happy: it's not all about acting.

If it seems incongruous to say that success in the business will occur if you stop focusing on the business, I get it. Actors often think they need to be self-centered out of necessity, narcissistic for survival. We spend hours of our lives and many dollars of our money having photos taken of just our heads. Then we float them online, in thumbnail form, in hopes of getting a job. Sometimes, that's the extent of a 'job application.' Sending someone a photo of your head.

In the time I've spent working in this business, I've discovered actors who read, go to museums, cook wonderful meals, learn to speak other languages, take piano lessons, travel, allow their curiosity to take them far, far away from themselves, and those are the people I think of as successful. Because what they've learned is that all that pursuit of the other, the unknown, the complex, will make them better at their jobs as actors.

In an ideal situation, an actor is paid to bring herself to a role, and create a piece of unique art. Whether in fleeting moments onstage, or in streaming clarity, at some point, the performance doesn't belong to the actor. It's given to the editor, and then the audience. Unless you're a stone statue, sometimes that's going to hurt.

So here's what I tell the actors I coach, and what I strive for in my own acting life: let it go. At every stage of the process, just let it go. Before you start memorizing lines, let it go. Before you audition, let it go. And most important, when the audition is over, let it go. Ego, expectations, judgment, just let it all go.

It's the one part of the process in which we have a modicum of control. It takes practice, like everything else. But I truly believe letting go and focusing on other things deserves just as much time and energy as the effort we put into our auditions and our performances. And in the long run, it's what will make you the happiest. The courage to let it go.

PREPARATION

Auditions are amazing and wonderful – until you get one. Panic sets in and the fear can be immobilizing. Suddenly you've forgotten how to be a human being who says words.

The next time you get an audition, think of something you love to do – hiking, shopping in a favorite store, meeting a dear friend for coffee – and schedule it for right after the audition. Put it in your calendar. Make it an event. Don't let that audition be the only thing on

LET IT GO

the horizon, because that's the quickest way to let it take over your brain.

Have somewhere to go or something to do after the audition. Don't just go blithely into the abyss of post-audition self-flagellation. Let it go. It's done. It's out of your hands.

If you're meeting a friend for coffee, ask about <u>their</u> day. Give yourself permission to live in the present. Obsessing about the audition isn't going to change anything, and it isn't likely to make your next audition any better. Let it go. Enjoy a hike. Hang out with a friend. Take a deep breath. Smile.

"You cannot try to get the job. Just go in there, have some fun, and do your version of that part. This is what I'm selling. If you want to buy it, that's cool. Have some adjustments for me? That's fine, I'll make some adjustments, but this is basically what I want to do. That's the attitude, sort of a 'f*ck it' attitude. Not f*ck you, but f*ck it."

- SAM ROCKWELL

Chapter 10

Get Outside of Your Box

"I became a writer, and a producer and a director out of, I felt like, necessity."

- PAUL REUBENS AKA PEE WEE HERMAN

ALAN ANGELO

How Acting Can Help You Help Others

Alan holds a MA in Theatre from the University of Albany, NY. He has performed in such noted venues as Glimmerglass Opera and Mac-Hayden Theater. His 150 on-stage credits cover a wide variety of genres, ranging from Shakespeare to historical dramas to musical theatre to children's theatre to dinner mysteries. Favorite roles include Pseudelous *(Forum)*, Fiorello *(Fiorello)*, Jean Sheppard *(A Christmas Story)*, Baptista in *The Taming of the Shrew*, and Mike Talman in *Wait Until Dark*. Alan has also appeared in independent films.

When I was in high school, I was one of those kids who didn't fit in. I played a saxophone, and that helped me find myself and develop self-confidence. I was going to be a music teacher. But then, after I went to one semester at Berkeley College of Music in Boston, I dropped out and I got into other fields.

For about seven years, I didn't play, but then I came back to study the saxophone again. There's always one person who can make a difference in another person's life. And my teacher, Dave Lambert, did that for me. Part of the saxophone training was to sing the note, sing a melody of a song, and that helps develop your ear.

He liked my voice and he said, "Why don't you take some voice lessons from Mrs. Bush?"

Eileen Bush. Another person who changed my life. After studying with her for a while, she said, "Try out for this play."

I got into a play, *Shenandoah,* for a dinner theater. I was thirty years old at the time. And I really loved it. You got to play characters in costumes, and you met different people from different walks of life.

We all had one thing in common, a passion for theater and creating characters and telling stories, because that's what actors do. We view life experiences through our characters. When you play a character, many, many times you bring part of yourself to that character.

Then I studied more voice and acting lessons and so forth. I've gone from community theater to professional acting, I do both. All I can say is, I have met wonderful people with wonderful stories, and it's like family. With film, I may do a bit part, and not even know who's in the cast. But when you're doing theater and you work with people over a period of month and a half, you develop a comradeship. Theater is a very collective art form – everybody puts in their two cents. It's just great.

I'm 72 now, so I've been doing it for 42 years. I've got about 141 credits under my belt. I go from one to another. Some might be a staged reading, some are ten-minute plays, some might be a full production. After I retired, I got my Masters in Theater from University at New York and Albany, and I also went full circle back to playing saxophone. I play in jazz bands, plus I do theater. I've never married, my art is like my passion in life. That's how I connect with people.

I did a play called *Thirteen Suits*. There was an incident in 2015 where a young man, Patrick Duff, was walking home in Half Moon, New York, and he was struck and killed by a drunk driver. Mrs. Duff was willing to forgive the person who killed her son, but when she learned the driver had left him on her windshield, and the accident was only reported an hour and a half later – and not by the driver, but by her sister – the question she had was, where are the good Samaritans?

The family wrote a group of poems and got somebody to make a play out of their story. It was remarkable. Theater is used by many people as a catharsis, to explain their feelings and their life experiences. Sometimes theater is a reaction. There was Renaissance art and then there was Renaissance theater. Theater sometimes comes a bit behind and comments on what's been going on in the world.

Acting is something you can engage in to express yourself, or to help other people. There's voice-over opportunities and on-screen acting roles in training videos that teach skills, like how to use public transportation or how to administer medicine correctly. They can even have rather dramatic scenes, like a video about what to do if there's a school shooter.

I substitute teach once in a while, usually in Special Ed, with other teachers. We sometimes act out scenarios to prepare kids for real life. Say a kid with Down's Syndrome will be working at McDonald's. What if an unscrupulous coworker wants to get him in trouble and says, "Help yourself to a soda," even though he's supposed to pay for it? You have to follow the instructions your employer gave you or you might lose your job. Through acting out scenes like that, I've helped train kids to make good decisions in the real world.

I'm also involved with the New York State Office of Family and Children's Services. We improvise a scenario that a caseworker might encounter. Their job involves difficult circumstances, so this gives them a chance to practice, to help train them to go out in the field.

I might play a grandfather or a child. A scenario might be that a baby has been left alone under the care of a ten-year-old, and this wasn't the agreement the caseworker had with the family. The baby is undernourished, has medical problems, and has to be taken out of the home.

If I'm playing the grandfather, the case worker has to call me and ask if I'll watch the child while they make an emergency plan with the family. That's how a scenario develops. I'll say things like, "Oh Jeez, I'm not sure about that. But okay, yes. I'll take my grandkid because I don't want her to go into a foster home."

There's a supervisor who takes notes while I'm role-playing with the caseworker trainee. The notes are often about asking open-ended questions, rather than a question that's leading to a certain kind of desirable answer. (By the way, that's good advice for an actor as well – in getting to know a character you're going to play, ask them open-ended, rather than leading questions.)

I've heard of organizations and companies that use acting and role-playing for mental health issues, alcoholism, and so forth. There's a law school near me that hires actors to help train students for the courtroom. I don't know exactly what it's like because I tried out, but wasn't cast. They were looking for younger actors. Which is another thing about acting: you learn to take rejection. You learn how to deal with disappointment.

Acting is a wonderful field. Some are hesitant to try it because they're afraid of rejection. You try out for a play, you don't get in and you think, *Jeez, I'm not good enough.* All I can say is, it took me a couple of times to finally get cast. If you really want it, just follow your passion. Remember that acting can be used to help others and not necessarily just for entertainment.

PREPARATION

First, find a good acting school in your area. Having lessons and instructions will help you. A lot of times, acting teachers have showcases that help you develop skills and practice performing for an audience. Classes are also an opportunity to make connections with casting directors invited by the teacher.

You can take acting lessons one-on-one, but in theater, acting tends to be a collective engagement, so if you're in a good small class of no more than twelve, with a good teacher, who has a good reputation, with your interests at heart, I think that's the way to go. Learn the craft, learn the trade, and bond with other people.

When you're ready to work, look outside the box of just getting cast in plays and movies. You may be able to get hired for some fulfilling acting adventures that have to do with art therapy, or helping people prepare for real-life jobs and situations.

There's a lot of creative ways you can practice your acting skills, and get paid for them!

VINNIE LANGDON III

But They Don't Make Movies Where I Live!

Vinnie Langdon III is an American actor and multi-award-winning filmmaker. He is currently a freelance director at a PBS television station. He has produced over 35 award-winning short films, produced 550 half-hour episodes of his own self-titled public access TV show that was syndicated on seven cable access stations across the U.S., appeared on multiple episodes of TMZ, Discovery Channel crime reenactment-based shows, worked behind the scenes of Super Bowl commercials and is a 2008 Graduate of Solano Community College's Acting Training Program. Today he works in the Tri-State Area: New York, New Jersey and Pennsylvania, and loves both acting in and directing short films. In 2022, he founded the Staten Island Summer of Shorts International Film Festival in Staten Island, New York.

When I started out as an actor, I had no connections. It was super frustrating and discouraging. I wasn't signed up with any casting companies. I had no agent. I was taking acting classes and that's as close to a 'set' as I could get in my hometown. Acting classes simply taught you how to get into character, memorize lines, perform. Then you were critiqued, and you would repeat the process.

Yes, I did school plays, I was in church shows and Boy Scout campfire skits, but I craved more of that Hollywood flare.

I was at the "in-between" stage when I decided I wanted to be a professional actor. I was too old to act in children plays. I was too young to audition for roles for adults. I seriously wanted to be a movie star! But Los Angeles was six hours south by car. I had to find my own way.

Any time I met a successful actor at a film festival or later in my career, on set, it always blew me away when I'd seek advice, that no one seemed to want to give out their "secret recipe."

It dawned on me early in my career that if I truly wanted to be a professional actor – maybe I needed an agent or publicist? To get my headshot and resume to as many casting companies as possible? To join SAG-AFTRA? How did this actor get on my favorite TV show, anyhow? How do I get started?

Whenever I had the opportunity to ask these types of questions, I always got the run around. You probably have too. Everyone seemed to answer the same way: "It just happened."

Back in the early 2000's, IMDb actually posted celebrities' management contact info without needing a paid IMDb Pro account. I would call my favorite child stars' managers, just to ask them for advice. They were intrigued, bothered, and surprised I was calling them for advice, instead of being some big-shot producer hiring their talent for a major motion picture. Ha. I laugh about it now, but I was really starving to know the answers I wasn't getting anywhere else. I wonder if these successful mentors did this to protect me from the harsh reality of how slim the chance is to make it to the top of showbiz?

I had to search for the answers myself. Again, I lived six hours north of Los Angeles. I was a minor when I decided I wanted to be an actor. For many of the casting calls in the San Francisco Bay Area, you had to be an adult – due to child labor laws in the entertainment industry – or have professional representation or real set experience. Apparently, having your Mom as your manager isn't considered "professional representation."

One of my first summer jobs out of high school was spending four years teaching acting classes in my hometown of Vacaville, California at a public library. I often explained to my students that the acting world is like a big figure-eight loop. You can't get acting work unless you have experience. Can't get experience unless you have representation. Can't get representation unless you have a full resume and reel. Can't make a reel without acting experience. Just like my thirteen-year-old self, I'm sure my students wondered, "How do I get my start?"

BUT THEY DON'T MAKE MOVIES WHERE I LIVE!

For me, it was carving a path through filmmaking. I wanted to be a movie star at the time, but there were not many filmmakers doing projects in my area. Sure, there were a few local event videography businesses, but my dream was bigger.

So I started teaching myself filmmaking. I did everything from picking up a camcorder, to spending hours learning how to edit with Final Cut Pro, to studying a screenwriting book, to working crappy part-time jobs to be able to afford all the tools that go along with filmmaking, like a lighting kit and audio equipment.

I began creating my own short films in my backyard. This gave me the opportunity to cast myself as fun characters I always wanted to play. Maybe I could be a punk-rocker pirate, or an Italian mob boss, or the quirky guy who gets the prettiest girl in his school?

Once I began making short films, I was not only learning the filmmaking process, I was able to build up my resume and the reel I needed to begin my true acting journey.

Making short ultra-low-budget (aka no-budget) movies with my family and friends, they were still considered experience. Yes, when you audition for a major production you won't put these fun little projects on your resume. But when you're starting out in your hometown, it's fine to do so, regardless of what anyone tells you.

And when you film yourself, you end up watching your own acting a million times during the editing, and you learn from your mistakes. Yikes, don't make that facial expression-! Don't step on other actors' dialogue. Your movements look too stiff and unnatural.

You do learn a lot from your performances.

Of course, you may have no interest in studying filmmaking in addition to becoming the best actor you possibly can be, and that is fine too. But if you have zero resources to start with, I can testify that it worked for me. I had some advantage from growing up in California, but imagine living in Middletown, USA, where the nearest movie production is being filmed several states away. I can imagine feeling discouraged and thinking running away to Los Angeles is your best bet. But you still have to build up your resume first!

Once I had a handful of unique shorts that showed off the variety of characters I could play – now I had a few resume and reel-worthy projects. Once I had four or five short films that I was submitting to film festivals, I had gained the confidence to audition for bigger productions outside of my hometown. I was a shy young adult who struggled for years not to be nervous when auditioning for films or television commercials. But after spending those early years working on my craft, my confidence to audition in front of cameras and strangers blossomed.

Sure, maybe no one reading this has ever heard of my first short film, *Magic Sunglasses*. or my award-winning film, *Permission*, that took home ten awards from international film festivals, but they gave me the experience that prepared me when I was ready to submit myself for bigger auditions. All this prior experience helped, like getting a call back for the feature film CONTAGION, after I handed my resume to a casting director in pouring rain at Warner Bros. Paid jobs, too, on television shows like Discovery ID's *I (Almost) Got Away with It.* If I only had a blank resume and no reel, I know for a fact I would've gotten lost in the rubble of the endless rubble of resumes and headshots submitted.

With my experience participating in numerous film festivals around the U.S., in 2022, I formed my own film festival in Staten Island, New York. It was a fundraising effort to help a non-profit church organization, and I know how vital it is to network. At the time, public places in New York were just beginning to open back up. Independent directors I know were starving to cast talent for their projects, and actors wanted to be booked! The only way to do that is by coming together to make it happen.

Film festivals are great avenues for networking. Some may think it's just going to watch movies all day, then leave. No. From rubbing elbows, to paying attention during the Q&A sessions, to the after-parties, it's all crucial for us. I can't tell you how many roles I booked because I shook hands with the person standing in the corner who turned out to be the producer of an upcoming production and needed some help.

PREPARATION

Perhaps creating your own short films and skits could be your starting point too? They don't have to be Scorsese or George Lucasquality, and it's easier now than ever. Put your finished content on YouTube – maybe you'll even find an audience.

If you don't have a lot of acting opportunities or a big filmmaking community in your town, you gotta make your own.

For filmmakers, getting an audience to watch your films can be difficult. My advice on that is to get your community involved.

If you make a film with just you and your best friend, not many are going to be interested. You have to develop a large pool of potential viewers.

For shooting locations, ask business owners. They have built-in customers already. If you film at their location, they will mention it to their customers.

Do your friends have a unique car or home? Put it in your film. They'll brag to their friends.

When I would make a film at home with a cast and crew of only five or so, I felt like all the pressure was on me to get the viewers. Actors would say, "How come we spent four weekends shooting this and it only has twenty views?"

You have to push it out. My more successful films had a larger cast or crew. Forty people know 40,000 people – so getting those views was not all just on me and my own network. It was a huge relief when I learned this. Filmmaking is not a one-man sport.

CARYN RUBY

How to Create a Showcase for Your Acting Through Collaboration

Selected for Blackmagic Collective's Filmmaker Advancement Initiative, Caryn Ruby co-created, produced, and stars in the multi-award-winning short *Vadgevertising* and the 15-episode web series *Baked Goodes*, named, "What to Watch on Marijuana's Biggest Holiday" by *Newsweek Magazine*. Her pilot script *Morrieville*, a Quarterfinalist in the prestigious Inroads Screenwriting Fellowship, won "Best Dark Comedy Teleplay" at the Houston Comedy Film Festival, where her sketch 'Poverty Tourism' was a Finalist for "Best Dark Comedy Microfilm." A professional script supervisor, Caryn has worked alongside Oscar and Emmy-award-winning crew on films currently streaming on Amazon, Netflix and Lifetime. She created and hosts the only podcast dedicated to script supervising, garnering 40+ five-star reviews.

As an actor, my favorite roles to play have always been the ones I created. Training and performing at world-famous comedy institutions *The Second City* and *The Groundlings* gave me the skillsets, experience, and confidence to write and create such fun characters as Leo Mann, misogynistic visionary creator of "Vadgevertising," entitled rich idiot, Becks, semi-famous shower-singer, Cheryl, and of course, perpetually-drunk girl, Stephanie – who I can't help but automatically embody whenever I take even a sip of alcohol.

Early on, most of my audition opportunities weren't that appealing. Plus, I had been creating all these characters and sketches that were doing no good just sitting on my computer. I wanted to be on set, not

HOW TO CREATE A SHOWCASE FOR YOUR ACTING THROUGH COLLABORATION

sit around waiting to be cast. Other people were making videos for YouTube, going to film festivals and building their reels, and I decided I could do that too.

While it is possible to create and put out content by yourself, through my experience of creating dozens of shorts and web series – some solo – I have found the most joy and by far the most success working with others, and I don't just mean when it's time to shoot, but collaborating from the very beginning.

There is a magic sauce to getting to the finish line with something you can be proud of: a common commitment, clear communication, and sincere compassion. Both *Baked Goodes* (15-episode web series written up in *Newsweek)* and "Poverty Tourism," (sketch that played multiple festivals) began with a simple declaration, "Let's make something together!"

Creating my own work in collaboration with others has been the highlight of my life and professional career, and you can do it too! You don't need to "wait for permission" or even a lot of money, just determination and the simple steps I'm sharing here. Whether you want to create a scene to showcase your talent on your reel, a festival film, video pitch, or just to participate in the creative process with others, for me, there is no better way to indulge in my creativity than purposeful collaboration.

PREPARATION

1. Common Commitment

Maybe you and another actor have great chemistry and want to create a scene for your reels, or your improv group wants to create a web series off of a scene you improvised in one of your shows. The first important step is to be sure that you and your collaborators agree on the same end goal/s. It may sound cliché, but it will cause less riffs all along the way if, when you start, you each, "Begin with the end in mind."

For example, if you want to play a cowboy because that, in your heart of hearts, is your dream role, and your partner wants to create a work of art to submit to museums, it *could* work. But it's much better if you both want <u>either</u> to create a work of art for museums <u>or</u> you both want to create a cowboy film.

On *Baked Goodes,* we were a team of five women who decided by group consensus to make a web series. With *Poverty Tourism* we wanted to make a comedy sketch video, and for *Vadgevertising* the goal was a short film.

Other than the differences between the end goals (sketches vs. shorts vs. web series), all the aforementioned projects followed a similar path. We started with weekly meetings that were basically a writer's room that became production meetings once a script was locked. After production, the weekly meetings transitioned into email updates with occasional meetings and sporadic phone calls about festivals and opportunities.

2. Clear Communication

Be honest with yourself about how committed you can be. Then get clear about what you're all agreeing to and which responsibilities you're each willing to take on.

Know your boundaries and don't say you'll do something you know you can't do, or have no intention of doing. If you say you're going to get the costumes, get the costumes. Don't say you'll do it if you don't want to or can't, then come up with an excuse for why you didn't. Trust me, nobody wants to work with a flake. Including you. If necessary, hold your counterparts accountable to the same standard. Once one person's integrity is missing, everything can start to fall apart.

It's a good idea to discuss financing before you even start. You don't want to get to prep and learn one person assumed you'd hire a professional crew and split the bill while another was going to ask their mom to shoot it on their iPhone. Make sure you're all on the same page, and talk about what you're each comfortable investing, as far as time, energy and money. Will you crowd-fund? Call in favors? Keep in mind, submitting to film festivals can get pricey.

Be sure to verbalize your understanding – or better yet – put a contract together. It doesn't have to be super technical or drawn up by a lawyer, but discuss and get clear on what expectations you have for yourself and each other. Be sure to think it all the way through the production process to the end result.

If your goal is for the film to play at Sundance, say so. Listen to everyone else's goals, and get on board or agree on a particular plan. On *Poverty Tourism*, Sofia and I both wanted to create a comedy sketch that we could act in, but she was mostly interested in using it for her reel and I wanted to submit it to festivals. We both ended up with what we wanted, but because festivals weren't her top priority, I volunteered to pay the majority of submission fees.

3. Sincere Compassion

Choose your partner(s) wisely. Looking back at all of my successful collaborations, you might think it was easy for me – and in all fairness, it probably *was* easier because of the volume of potential candidates in Chicago or Los Angeles – but what you don't see is literally dozens of attempts that were never completed. My computer probably has a terabyte of good intentions and incomplete projects.

Not unlike in other areas of my life… I spent a lot of time trying to "make it work" with the wrong people, or grew frustrated by attempting to do everything myself. In the past, I more easily tolerated disrespectful and less committed people because I was so eager to collaborate and continue creating.

That said, you do need to be flexible with your team and be willing to reschedule or recast when necessary for legitimate reasons. You're investing not only in the project, but in the relationship. Really think about who you want to "get in bed with" as they say. Problems are going to come up, because that's the nature of production, but the real question is how will you and everyone in your group handle it? Being on the same page from the beginning, having an open line of communication, and being sensitive to each other's needs is a winning formula for success!

WINTER BASSETT

So What?

Winter Bassett has been acting, singing, and dancing since the age of three. She grew up in Oceanside, San Diego and spent her entire childhood going from theater program to theater program all over the county. She received a scholarship for Musical Theater and got her degree at a liberal arts school in Orange County. She always knew she wanted to be an actress and couldn't be more grateful to her parents for supporting her dreams and cheering her on. She now has a blossoming career in film and TV, and recently secured distribution for her first feature film, which she co-wrote, co-produced, and starred in, LOST JOY.

During the pandemic, I needed a creative outlet, so I decided to post a video. I thought it would be fun to do a spoof: "The Girl with the Wrong Guy."

The first video blew up on TikTok, it got a million views overnight. I was like, *Okay, this is fun!*

People asked for Part Two and I wondered what that would be. I made a Part Two, and it ended up turning into a whole twelve-part thing.

What's funny is that when I started making those videos, I started getting better at auditioning. In fact, I booked my first network gig. I think it was because I was so excited about my little TikTok story, I wasn't focused on nailing the audition and being "perfect." What I was doing on TikTok was just for fun, laughs and giggles, but while I had this separate stream of creativity going on, my auditions started getting looser and more comfortable. It felt like, <u>*So what*</u> *if they don't choose me.*

That was a freeing new experience. Like a lot of actors, I'm kind of a people-pleaser and that can get in the way. I feel like an actor needs

SO WHAT?

a safe place in which to operate without thinking of a thousand different things, including how to please their coach. You need to come from a more relaxed place.

When I have a new student, I let them know, "I'm on your side. I'm coming at this from an actor's POV too. If it doesn't make sense, that's fine. Let's find it together. I would rather you feel comfortable than try to please me, because I'm just the middleman. I'm not the casting director or the director, I'm not the one you have to please. Let's figure it out together."

I love empowering acting students with more of a "So what?" attitude.

My number one biggest piece of advice is to have multiple streams of creativity because it helps you get to a sweet spot of "So what?" When you have your own creative outlets, it frees up your other acting work a lot, because it takes the pressure off. Rather than worrying about how you've got to nail an audition – *If only I can just book this!* – you can go into it without being attached to the outcome.

A side benefit of multiple streams of creativity is it helps you find your people. Having a good collaborative support system is so valuable. And one day, one of you is going to make it big, and they're going to want to bring their core group along with them. I plan to continue creating my own works, both comedy and drama, while collaborating with kind, like-minded individuals.

Anyhow, the other biggest thing that has helped me, is when I figured out how to relax with breathing exercises before a scene or an audition. I have a lot of energy, so I tend to go a little overboard sometimes. An acting teacher told me to focus on breathing techniques.

The very next day I got an audition for a Netflix movie. Until then, I never got past the first round, but this time, I got all the way to the end. It was between me and one girl for the lead. I didn't get it, but I got to the end, and that was quite an accomplishment. I'm positive it was because I took the time to do breathing exercises, to fully relax and just, "Let it go."

You can prepare, you can learn your lines, you can practice. The relaxation is where we actors tend to get tripped up the most. Because you want it so bad. You're trying to please the director, you're trying to please the casting director, you're trying to please yourself. There's so much going on that whatever you can do to just physically chill out, that's what I found to be the most beneficial.

I don't know how many times I've walked into the room and felt intimidated. Now I tell myself, *You're just going to do your thing, and if they don't get it, <u>so what</u>?*

That attitude does take practice. Not caring about the outcome doesn't mean you don't want it. or you don't respect it, or you're not putting your all into it. But you can't let caring too much deter you from your work. When you're trying to do what you think they want, that can wear you down, it chips away at you.

They are not looking for perfection in an audition. They're looking for you. If you do mess up, they're just looking to see how you handle it. Are you going to crumble? Are you going to say, "I'm so sorry"-? (People-pleasing kicking in.) If you can keep going, they're going to remember you because you recovered like a pro, not because you messed up.

So as soon as I figured out how to relax and stop trying to do it the way I thought they wanted me to, I started to:

1) get more callbacks,
2) have more fun in the audition,
3) mot take it personally if I didn't get it, knowing I gave my all.

I think feeling relaxed goes hand in hand with being so prepared that you can play and have fun. Memorizing the lines is obviously a big part of it, but anyone can memorize lines. It's what you do with the lines and how you put yourself into the role. The more relaxed you are, the more you can have fun putting your own imagination and your real self into it. When you come at it that way, they're more likely to see what you can do, which is what they want to see, and what makes you stand out.

It also helps a lot to recognize that whatever they decide is not a reflection on you. There's a lot of competition and you just weren't who they picked this time. <u>So what</u>?

If you can get experience on the other side of casting, you'll learn a lot. When you see how specific it can get, you realize, *it's not because this person wasn't talented, they were great, but they didn't fit the look as well,* and you'll be more forgiving of yourself.

SO WHAT?

Many times, I have been the one casting roles. It could come down to two little girls who were both great. For whatever reason, we went with one and not the other. Maybe that perspective allows me a little more freedom in my own auditions to say, "So what if I don't get it?"

This is all from my own experience, years of trial and error, and experience can't be taught. It does take time. I've had horrible auditions and many times where I was sure they hated me. I have so much respect for actors who have been at it way longer than I have because, boy, do you have to build a thick skin.

PREPARATION

Breathing techniques and cultivating your own creative outlets will go a long way to helping you find your relaxed sweet spot and "So what?" attitude.

Getting some experience on the other side will also help, while teaching you so much that can make you easier to work with as an actor – and more employable.

1. Gain Experience on the Other Side of Casting

Reach out to casting directors and ask them if you can be a reader for some auditions. If you get that opportunity, you will learn so much. You'll also have the chance to get to know a casting director, but don't go in with that angle of, *What can I get out of this?* Just do it to be of service to other actors, and to learn.

If you go in with the right mindset, you're going to get so much more out of it. So what if it's on a volunteer basis? The knowledge you gain will be invaluable and will help take the pressure off next time you go to an audition.

2. Work a Crew Position at Least Once – Try Being a Production Assistant

Another advantage of creating your own work is it gives you an appreciation for how much goes into any production. And gaining experience with a larger production and crew will make you easier to work with as an actor, because you'll understand even more. For one thing, it makes you more respectful of everyone's time and effort.

If you're only acting, you can get caught in your own bubble or oblivious mindset. Sometimes actors get in their heads that they're the most important thing on set. For example, the actor who insists on staying in character every minute – walking with their prop crutches to the bathroom – turning a quick break into forty-five minutes. They may think they're creating a more powerful performance, but really, they're just wasting everyone's time.

You'll see how important it is to be very prepared and know your lines. The director is under a lot of pressure to make the day of shooting and a whole team is counting on you to be ready to help make that happen.

Guess what, the grips have been there since three or four am. They're exhausted and want to go home, and that is not a "<u>So what</u>?" – because they matter too.

STANZI POTENZA

Comedy Is a Necessity

Stanzi Potenza is a Boston native now based in Los Angeles. She is a trained actor, comedian, and digital creator with a rabid fan base of over five million. Stanzi is known for her viral sketches and comedic commentary, and she is the co-host of the popular weekly podcast Late to the Party. Her other piece in this book is "The Hill of Embarrassment" in Chapter 1.

In his special *Make Happy*, Bo Burnham said, "Come and watch the skinny kid with steadily declining mental health, and laugh as he attempts to give you what he cannot give himself."

That is something I relate to, a lot.

People ask, "How often do you break character and start laughing while you're filming your videos?"

I don't. It's kind of strange. I'm not having the same experience as the audience.

When I'm coming up with material it's like putting together a puzzle. I'll start with an idea, a rough outline of what I want to do. I figure out the motives of a certain character, how to get a certain emotion across or deliver a line a certain way – that is kind of like putting the pieces of a puzzle together.

Then the punch line is putting the final puzzle piece into place. Whether writing a standup routine or a sketch, I'm navigating this joke and how to deliver it, and the punch line is like delivering a "final blow."

I feel like comedy is a necessity, especially in dark times. People need a laugh in order to escape. It also helps when a comedian works serious stuff into their comedy and adds a comic spin to heavy things going on in the world. It's a way to get people to engage with serious topics. There are plenty of comedians who've been able to engage with those discussions and put a spin on dark things that makes them more digestible.

You have to find light in the darkness. A lot of people don't want to engage with darkness if they don't have to, and that's understandable. Still, we have to think and talk about difficult things, because it's the only way we're going to solve them. Humor is the easiest gateway for people to understand a controversial topic a bit more, and to present a perspective someone might not share.

My first series was *Civil War Love Saga*, about a lesbian couple navigating being in a queer relationship at that time in history. It was very silly and it got a lot of people watching who just loved those characters. Then I started my *Heaven and Hell* series – I was talking about abortion, politics, religion, racism, sexism, the patriarchy, white supremacy. Those are all heavy topics, but I presented them through a comedic lens.

Comedy is such a useful tool to present an argument, because people don't like to be lectured. I think it's more effective at winning people over to a point of view than arguing with them. Every now and then, I'll get someone in the comment sections that says, "I didn't think about it this way and now I'm sort of seeing it differently."

People also tell me they see themselves in the characters I come up with – they feel seen and heard and validated. So I think I'm getting across the message I want to get across, in sketch comedy form.

TikTok is a floodgate when it comes to finding those conversations, because people are making these sort of "think piece" videos all the time, and a lot of them are really tone deaf. To me those are perfect pieces of content to respond to in my own way.

Dealing with Haters

On the internet, it's kind of inevitable that you're going to get some negative response. One of the reasons I don't care so much about receiving hate online is because I know people will find any reason to not like you, no matter what you do.

Miss Rachel is an online creator who is very big with young children – like toddlers. She made a video saying she was she going to make donations to help starving children. People got really mad at her about that because of where the funds were going. Then she made a video crying about the backlash, and it was like, *How are you going to bully Miss Rachel? She's the nicest person in the universe and she wants to help starving children.*

If people are going to be mad at someone like her, they can find any reason not to like you and me. Some will say they don't like seeing your face, they're going to say they don't like the way you look or the way you talk. They're going to say whatever they want. And if people are going to be like that on the internet, then the internet is a very unhinged place. So you might as well just talk about things that matter to you.

I grew up in a household where we were encouraged to speak our minds. My mom has been on the local news three or four times because they find her at rallies and protests and she's very outspoken. That definitely made me and my sisters outspoken too. I wouldn't be the creator I am today without talking about certain things, and I am very passionate about these topics.

As long as you stay true to your beliefs, I think that's all that matters. As long as you genuinely care about the message you're trying to get across, I think you can brush a lot of those insults off your shoulders. By the way, a lot of these anonymous haters on the internet are 14-year-old kids.

I knew going into this kind of career that you have to expect to receive a lot of criticism, whether it be about personal beliefs, or your physical traits, which is crazy. You do have to have a kind of tough skin to be in the industry, whether it's acting in traditional media or online, because you're going to get some criticism either way. (See my piece in Chapter 1, "The Hill of Embarrassment.")

Many will say, "Don't give any attention to these people."

When I get hate, sometimes I find a way to make a funny spin on the comment. I think that's a more interesting way to go about receiving it, and then you're making money off of people's stupid hate comments. For me, that is a huge win.

Online Can Take You Offline

As I was posting my series, I kept gaining followers and traction across all my social media platforms. Then I started my first podcast. Then a touring company offered me a live show, and that's how I got signed to UTA. Then I was thrust into the world of stand-up comedy. I completely bypassed the stand-up route most people have to go through – open mic nights (which are such a humiliating process), then getting invited to do tight fives and building your way up.

I wrote a 45-minute stand-up show and was sent out on my first tour. I loved doing it, and people were impressed because they don't necessarily have faith in someone who starts online, but I had a background in live theater.

Now I have an acting agent and am doing auditions for film and television, and continuing with live comedy touring. So I'm moving into traditional media spaces, which was always the goal, it was just a crazy process getting here.

Expanding Opportunities and Taking It Step by Step

When I was a kid, I didn't see myself represented in the comedy space. When you don't see yourself represented, you assume those spaces aren't meant for you. That goes for women. That goes for people of color, people of different gender identities, and people with disabilities. When you don't see yourself represented, it sort of gets ingrained in your brain that those spaces aren't meant for you. It's hard to imagine those spaces being inclusive to you when you don't see or know anyone like you who is in there.

When I was a kid, I thought about doing stand-up, because I knew I was funny. But I didn't know a lot of female comedians. As I got older, I started recognizing more female comedians in the stand-up space and film and television. Eventually I thought, *Okay, I can do this, because I see other people doing it.*

I got some confidence about being funny from performing other people's material. It was taking my first playwriting class in college that made me realize I could write funny too. That was a really big turning point that gave me a lot more confidence when I started doing TikTok, because I wrote my own sketches, and it was a way for me to perform my own material without having to be in front of a live audience. I would have been devastated if I wrote a play performed in a theater and no one laughed.

I'm not saying it's easy to post a video on the internet because, you know, you're posting it on the internet, which is full of horrible individuals who are going to write heinous things in the comment section. But it did feel better to me doing my own comedy online first. I was posting content, a lot of people found it funny, and I got a lot of validation from that.

That made me feel confident enough to start my podcast, then do my first live show, then write the stand-up show and perform it for live audiences. I had to sort of find validation and gain confidence each step of the way.

Now I meet so many women who are really funny, really good at character work and sketches. Turns out, many of them are funnier than a lot of the men.

I'm not saying there aren't funny men, one of my best friends is a male comedian I met through TikTok, and he's one of the funniest people I know. (He does admit he's not as funny as me, wink. Anyhow, we work very well together.) What I am saying is that I now recognize that comedy is absolutely a space that belongs to women as much as it does to men.

PREPARATION

Inspiration is everywhere. If you want to create your own content, make sure you're thinking in that way – always seeking out inspiration. If you keep your eyes peeled, you're going to find an unlimited source of ideas for creating your own content, whether it's comedy or not.

I find inspiration online in conversations people are having, but it could also be things I've been through in my personal life. When I first started doing stand-up, I had a bit about a holiday my parents made up for me called "Middle Child's Day" because I was the middle child and they felt like they were neglecting me.

There are so many personal things you can explore. Then, if you want to, you can expand into broader horizons like political and social dynamics and current events.

A huge part of my inspiration comes from daydreaming. Maybe you're in the shower daydreaming about a conversation you wish you had, or you wish had gone differently. You could make a sketch about that conversation – and this time say what you really wanted to say.

Whether you want to create your own content or bring to life a character in a script, there's inner inspiration that comes from daydreams, imagination, plus things you observe happening around the world. You have these thoughts and deep feelings, and if you don't know how to navigate them, you can make something funny or weird out of it, or channel those feelings into a character.

For me it doesn't have to be comedy. If I'm feeling weird and bad and existential about the world, I'll make a weird existential video. However it is I'm feeling, I'll turn it into a video. When I share it, I get all these people saying they feel the same way. That's sort of like healing my own thoughts while also helping others navigate those feelings themselves.

I spend a lot of time looking for: *What is driving a wedge in society? What are people arguing about right now?* I think about what I can add to the conversation, and also feed my audience what they want to see. When I have a strong emotional reaction, rather than yell about it, I try to find a way to take that reaction and mold it into something creative and funny.

For example, there's a conversation on TikTok started by this guy who asked a bunch of women if they would rather be lost in the woods with a bear or a man. A lot of the women said they would rather be lost in the woods with a bear, and a lot of men got very pissed off. Then women were like, *Don't you know what harm men can do to us?*

Conversations like that can get pretty heated. I may see something and feel strongly about it. I could yell at someone in a comment. But I don't consider that a win. Making a well-thought-out, funny response feels more validating.

I did make a sketch video about that conversation, which is kind of strange, because I actually have a weird fear of bears. There's no logic behind that, because I'm an indoor person and don't go in the woods. Yet even if I did, statistically speaking I'd be more at risk of being killed by a man than a bear.

So, when you see something that pushes your buttons, ask yourself:

What is my own take on this?

How could I get my point across in a way that would be funny and engaging?

How can I make people think about this topic a little differently, while also being entertaining?

"Actors are agents of change. A film, a piece of theater, a piece of music, or a book can make a difference. It can change the world."

- ALAN RICKMAN

DEVELOP A SUSTAINABLE CAREER

"Do your job and demand your compensation – but in that order."

- CARY GRANT

Chapter 11.

Understand Your Medium – The Craft and The Business

"Theater acting is an operation with a scalpel, movie acting is an operation with a laser."

– MICHAEL CAINE

MARK PELLEGRINO

Life, Luck, Law, and Logic in Art

Mark Pellegrino continues to work in popular TV shows like *American Rust, Supernatural, Dexter, The Closer,* and *Lost.* He appeared in the movies NATIONAL TREASURE, THE BIG LEBOWSKI, CAPOTE, BEVERLY HILLS COP 4 and David Lynch's MULHOLLAND DRIVE. Mark taught the Meisner technique at Playhouse West for over seventeen years, and currently co-teaches at Playhouse Paris with his wife, Tracy Pellegrino, and his dog Frankie. Jiu Jitsu is his church.

When I was a young man, I had no connection to acting at all. Actors didn't mystify me and movies were just things I watched with friends on the weekends. My real passion was the ocean and ecology. So up until the age of twenty-five, I might not have been able to tell you why Marlon Brando mattered in the grand scheme of cinematic history, but I could tell you everything about the day in the life of a great white shark.

The fact that I abandoned marine biology for acting, or something I was passionate about for something I knew nothing about, and did well despite being a rube, is not necessarily definitive proof that luck determines a lot in our lives, but it's a strong suggestion.

My life has been full of those suggestions.

Here's what happened, Occam-Razor style: I got bored with college, fell in love with a girl far more interesting than my classes, and dropped out to devote my time to her. Crazy? You don't know the half of it.

After that dark comedy had run its course and the girl was gone, I had nothing to do. And a 21-year-old dude has to do something. I mean let's face it, by twenty-one, the world of adulthood has been pressing in with its own sense of propriety for three years, and a young man adrift has two choices: continue to drift, or grab onto something with a semblance of direction, and get on with it.

It was at this point that I found myself shopping at the Topanga Mall when I spied with my little eye an ad for a modeling school.

I'd never considered modeling as a career, but it sounded easy, and it was something to do, so I went.

I remember very little about the whole experience, and I've forgotten entirely whether or not I ended up paying anything, (I probably did, schools like that are tailor-made for rubes like me) but I remember the school was offering a special: a free commercial workshop class, taught by a working commercial and soap opera actor by the name of Bob Hover.

Who was Bob Hover? No idea. What qualified him to teach a class in 'commercial acting'? Also, no idea. But the class was free and it was something to do, so I went.

After a few commercial scenes and a monologue from *Spoon River Anthology,* Bob thought he saw enough in me to introduce me to an agent. I thought that was pretty generous, considering any time he said I did a scene or monologue well, it felt just as awful as when I did badly. But an agent seemed like a damn good thing to have if I was going to take this any further, and I had nothing to do, so I went.

Now this agent (who will remain nameless as he is still alive) wasn't a good guy and didn't really have the power or reputation to advance my career much, but he did give me a list of acting schools.

I didn't know it at the time, but on that list was a school that would change my life. I only picked the school (Playhouse West) because it was relatively close to my house and super cheap. But it would be at this teeny stage in Studio City where I would discover the magical process behind good acting.

My mentor and the owner of the school, Bob Carnegie, was young and fiery. He had an intense passion for the craft of acting (which he instilled in me) and a palpable distain for all things Hollywood (which he also instilled in me.) His insane dream was to create a Group Theatre right there in Studio City, California.

At the time I didn't know what the Group Theatre was or why he was so obsessed with it, so I set about learning and, after a short while, I got swept up in the contagion of purpose and passion.

And that's a good thing, because purpose and passion are two things a man adrift doesn't have.

No longer rudderless, I immersed myself in discovering the craft of acting from the Meisner point of view. I did classes two times a week and rehearsed exercises, and eventually scenes, every day, sometimes as often as four times a day.

I read plays, literature, history and philosophy. I noticed that the reading list for this dinky little theatre school was more comprehensive than anything in my aforementioned college curriculum. It looked like I was gonna get cultured whether I wanted to or not.

C'est la vie.

Turns out Calvin Coolidge was right, effort beats talent any day of the week, and when you're working at something as hard as I was working, something's bound to give.

I started to get work.

But the work was troubling. Not that it was bad (it was, but that's a whole other story), it was the experience of a great disparity between what I could do in class and what I was doing on set that felt bad.

Part of that disparity was in the parts themselves (though I was too young and inexperienced not to personalize it.) You see, I'm 6'3", blonde and muscular, which suggests a certain type to Hollywood. This type was not me though. And because my type bore no resemblance to myself as a man, I felt a rift in my work that I was unequipped to bridge.

There's also the fact that a classroom and actual sets are very different worlds.

Class was a self-contained unit which, more or less, had the perfect conditions for decent acting prepackaged in.

The set was the exact opposite; a place that dares you to have a human moment and does everything in its power to undermine that remote possibility. It's a chaotic, noisy place with time constraints, distracting technology and the necessity for results – the kryptonite of good acting.

An actor cannot enter this realm of the bizarro sans a strong sense of himself and what he wants. That's like going into a zombie horde without a melee weapon.

Unfortunately, I had developed neither quality in real life, and acting school could not supply me (or anyone else for that matter) with an artist's self-esteem.

That self-esteem, where you think highly enough of yourself to make your own peculiar acting conditions happen in any situation, comes with time, failure, learning, internalizing what matters, and letting go of what doesn't.

Sanford Meisner himself wisely said it takes twenty years to be an actor. Well, it ain't the technique that takes that long to master, you learn that in two years; it's developing the artist's self-esteem that takes all that time.

I guess that makes the acting journey primarily one of self-mastery, and that applies not only to the internal workings of the actor, but also to controllable externals.

Controllable externals: the world of the actor is not just a work element, it's a social element as well. For a number of years, I didn't understand this. This blindness was due in part to my radical anti-Hollywood teacher who taught me that only the work should matter. But it wasn't all him.

That outsider attitude fed directly into a natural social awkwardness I'd had since I was a kid. (If you suffer from the same issues, get over them.)

The social element of TV and film acting is very important and probably exists for a lot of reasons, but practically speaking, it's because you, as the actor, must work in collaboration with others for long periods of time. Always.

It follows, therefore, that such close proximity to other creatives over extended periods would inspire people to look at more than your acting when they're evaluating you. *Do I want to live with this guy for the next six years of my life?* – is a legit concern for any producer watching your work. Once you understand and internalize this truth, it changes your whole approach to the work process.

For me, that translated into a more sociable audition process, which, ironically, enabled me to let go of my technique (a vital realization), to enter auditions with a spirit of play and suggestibility (another vital realization), and to trust myself more.

Self-trust. Playfulness. Suggestibility. Ease. More than technique, these are the necessary ingredients of good acting. And they are the results of self-mastery.

I've been fortunate in my journey to have worked with lots of very good people, who, without even trying, taught me that everything has laws that must be abided by. And at the risk of sounding overly simplistic, if you want to achieve some level of success (in anything really) you need only concern yourself with whatever laws command your task.

So there you have it. A life in brief with some (hopefully translatable) revelations. A life composed of major turning points that could've gone one way but went another. A life composed of one part luck, one part stubbornness, and two parts hard work. A life that, in retrospect, is better than I knew.

PREPARATION

What are the laws of good acting?

<u>Really Do</u>

Acting is doing. And when you really do something, your body doesn't know the difference between fantasy and reality, it knows what you're really doing. It's the law of the body to react to reality.

<u>Really Listen</u>

Since the fundamental problem for the actor is self-consciousness, really listening takes the awareness off of yourself and places it on to someone or something else. When your attention is externalized and you are caught up in your action, you're not self-conscious. When you're not self-conscious, you are free.

It's a law of consciousness that when it is occupied, the great well of the unconscious and subconscious become the pallet with which you can paint your scene.

Use Logic

On the one hand, we actors are taught to distrust logic while performing, but it must be present in all that we do, as it must be present in every element of a narrative.

Weed out the (accidental) contradictions in the story and the character, and both will take you away of their own accord. Logic is a law of story and storytelling.

Have a Spirit of Play

We forget when doing something as deeply taxing as *Hamlet*, that it's a 'play', and that the spirit of childlike play is at the heart of everything we do. From *Antigone* to *An Enemy of the People,* a spirit of play is what makes all acting experiences, even the emotionally tough ones, deeply rewarding and creative experiences.

Don't Fear Playback

You can't see yourself when you work. That's why we have a third eye in the director. It's a sad fact that you can feel a thing to the ends of the universe, but if it ain't reading, it won't show.

Jeff Bridges, one of the least self-conscious actors I've ever worked with, watched every scene he did in playback. That got me in the habit of doing the same, when I can. Far from making me self-conscious, it enabled me to get a perspective on what worked and what didn't.

Do what works. It's a law of acting, and life.

Art is What's Necessary

Rod Steiger taught me this. I agree with it in the mechanics of acting, and in the mechanics of narrative storytelling.

With respect to acting, the script is the road map. Follow it and you'll get to your destination.

With respect to narrative, we come to our characters in the heat of crisis. It's their resolution of that crisis that composes the story. The narrative's world is NOT the everyday, it is an intensely focused world where the stakes are very high, and everything in that world MUST HAPPEN, and every action taken MUST BE TAKEN. It's a law of art. Art is what must be there.

Find the Humanity

This is particularly relevant when playing supernatural characters or villains (although an actor NEVER views their own character as a "villain".)

I have been fortunate enough to play both character types simultaneously: villains in the supernatural realm. In each case, the problem is the same: take a being who does 'bad' things to get what he wants, and find the humanity that drives those actions.

The audience has a sense of good and evil and will judge you accordingly, but you, as the actor, cannot sit in judgment against yourself. You have to find the humanity in everyone, or you'll play a caricature.

For example, Bishop (in *Being Human*) was not the evil vampire boss of Boston. He was a man who had to hide his nature from the world, and live a lie in order to survive. This is almost a universal sentiment for anyone who finds himself on the outside of any "in" group.

To continue: Bishop wasn't the evil vampire boss of Boston, he was the leader of a deeply oppressed group who had dreams of setting himself and his people free.

More? He was a father who hurt his son and yearned for that lost connection. Far from being a villain, he was a rebel who wanted what any other person in the world wants: to live free and be happy.

Likewise, Lucifer in *Supernatural* was not the devil. He was a scorned son and brother who was ruthlessly betrayed by a father who didn't care about him, and by a family of conformists who preferred status in their father's eyes over truth and justice. He was the original rebel against arbitrary authority. What could be more noble?

PAUL BARRY

Stage vs. Screen

Paul Barry was a professional actor who had a co-lead role in the series *Love is a Four Letter Word,* and appeared in *Underbelly, The Cut,* and the TV movie *The Mystery of Natalie Wood.* As an acting coach for twenty years, he taught over 5,000 students from around the world in both Sydney and Los Angeles. He wrote the acting book *Choices* and sixty articles for *Backstage*. Paul wrote and directed many projects for stage and screen and founded a video production company that operated in five cities across two countries. Turning his attention to helping coaches, consultants, and business owners think big in business, he gave the TEDx talk, "The Opposite of People: The Transformative Power of Counterintuition." He is now CEO of an AI-powered habit building app called Habit Driven. Paul spends his spare time hosting professional mixers and exploring the great outdoors.

There is little difference between acting for stage and acting for screen.

This contentious statement has fired up many students over the three decades that I taught acting for stage and screen. I wasn't always well-equipped to support my thesis, but now, I am excited to give you the tools you need to test the results of my assertion for yourself.

It is an entrenched belief that acting for stage is an entirely different animal than acting on screen. The acceptance of this as a rule by so many leads talented actors to avoid one in favor of the other, simply because they fear (or worse, are told) that they will not be able to master the skills required to be great in that medium. It is my experience that the people most certain of these so-called differences are experienced in either stage or screen only, or lack experience in both.

STAGE VS. SCREEN

Experts in both mediums don't take such a simplistic approach.

The word "differences" by definition separates the two as disciplines, and forces a gap between them. It's harder and more time-consuming to learn two entirely different skills than to master only one.

But what if, rather than <u>differences</u>, we thought of them simply as <u>considerations</u>? As such, they may be differences, but then again, they may be tools for enhancement or simplification of the skill you currently possess.

I believe that you will soon view the following five considerations as empowering departure points for exciting discovery in your acting, rather than insurmountable differences that prevent you from becoming a master of acting across multiple mediums.

<u>Visibility</u>

Actors on stage frequently receive notes relating to being seen, so let's start there.

"I can't see you."

"You're standing behind her, move out to the side."

"If you can't see me, I can't see you."

And so on. Being seen is apparently an important aspect of being on stage.

But it's also important on screen, right?

My question is, who cares if you can be seen on the stage right now? Is your character important to the plot at this very second? Will the audience's understanding of the play be impaired if your character isn't visible every moment?

If so, why don't audiences grow more and more confused as the film editor cuts between actors in a scene? Surely, if we need to see all the characters in a stage scene at the same time, we must need to see all the scene's characters on screen at the same time.

If not, then why must we see all the actors in a scene on stage at all times? The answer is, it's not that important in every case.

Seeing a character is important only when they and their action or reaction are essential to the plot and story. Otherwise, I would argue, the character doesn't need to be seen. In fact, if they are not essential in this moment, I would prefer not to see them until they are necessary to the story. Actors needing to be seen on stage simply because it is aesthetically pleasing, or because tradition dictates, are not compelling reasons. The same is most definitely true on screen.

The first of five considerations (as opposed to differences) that I'd like you to absorb into your acting practice is visibility.

Do I need to be visible to the audience in order to support the plot and story at this moment? If not, don't worry about it.

Audibility

"Speak up, I can't hear you," and "Project to the last row of the theater," are common notes from stage directors.

Conversely, "You don't need to speak so loudly, the mic is right above your head," is what actors starting out on screen hear a lot.

You'd be forgiven for thinking that the rule is to be loud on stage and quiet on screen.

But following that rule, you'd be incredibly confused as to how to perform in a street scene on camera that requires volume, or an intimate bedroom scene in a fifty-seat theater. Obviously, context plays a part too.

You see, these are less rules than they are considerations. It is essential to consider if one is able to be heard in an important moment, just as it is important to consider if one is being seen. Volume must be taken into consideration, but it also depends on the noise in the performing environment, the technical or venue limitations, the context of the scene, and the emotional intensity of the moment, among many other considerations.

Imagine two characters in a crowded high school corridor speaking about whether or not one of them is pregnant. Wouldn't it be obvious they speak quietly, since they're on camera? It might also make sense in the context of the scene, but for some reason – could be placement of mics, comedic reasons, or something else – they speak at a loud volume.

To simply raise your voice on stage and lower it on screen will fail to serve you as an actor in either medium, and it may leave you believing that perhaps one or the other is not for you.

Veteran multi-award-winning screen actor Jack Nicholson once said that he doesn't change anything in his performance depending on the size of the shot. If it's a whispering moment, he whispers. If it's a shouting moment, he shouts. Physically, he does the same thing in the wide shot as he did in the medium, which is the same as he does in the closeup. Many would suggest that Nicholson would be inconsistent on stage for that very reason, but all I would say is that his size and volume must be considered, and that is all. Once considered, they may need changing, but they should not be changed simply because the medium is different.

His performance should be allowed full and free expression, and any tweaks should be made after exploring it, not before.

We live in a world of incredible technology, after all. Even the amphitheaters and masks of ancient Greece were designed to amplify voices and minimize the need to 'project to the back row,' so surely we can move beyond tired old traditions this far into the twenty-first century.

I have performed on stage with a mic, and I have acted in many small theaters, which meant a whisper could be heard clearly. Conversely, I have performed in an intimate environment on screen where the mic can't get close enough due to lack of space, so I was instructed to raise my voice. In such instances, you will learn on the job and give what the situation technically dictates, but the one thing you can and should learn in advance is to not set anything in stone based on supposed rules that, ultimately, have many exceptions.

Proximity

For on camera work, actors are often told to stand uncomfortably close to one another – the aesthetics of the shot being the reason. On stage, the opposite is common, the reason being to 'fill the stage', which is just another aesthetic driver. In both mediums, the opposite is also true at times, rendering any such rule incorrect more often than any 'rule' should be.

Actors on screen sometimes need to stand far apart in an intimate scene, especially if the camera is on a long lens. Actors may be called upon to stand close together on stage at times if they are within a limited set size or small lighting pool, and stepping outside of it would plunge them into darkness.

As you can see, one must always consider the need for being in close proximity to the other performers, or whether some distance is, in fact, ideal. It is this consideration that's missing from most discussions of the so-called differences between acting for stage and screen that compelled me to dedicate so much time to this topic. (I hope it is becoming clear why considerations are so much more important, and useful, than rules.)

Aside from the pure technical consideration of proximity on stage and screen, there is also the very real effect that proximity has on the audience's understanding of the relationship between characters and things.

When a policeman enters a room, you don't typically stand very close. You give them room. When your lover enters, you don't normally move away from them, unless of course you are using the breaking of our expectations to make a point about the relationship.

A criminal getting in the face of a detective may make for a surprising and compelling scene, and someone flinching and withdrawing from their lover can raise interesting questions.

Juxtaposition

Directors of both stage and screen often use the "size" of the performance and volume (colloquially referred to as "color and movement") to compensate for lack of actual nuanced differentiation in storytelling.

A classic experiment in juxtaposition, first explored by the legendary filmmaker Sergei Eisenstein, is to film an actor's neutral face and intercut it with images of a hamburger, an act of violence, or children playing with a puppy in a field.

Based on the context – the nature of the image juxtaposed with the actor's neutral face – most viewers interpret the actor as being hungry, horrified, or smiling, even though the same shot of his face is used each time.

You can perform a similar experiment on stage by simply switching a light on and off, or deploying the opening and closing of a curtain in between tableaus.

On stage, an actor playing hopscotch stage left as another simulates slitting the throat of a pig stage right has such power to affect the audience, that large movements and loud volume would almost be redundant in the storytelling. In fact, they might simply get in the way.

Or not. The point is, it's not a rule, it's a consideration.

Both stage and screen require us to consider how we juxtapose images and scenes to tell our story appropriately, regardless of the budget. However, actors should not carry that burden, because it is largely the job of the writer and director to define such things.

When we as actors trust that the powerful juxtaposition of images and scenes is impacting the audience, we feel far less like the onus is on us to emote, shout, or run around the stage, attempting to elicit an emotional response in the audience.

Frame

One thing often cited as a major difference between acting for stage and acting for screen is frame size. An extreme close up on screen focuses all our attention on one thing, perhaps an eyeball. If the goal is that nothing else is seen, by directing us to exclusively concentrate our attention on the eye, then we can achieve similar results on stage too.

Stage uses framing much less often, and I think it's a shame. It comes down to lack of budget, technical ability, or simply failing to consider it. Many stages are well and evenly lit, perpetuating the belief that stage and screen are very different, when it's simply a lack of the use of frame in stage direction (or poor lighting budgets.)

Yes, an extreme close-up on screen is incredibly difficult to replicate onstage (without simply projecting an image) since the human eye appears very small inside a large theater. However, as long as an audience member is able to physically see that eyeball from their seat in the auditorium, a wink will be obvious (in the absence of distracting light and motion elsewhere onstage.)

Magicians, in particular, are excellent at directing, or more specifically, mis-directing, your attention. Even on a massive stage, our focus can be so directed as to completely miss a large elephant being moved before our very eyes. If we are focused exclusively on a very specific thing on stage, it is the equivalent of a close-up on screen: all else becomes unimportant.

There is a seminal Samuel Beckett play called *Not I* which shocked the audience with an almost pitch-black stage with only a shadowy figure off to the side, and a pinpoint spotlight on a woman's mouth center stage. Despite the audience sitting at various distances from the actress, what else could we call this but a close-up of a mouth in darkness? We have effectively 'framed out' everything but the mouth, giving the audience nothing else to focus on.

Clearly this is an extreme avant-garde technique for focusing attention, but it does prove that, even to lesser extents, framing on stage can be done with light in much the same way it is done on screen with the boundaries created by a camera frame. If the actress in *Not I* followed the rule to be big and loud on stage and small and quiet on camera, it would ruin the entire experience.

One must consider the frame when preparing to adapt one's acting, rather than simply changing it for the medium.

Though there are certainly technical aspects to adapt to between the mediums of stage and screen, including but not limited to, live versus pre-recorded, performing scenes in or out of story sequence, one take versus multiple takes, rehearsal or lack thereof, my aim here is to encourage you to see those things as different in the way driving an automatic car is different from driving a stick, rather than riding a bike vs. piloting a rocket ship to Mars. And just as there can be natural, believable behavior on both stage and screen, the phony stuff stands out like a sore thumb – regardless of the medium.

Yes, they are different. No, the differences are not insurmountable. The so-called rules that allegedly separate stage and screen actually contain creative opportunities for discovery. But only if we take the time to consider them.

PREPARATION

1. Visibility

Watch any film or television episode and tell me if you can still follow the thread without seeing every single actor in a scene on screen at the same moment.

Then choose one scene from a film or TV show where one of the characters was not on screen for quite a while (even though they were

STAGE VS. SCREEN

present), then appear on screen for an important moment. Hopefully, you'll soon understand that visibility is great when necessary, distracting when unnecessary.

Think back to a play you've performed where the director instructed you all to move to a position where you can be seen, only to discover that it was for purely aesthetic purposes, and nothing to do with your reaction being essential. Put yourself back there in your mind. Clear yourself of the clutter of cliched directions and phony traditions on stage, and ask yourself, *Would it actually have mattered if nobody could see my character until the moment I did or said X?*

From now on, pay attention to wide shots in film and television, especially those times when there is an establishing wide shot with actors all standing around awkwardly, not really knowing their place or what they're doing.

Aside from being a healthy experiment for your imagination, I believe you will find that much of the stage direction we receive is due to traditions and old rules rather than any practical purpose. You can be the vanguard of the new order of actors, whose performance arises out of a deep understanding of the art, rather than shallow artifice.

2. Audibility

Go to a theater and watch a show. Notice if everyone on stage is raising their voice and 'projecting to the back,' even in intimate moments. Ask yourself if it was 100% necessary in order for you to hear them. Is it possible that better acoustics or amplification could have done the work for them? Could slightly more disciplined vocal training and modulation have done the trick to avoid all the shouting?

Watch a television show you enjoy and pay particular attention to scenes in which people are in public places having private, intimate conversations, but still speak as though they are alone. High school movies and TV shows are good (bad?) for this.

Loud in theater, quiet on camera is yet another consideration, not a rule, when it comes to the two mediums. Begin an exploration about how loudly people speak in real life, and see what you discover.

3. Proximity

Set your phone up on a stand and ask a friend to get into frame with you. Your goal is to perform an entire scene without leaving frame.

Now move the camera behind the shoulder of one of you, so that you primarily capture the performance of only one actor. Likely, you will soon see that the actor not featured (ie: with their back to the camera) will need to move a little farther back in order to avoid obscuring the featured actor.

Then, find some time to stand on a stage and define three different spaces, such as a bedroom, an office, and a park.

As you act in the park environment, notice how you would dearly love to move more, but the parameters of the world you've created simply don't permit it.

Finally, learn a short half-page scene with a friend and perform it in several ways, in both these stage and screen environments:

    a) Very close to one another

    b) Very distant from one another

    c) Alternating, from close to far from one another

You will see that the lines take on different meanings depending on your proximity, as well as when you choose to move closer, to or farther from, your scene partner. Such is the power of proximity in acting, regardless of the medium.

4. Juxtaposition

Watch any film or television episode toward the very end, when there is a climactic moment and the editor cuts between scenes as the story builds to the conclusion. Much of what you feel as a viewer comes down to the juxtaposition of images and sounds, not exclusively to the performance of the actor running through a hundred emotions.

Attend a production of *The Phantom of the Opera*, *Hamilton*, or any large-scale stage production, and appreciate how cinematic they are in that respect. Fast cuts between scenes, augmented with sophisticated sound systems, lighting rigs, and visual effects, make the concept of juxtaposition more obvious.

STAGE VS. SCREEN

5. Frame

Watch the YouTube clip of Samuel Beckett's play *Not I* in which Billie Whitelaw, the actress of the original production directed by Beckett himself, describes the experience and its effect on the audience. It is a rare example, yes, but I'll wager you'll begin to see instances in great modern theater where similar techniques are used to some extent.

Go see a play, or think back on one you've seen, and ask yourself if the entire stage needed to be lit the entire time, or if the director just failed to direct the audience's attention.

"In a close-up, the audience is only inches away, and your face becomes the stage."

- MARLON BRANDO

CHRISTOPHER M. ALLPORT

Acting is Technical

Christopher is a Hollywood native who performed in movies including HOCUS POCUS and PIRATES OF THE CARIBBEAN 3, the series *Peter Pan and the Pirates,* and the short film *The Man Who Would Not Shake Hands*. He has also performed extensively on stage and as a recording artist. Christopher penned the novel *Senja Chronicles* with co-author Fansu Njie, and wrote, directed and starred in the award-winning feature film EMILY OR OSCAR. He is completing a feature rock-u-mentary chronicling the legendary Gold Star Studio from 1950 to 1984, and composed the orchestral suite, *Song of Solomon*. (His other contribution to this book is "Craft, Career and Content" in Chapter 1.)

Film acting is extraordinarily technical, especially when compared to theatre.

If a director asks you to do something, you must do it, not judge it. Taking direction requires you to listen closely and understand what is being asked of you. Compare the direction with what you already have created in your mind. *Is it the same? Is it different? Do I need to scrap my ideas, execute them, or merge them with new ideas?* Those are questions that you should ask yourself before taking action.

"I would never do that. My character would never do that. It doesn't say that in the script."

These common 'head speak' phrases that pop into an actor's mind when pushed to change an approach are dangerous attitudes that will not serve the collective creative purpose, and therefore will not serve the actor's own career.

Most likely the director will have a broader perspective on the project that you have not yet envisioned. And chances are, if you're just memorizing lines, you haven't done enough detective and imaginative work to envision underlying story points and character motivations for yourself.

"I'm just not feeling it," many actors lament when disagreeing with a direction.

You must understand, however, that the production doesn't care what you're feeling. We care about what the audience is feeling. In this team sport that is our job to craft together: an emotional response from an intended audience.

That is accomplished through your actions. Your internal feelings as an actor belong to you. So, they can be whatever you want or need them to be for you to evoke the emotion from somebody else. But you must not be hung up on your feelings. The word "acting" itself comes from the word "action," not feeling.

Understand the Writing

Action is written in the script, so you need to do it, not feel it. The term 'actor' refers to action! It's your job as an actor to find a way to deliver a performance of actions. Directors care more about what the action is than how you feel about it.

Say your character needs to exit a door, but you don't know why. I have heard actors say this before, "I'm not sure what my motivation is."

Who cares? If you're told exiting the door is the action, it becomes your homework to create the motivation or reason to leave the room. You have to trust that the reasons for every action are somewhere in the script, even if they're not spelled out. It's your job to figure out the motivations.

Productions do not offer the luxury of explaining the entire story to you. That is part of your work, and what you must do. If you don't understand the script, you're not doing your job.

Since the only elements written in a script are actions and lines of dialogue, it's up to you to figure out the reasons for your character's actions. Internal feelings are open for your interpretation from what's on the page. You can infer the 'why' for any action, in whatever way works for you. That said, you must be open to reinterpretation when presented with new information, approach, or direction.

The writer is the story architect. If you're on a big project, rest assured that writer is likely rather intelligent with a massive knowledge of their craft. There may even be a team of writers sitting around a table figuring out how every story element works. That team is serving the overall vision of the lead writer.

Again, it's your job as an actor to be a detective. It's not just, "What are my lines?"

You also will want to understand how your character fits into the story. You need to be open to how your character actually fits, after reading the entire script or sides that were sent you – as opposed to how you thought it was going to be. Excitement over booking a role may trigger fantasies of grandeur. Do not approach a job like this. Instead, thoughtfully enter the production – listening much more than speaking.

If you're able to understand and summarize the entire story, then you can understand how your character and your character's arc fit into that story. Once you understand how your character's arc fits into that story, it becomes much easier to memorize lines, because the lines make sense in the context of the whole story. You are simply responding to things that happen or things that are said by other characters, because the writer(s) already thought about what would make sense.

As an actor, if you trust that those lines and descriptions are indeed things your character would say and do, you can stay focused on finding the clues as to your character's motivations. All of a sudden, you'll have a much deeper and clearer understanding, and you will also enter a new world of castability.

Work with Your Director

Acting is a team sport. Your director is your coach. When you're working with other people, they are all there to give you something. However, you're not there to take. Your role is to receive collaborative input and to give something back.

Meet these collaborators where they are. Because ultimately, it's not about you; your performance is about the project. Productions don't actually care how big of a role you have, or how big of a celebrity you are. And the director knows how all of the scenes and characters fit together much better than you do.

I've had actors challenge me while I'm directing, and sometimes there's something to glean out of that, so I do listen. However, time is of the essence. In general, it's a better bet to merge your perspective with the direction, and then execute that. Challenging producers and directors can often lead to your services no longer being needed.

If you're an actor with a great idea, the best way to present it is, "May I demonstrate my take?"

Show them, only if they give you a green light. Do NOT go through a stop sign. Ultimately you need to respect the production's decisions. Even if the director didn't consider or listen to your suggestion, and you as the actor think they're totally wrong, it does not matter. You are being paid as a professional to set your own opinions aside and deliver what production is asking of you.

Understand Production

Here are the main phases of production in its totality:

Idea	(creator)
Script	(writer)
Pre-Production	(producers, director, cinematographer, location scout, designers)
Casting	(casting directors, actors, producers, director, creator)
Production	(producers, director, actors, crew)
Post-Production	(editor, director, producer)

As you can see in the six phases of production listed here, the actors are really only involved in one third of the total process. The old adage is that the actors are the last people hired and the first to be let go as the production phase is completed. It's good to understand your place in the process.

Each crew person has a role to play. I think it's important to note the broad spectrum of crew positions behind the camera, to understand what each person is doing, and why.

For example, as the actor, you need to repeat your lines at a similar volume and follow the same blocking every time, because the boom operator has to follow you with the microphone, <u>and</u> the camera operator has to follow you on the dolly, or to do a rack focus or a pan or a tilt, <u>and</u> all the other professional performers will be repeating their own actions. All of these actions must be cut together by the editor.

Even if a performance is great, if the actions don't match between the master shot and a medium or close up, chances are the take of that great performance can't be used.

On a film or TV show, <u>continuity</u> is more important for the overall project than what you feel like doing in the moment. You're helping to create a story out of sequence, therefore your precision and continuity are vitally important to the editor being able to put the scenes together in post-production.

A broad example would be taking your shirt off in one take and leaving it on in the next. Part of one take and the other take cannot be cut together, because the image would not flow continuously. More subtly, if you use a fun gesture or facial expression, but don't implement it at the exact same time in your delivery from take to take, the editor will have a difficult time lining up the shots.

Believe it or not, the editor is the one who can make or break your comedic timing. So once you have come up with a bit that's approved by the director, don't vary from it. They may be repeating a take for a slip up somewhere else in the scene and are expecting you to repeat exactly what you did.

Understand Editing

"Cut. That's great, guys. Let's get the punch-ins and then do the turnarounds," I said one day on set.

"I don't think we need those shots," an actor blurted out – out-of-turn.

Excuse me, you have no idea what shots we need, I thought, before handling the situation – hopefully diplomatically.

This encounter was an example of an actor stepping out of their lane. It turned out the motivation for this disruption had to do with the actor wanting to leave set early to get to another audition. Sorry, wrong answer. You don't need to book every single job out there. Focus on the one you are at right now!

There's a great book by Academy-Award-winning film editor and sound designer Walter Murch, called *In the Blink of an Eye*. It is so revealing of editing technique that I cannot recommend enough that every actor read it. In fact, it is required reading in my master classes. From this book, you are examining how your performance will be controlled in post-production. Once you understand this, it is much easier to disabuse yourself of your own ego.

Without such perspective, an actor's ego might think, *My performance is really good. It doesn't have to be controlled in post-production.*

Sorry, that's incorrect, and a dangerous attitude to throw out the window immediately – because it's not going to work. Like it or not, your performance is very much going to be controlled in post-production. The shots fitting together in editing is how the emotional tone is controlled by the director and editor, ultimately in preparation for consumption by an audience.

So… what can you do to control the way your performance is edited? Walter Murch's award-winning film editor's perspective will give you deep insight into how editors work with your performance.

For example, they often will place a cut right before the eyelid starts to droop for a blink. That's how you maintain the tension of a scene and audience engagement. They would only keep the blink if they're trying to make a point with it. When you watch a performance one frame at a time or in slow motion, this starts to make sense.

Walter Murch says that the blink, which you, the actor, might think is random, isn't so random. Part of your psychology, the blink tends to indicate a pause, change, disruption, or end of a thought. It will often happen if you're nervous or went up on a line. So blinking is very interesting. With that understanding, you can get into very technical on-camera work, such as holding your eyes open at the end of a scene, or blinking intentionally at a particular moment you choose for the delivery of a particular line.

This is an example of a technical extreme in acting. To succeed, you must blend technical wizardry with your acting foundation or method. Meisner, Stanislavsky, Strasberg, Chekhov, Hagen or Adler – each method has something to offer actors, so don't rely on only one. Your best performances will be influenced by a multitude of schools of thought, and the implementation of a variety of practices.

So, whatever your approach, weave it together with technique – like hitting the same mark precisely for multiple takes in a row, along with a general knowledge of filmmaking. It's the weaving together of all of it that will make you successful. And you need to do this without stepping out of bounds, because you're there to do a specific job. Magic happens when you're able to stay in your own lane while intertwining all of that together.

PREPARATION

1. Take the time to understand the story as a whole.

The first thing I do when I get a script is read the entire thing without taking out a highlighter and looking for my lines. I'm not interested in my lines at that moment, because focusing only on what applies to me will not help me understand the whole story, which is what I need to do.

2. After you have a good grasp for the story, start writing!

Summarize your character's journey to make sure you understand it. Discover plausible motivations for your character's actions.

3. Write down how each scenario makes you feel and how it makes you react, given the context of the story and relationships.

4. Learn about filmmaking in general, especially the primary job functions.

You'll gain a lot more respect for the professionals around you, and understand how to work more efficiently and effectively with all the technical aspects on a set.

5. Did I mention you need to read *In the Blink of an Eye* by Walter Murch?

You'll discover so much you'll be able to apply to your on-camera performance.

ROXANNA LEWIS

Casting Performers Authentically – I'm Looking for You, So Be You!

CEO of Roxxiedanz Productions, Roxanna Lewis helms film and live productions that entertain, defy stereotypes, and amplify resilience with globally-inclusive themes of those who have been traditionally unrepresented. She works with remarkable artists of all backgrounds and body types to include people who are neurotypical and neurodivergent, paraplegic, wheelchair users, d/Deaf, and blind. She's received support from The Community Foundation (NEA partnership) and The Flutie Foundation for her film, *Mandy's Voice* starring Rachel Barcellona. As a 'life changer' for the powerful WE Believe event, Roxanna has presented to live audiences of 8,000+, and live-streamed to 1.6 million across North America on "The Healing Power of Creativity and The Courage to Follow Your Dreams."

Just about every performer I've ever known has experienced the overwhelm that comes with booking a job, more specifically, the casting and audition process. In fact, some talented individuals let this fear keep them from even trying. What I want you to know is that slogging through discomfort and insecurity is a standard part of the creative process – you're actually right on track. Ultimately, it would be a very positive thing to enjoy the audition process, which is absolutely possible through effective preparation and showing up as yourself, just as you are. Believe me, some fabulous casting director out there is looking for exactly that – YOU.

During the dream-come-true experience working with Emmy Award-winning actor, Ben Gazzara, on his autobiography, *In the*

Moment: My Life as An Actor, I asked him how he dealt with the intense pressures of auditions.

Ben looked me square in the eye and said, "What are you talking about? I don't do anything different. I just act like myself in that particular situation – they either want it or they don't."

Simple. Clean. Confident. Wow! Having carved out an awe-inspiring career spanning over fifty years in TV, film and on Broadway – this honest approach fortified with training and tenacity certainly worked for Ben, and countless others.

Learning this lesson from a different angle, I was once brought in to audition for a role on *Law & Order*. I later found out from the casting director that the character was originally written as a Hasidic Jewish male, late 40's, and there I was, an eastern European/middle Eastern young ingenue, late 20's…. Well, I gave it my all, got close, but didn't book it. This could have been internalized as a total failure. However, that same casting director ended up calling me back for other projects – that I did book. That's what you want, to grow from the "No," and morph it into a "Yes," by exuding genuine confidence, developing plentiful opportunities and lasting relationships.

As an only child, I had a powerful imagination and was heavily influenced by the tight-knit, multi-generational immigrant home in which I was raised – my elders tirelessly dedicated their lives to human rights and social activism. Thankfully, as a young girl I awakened to the notion that every single person wants to be met where they are, have their uniqueness recognized, and endeavor to live the fullest life possible. These inalienable rights transcend time, culture, and stereotypes. These basic tenets of humanity require respect, compassion, and a modicum of interest in one another to create the heart-space to understand that which is less familiar. Becoming an artist, a sculptor of characters, an architect of stories, and a designer of worlds helped me embrace who I am.

I am obsessed with the endless ways one can create stories through the manipulation of words, visual design, physical movement, connection through relationship, and use of environment. Productions with Gallaudet University, choreographing and performing internationally with Infinity Dance Theatre (NYC), and contributing as a featured choreographer on Broadway in Christopher Reeves' *First You Dream*

CASTING PEFORMERS AUTHENTICALLY – I'M LOOKING FOR YOU SO BE YOU!

were not only groundbreaking endeavors at the time, but my springboard to passionately and organically champion the importance of finding and working with performers with a variety of lived experiences.

Entertainment decision-makers have recently experienced a seismic shift towards authenticity in casting. My entry into the world of filmmaking and TV through the side door as a choreographer and theatrical director has held some distinct advantages. I've worked with extraordinarily talented artists from all over the world, including neurotypical and neurodivergent artists, disabled artists who are paraplegic, wheelchair users, d/Deaf, and blind.

Our diversity is what makes us strong as creatives and storytellers. Living boldly, just as you are, is more important now than ever.

As a writer, director and producer, I seek out that exact boldness on both sides of the camera. As the daughter of a parent on the spectrum, I produced and directed one of the first narrative films ever made about a non-speaking girl on the spectrum – through authentic casting. We auditioned a large number of very talented actors from Florida, Atlanta, and Los Angeles, but the puzzle pieces weren't fitting. Something was missing from the story: authenticity. The message of our movie could have been lost due to a fundamental flaw in depicting the character's neurodivergence inaccurately.

At the time, only two percent of films were cast with people who actually embodied the disability being presented on-screen. We did so, not only in front of the camera, but also in forming our crew and producing team. *Mandy's Voice* held up a mirror to our larger societal predispositions and prejudices against the 'other' or, as some might say, 'Those who aren't like us.' We didn't aim to hit a mark or fill a quota, we simply did what was right for the story.

Authentic casting continues to be challenging in Hollywood and beyond. Characters who represent people with disabilities are already hard to find on screen: According to *The State of Disability Representation on Television: An Analysis of Scripted TV Series from 2016-2023*, a study of 350 scripted TV shows produced in the U.S., data reveals that only 3.7% of TV characters have a disability, on average. And of these characters, almost 80% of them are portrayed by actors who do not have the same (or similar) disability.

This said, statistics are the past. You are the future.

I believe – I know – that no matter what category of happy marathon-binge-watching geek we might fall into, audiences are ready for more choice. The choice of visibility, bold voices and people of varied life experiences in film and TV increases the number of relatable and fascinating stories which shape societal attitudes and public policy.

As a human-being first and filmmaker second, it is my nature to create opportunities with and for those who have been historically undervalued and kept out of the larger conversations, and to tell remarkable stories that reflect everyday people in our real-world communities. I recall saying, "We don't need thousands of people to audition, we just need the right few. We're looking for them, and they're definitely looking for us, so let's put it out there!"

My takeaway for *you* is YES, we act to portray a variety of characters, and those characters thrive when the real you is a kernel within each character you portray. Authenticity intertwined with skill is paramount!

It is now common practice to ask the question of writers and directors, "Why are you the one to tell this story?" Today, the actor is an important player in this conversation too.

While doing a shoot for PBS with Dr. Maya Angelou, she so humbly asked me, of all people, whether I thought any of her work made a difference in the world at all? The matriarch of hope and inspiration wondered if she belonged, and whether her words mattered?! I was absolutely dumbfounded. Her high potency impact still ripples throughout our society in all directions. Yes, she absolutely continues to matter and so does her work, and *so do you*. Follow your dreams, share your talents, and let your artistry shine. I hope to see you at a casting call soon ;)

PREPARATION

No matter what your story is, here are some tips to get your acting career started. Above all else, prepare and hone your skills. Take the leap and commit to regularly attending quality acting classes. Acting classes are intended to be a space where you can excavate and understand your inner workings, while simultaneously honing technical skills to carry you through your career.

Go the extra mile and learn the craft of improv acting – you'll learn how to think fast and have fun in any circumstance, and you'll laugh your ass off along the way.

Be sure to research the company that's bringing you in to audition; being familiar helps you feel more relaxed. Take the time to understand all aspects of the character and story or project for which you're auditioning. Emmy Award winner Henry Winkler, who played The Fonz on *Happy Days,* learned of his dyslexia during his time on the iconic sitcom. He offers the advice that if you're not a strong cold reader, memorize the script in advance, if possible, and be prepared to improvise (good thing you took those improv classes!).

Basic must-do's before an audition start with getting enough sleep the night before so your concentration is solid and you can be fully present in the moment. Similarly, take the time to plan out your eating schedule and any medication you might need to take prior to the audition. You want to show up in your top condition.

When you're called in to audition, know that the person auditioning you is hoping that you are 'the one.' Enter the audition space knowing they want to hire you – even if they don't say a word or look at you. The only thing you need to do is think and react as your character would.

Actively tune into your senses so your whole being feels energized and ready for your moment to shine. What works for you? How about tuning out distractions with a good headset? For those who like music, whether in a busy hallway or home for an online meeting, something that may help you focus while waiting is to listen to your favorite (or your character's favorite) music with earbuds or a headset – just make sure it's not too loud as to disturb your neighbor or to make you miss your name being called.

Another option to settle those excitement butterflies, may be to play with a fidget spinner or look at a few of your favorite photos or artwork. Also, remember to bring water to hydrate. It's a great idea to create your own Actor Toolkit Bag for those last-minute auditions.

During the audition, if you happen to receive a note or suggestion from the director, apply it right away, even if it doesn't seem to make any sense. The director is purposely observing whether you can take and apply direction. Always end the audition in good spirits and offer a warm, "Thank you very much."

So, you rocked the audition (or perhaps not). What's next? Celebrate just showing up! There is something to be gained from every single experience. If you don't show up to an audition, then there's zero chance of getting the role. The more you audition, the more you book jobs, the more jobs you book, the more relationships you build, and the more opportunities you create. So, get back to business and continue your training. Acting is all about the process, not just results.

For any actor, "Nos" are a lot more common than "Yesses", so remember, it's just a numbers game. The most useful thing you can do is to find a positive lesson from each experience and apply it next time. You showed up and followed through – celebrate this win. Above all else, don't take a "No" personally, and don't give up.

If you received a "Yes" and got the gig – congratulations!

It's important to learn about your new workplace. Find out about its accessibility and be sure to give yourself extra time to arrive on time.

Have fun familiarizing yourself with the director and their work. Watch/listen/read interviews and articles about them so you're comfortable starting the process together.

When that fantastic day comes that you meet the director, be open, be yourself and don't be afraid to politely ask questions. When the timing feels right, inquire about the lighting and sound elements for your scenes so you can prepare as needed. Inquire about potential quiet spaces you might use to review lines or rest during breaks.

Each project is different, the flow between actors and crew is symbiotic and has a learning curve, so be professional and respectful of others who are working hard to make you, the actor, look good. Most of all, have fun, and be YOU!

CASTING PEFORMERS AUTHENTICALLY – I'M LOOKING FOR YOU SO BE YOU!

Resources

Here are some resources to start your research on disability in the entertainment industry:

GADIM (Global Alliance for Media and Entertainment)

abilityE (abilitye.com)

Reelabilities Film Festival

Easterseals Disability Film Challenge

Alliance for Inclusion in the Arts

NADC (UCLA National Arts and Disabilities Center)

RespectAbility (Disability Belongs.org)

Chapter 12.

Collaborate & Play Well with Others

"For me, our job as artists is to serve the story, serve the director, and serve the fellow actors. And if you do that, by osmosis you're serving yourself because you'll get the best out of yourself."

- DAVID OYELOWO

LYNNE BURNETT

What I Learned from Martin Sheen

Lynne Burnett is a writer, director, producer, actress, and the founder of the film industry networking nonprofit, Coffee Chatter. She wrote, produced and co-starred in the short *Diamond Real Estate*. She wrote, produced and appears in the short documentaries *The Negro Speaks* and *Coffee Chatter*. *Coffee Chatter* has won awards at numerous film festivals including Santa Clarita International, Silver Screen, Paris Awards Film Festival and many more. She appeared in the feature films SPRING, CLASS DISMISSED, THE MOVIE, and the TV series *Class Dismissed, Kenan & Kel, The Bold and the Beautiful* and *Girlfriends*. Lynne earned a Liberal Arts BA at IUPUI, Liberal Arts and a MA at Brandman University.

In 2011, I needed a job. A fellow actor friend of mine worked at Warner Brothers Studio and helped me get a security guard position. My duty was to check IDs and search car trunks for weapons or suspicious items that could be deemed harmful to WB and pedestrians on the lot.

Guess what, many celebrities are not big fans of having to give a security guard their driver's license or identification – it reveals their correct age.

The polyester security guard uniform is hot as hell. You're outside, on your feet all day, searching trunks, looking for potentially dangerous items, and trying to read people as they pass through the gate was stress enough. The last thing on my mind was calculating how old an actor might really be.

Thousands of actors have graced the Hollywood studio lots and, like it or not, each one of them had to show identification to gain entrance.

Except for one. I was surprised to learn that in the entire history of all cars that passed through all the studio gates over the years, there was one star who was universally exempt from showing a photo ID – just one! That was the late, great Elizabeth Taylor.

Man, oh man, talk about Hollywood star power. While I never had the pleasure of meeting her in person, I would have been honored to wave Elizabeth Taylor onto the lot.

Many wannabes and up-and-comers drive on the lot with a condescending attitude toward the guards as they impatiently explain how important they are and shouldn't have to show ID, even making quite a fuss. I admit it, at times I was tempted to inform them they were no Elizabeth Taylor.

On the other hand, genuinely accomplished, instantly-recognizable star Martin Sheen had an excellent reputation among us security guards as always being kind, polite and patient. No yelling, no arguments, no, "I'm better than you are" attitude.

I always wore make-up and two-inch heels. I was polite, smiled and waved hello to everyone. Even though I was currently a security guard, I too wanted to be a successful actress – many of the other security guards called me "Hollywood." The fact that Martin Sheen treated me personally like royalty made me feel good, and it made me admire and respect him even more.

Inspired by his example, I stepped it up. I treated every executive as if they were king or queen of the studio, and did whatever I could to ensure each starlet and muscle man who entered the lot was going to make it to the top.

PREPARATION

Even if we hadn't known who he was, we could have easily identified Martin Sheen as a worthwhile individual just by the way he carried himself and how he treated everyone with respect, no matter who they were.

So, if you want to be recognized as someone who would be great to hire, or continue working with after a first job, don't act like a diva. Be like Martin Sheen and show genuine respect for everyone, no matter who they are.

WHAT I LEARNED FROM MARTIN SHEEN

If you make up your mind that all people deserve to be treated like stars, whether an actor, an extra, an executive, a custodian, a gardener or a security guard, you'll be on the right track. With a "do unto others" attitude, you will naturally treat each person you meet with kindness and respect – regardless of their apparent station in life.

After all, in the entertainment industry you never know what hidden talents people have. A security guard you meet today could become a director you want to work with tomorrow.

"I just make it my business to get along with people so I can have fun. It's that simple."

– BETTY WHITE

MARA MCCANN

Creative Collaboration

Mara is a producer, actress, entrepreneur, expert strategist and start-up advisor. As an actress, she has upcoming roles in films and series, including a new pilot with *Parks and Recs* actor, Jim O'Heir, and a leading role in a thriller with a two-time Emmy-winning production company. She is also producing projects with Emmy-award-winning and Oscar-nominated development teams. Mara is an advisor at SXSW Tech Pitch Fest, and Founder of Zhive Media, a media resource hub for Gen Z girls + thems. She has coordinated numerous film and tech events from Sundance to Tribeca Film Fest, and received grants from organizations that include the NEA, NEH and Third Wave Foundation of New York. Previously she was on the strategic development team at one of the top innovation labs in New York.

With collaborators, it's important to talk about the nature of the collaboration and the project from day one, especially to find out what the other person's goal is for the project.

I think a lot of times we make mistakes when we assume that we and other people who are interested in the project all have the same goal. That's how a lot of trainwrecks can happen.

Whatever the situation is, in any type of creative collaboration, if you start at the beginning with anybody new, and especially with someone you already know, whether it's a writer, director, or another actor, never assume you know their goals if they haven't laid them out. Find out what everyone's goals are. Otherwise, you might find out later that they were planning to do summer stock while you're dreaming that this play is going to be on Broadway.

When there's not a shared goal and vision for the project, that creates problems.

CREATIVE COLLABORATION

When there's multiple collaborators, if there's not a shared vision it's possible that one or more of you can see it a different way and adjust to a shared vision, but first, everyone has to know and agree on what that vision is.

You could be thinking, *I love this script, this is going to be on the big screen* and you meet with a director who's thinking to make it into a web series, but didn't bother to mention that. You might be fine with it as a web series – after all, it's faster and easier to get made, but if you were thinking *movie* and find out on the first day of shooting it's a web series... it could have a negative impact on your working relationship with the director.

On the other hand, when you find alignment on goals, your creative project can prosper.

So suss it out from the very beginning, because then you can make sure you're with people who are as invested as you are in the same goal. Establishing clarity creates alignment between collaborator and synergy for the project – when everyone agrees they want the same result it can generate positive momentum.

PREPARATION

In a first meeting with anyone about a project, have a conversation in which you both answer the questions:
What is your goal here?
What is your dream for this project?
Take time to see if what everyone says matches what you want.

Be open, you and your collaborators may be able to adjust to each other. Maybe they had a different vision and when you share yours, they like it better than their original concept for the project. Or vice versa.

LISA SAWICKI

How To Cope with Difficult Personalities

Lisa owned the publicity agency Lapides Publicity Group for 35 years, taught acting classes at John Casablancas Acting Center, and performed in three major car commercials. She co-created the award-winning music and character development/education program *Youth Under Construction,* with her husband David Sawicki, before becoming a certified life coach. Lisa is a public speaker sharing topics relating to healthy boundaries and managing and thriving in the human experience. She holds a Bachelor of Science in Communications from Boston University.

This is about how to cope with other people's offensive and difficult personalities as an actor; how to build the "muscle" of self-preservation skills.

It is a tremendous skill to allow yourself to become a whole other personality while acting. Actors can be highly sensitive people, and it makes so much sense, because you must be empathic and vulnerable to truly understand and portray other personalities and experiences outside of your own authentic self.

Being a working actor includes having to live through a lot of rejection, sometimes insulting and tough directors, and all the other hundreds of people you work with in some capacity who may or may not have kind personalities, as well as all the social media critics and public scrutiny – which we know can be not just insulting and humiliating, but downright annihilating.

It is imperative that you know how to handle offensive and difficult people, as well as public scrutiny and humiliation. Unfortunately, it comes with the job, so you must learn healthy self-preservation skills.

The reality is, there are times when we all must put on a 'performance' in order to deal with challenging or toxic people and loaded situations. That's why having great acting skill can be a help when dealing with this kind of stuff – you actually have an advantage over people who do not know how to "play a part."

PREPARATION

Self-Preservation Skills for Actors

1. Always come prepared.

Know your lines and any planned directions. Be prompt, well-rested, well-fed, well-rehearsed, and arrive at any rehearsal or production with an open and strong state of mind. The more confident you are of your work in the assignment at hand, the better. Make sure that you feel grounded and open to learn and receive valid direction.

2. Do *not* take unfair attacks personally.

This can be extremely difficult, because most great actors are highly sensitive and are often people-pleasers. You can only do your best, and no one deserves abuse.

In the entertainment world, perhaps more-so than in the general population, you're likely to experience some level of abuse due to inflated egos, excess competitiveness, or even sadism, which may arise from others' own emotional wounds, deep insecurity, and simply because, 'Hurt people, hurt people.'

You need to accept this reality at a core level. You need to recognize that people who behave this way are damaged. And you need to safeguard yourself from attack. You don't have to be best friends; you just want to safely get along with them.

3. Keep your radar up when dealing with difficult or toxic people.

Keep it professional and cordial with anyone who has a tendency to 'behave badly.'

Don't get too personal. Do your best to make sure your conversation and messages won't provide ammunition for them to attack you down the line. Try to stay ten steps ahead so they won't have a chance to throw you in a ditch.

Not easy, but practice makes it better. Always have compassion and respect for yourself and others in your communication and actions. Be able to quickly admit if you make a mistake or misstep.

Let them know you appreciate their strengths and whichever qualities they have that you genuinely respect or admire. Damaged and insecure people feed off of praise and may well calm down when they know you respect and admire them.

4. Calm yourself down first, before responding to put-downs or intimidation.

When someone treats you unfairly – with put-downs, intimidation, threats or bullying – pause and take a few breaths before responding. Avoid the temptation to defend yourself.

People want to be heard and understood, so do your best to hear and understand the request, even if it was delivered in an unpleasant way.

Identify if you have any legitimate questions around the direction, what is needed, or any blaming or insults. Ask your questions in a CALM VOICE if at all possible.

Let others know that you want to do a good job for them <u>and</u> that you need to know what they want you to deliver. It may be helpful to ask for a bit more context around what they feel is lacking, or how they see the role or the scene, so you can get a better idea of how to embody what they want to see.

5. Avoid attacking back.

If anyone attacks you inappropriately, it's natural to feel angry and go on the offense. However, if you lash back at someone with a difficult personality, it will likely only get worse, so do your best not to respond with an attack back.

If you're steaming mad, ask for a five- or ten-minute break so you can cool down before responding.

If that's not an option, do your best to keep your voice calm and neutral as you move forward with questions and suggestions for solutions.

Your best option is to remain the mature and fair-minded adult in the room. If you lose control, you will also lose your power in the situation.

You can say things like:

"I can't listen to you or respond intelligently when you're screaming (or attacking me)."

"Can we take a small break, so each of us can cool down and come back together to solve this?'

"I really want to do this exactly how you want, and I need more instruction and precise direction from you. Let's please work as a team. I want this to work."

Regardless of how they respond, you must try to keep your cool. This is the best you can do.

6. Focus on the big picture.

Remind yourself of your good intentions and deliberate purpose with every situation you are in. It's not possible to completely avoid difficult or negative people so, instead, have a realistic goal of gaining skill in emotionally navigating difficult waters, rather than being drowned in emotional overwhelm.

You can be a winner in even the most challenging situation through your sincerity and a demeanor that radiates your own self-acceptance and self-love.

7. Be great at what you do.

Being an actor is not for the faint of heart. You may have to give a great performance even when your heart and your whole being feel hurt or angry over circumstances with a difficult person.

Just like the more you learn and practice your craft the better actor you will become, navigating challenging conversations and situations will also get easier with practice.

KEVIN E. WEST

Processing Direction

Kevin E. West is a veteran actor with over seventy IMDb credits, including guest starring roles on the TV series *The Righteous Gemstones, Hawaii 5-0, Criminal Minds, Bones, Castle, CSI: Miami, NCIS, CSI, Justified, Lost, 24* and *Alias*. He created The Actor MBA and founded the award-winning organization The Actors' Network, the most endorsed business organization for actors in U.S. history, with consecutive *Backstage West* "Readers' Choice" awards. Kevin authored *7 Deadly Sins the Actor Overcomes: The Business of Acting and Show Business,* and was featured in the audio program, "The Actor's Guide to Getting the Job." He also created the interview series ActorBizGuru, voted #1 online educational resource by *Backstage West.* Kevin has had speaking engagements at WGA, SAG-AFTRA, UCLA and Film Institute-Stockholm.

"Aaaaaaaand cut!"

The director walks over to you and says, "That was great. Now let's do it again, a little faster," then walks away.

Oftentimes, when working professionally in film or television, you'll have somewhere between thirty and ninety seconds to process that direction. Sure, it is possible there could be a momentary issue on set, or the director has a brief chat with the DP (Director of Photography, aka the Cinematographer), but more likely you will not get a lot of time to make an artistic and organic adjustment.

Most acting coaches and teachers initially focus on teaching you how to use yourself (aka your physical-mental instrument) to achieve a professional level of acting truth. In addition to classes and training, most actors begin working in theater, which provides an artistic and mental pattern of acting in a start-to-finish linear fashion.

Even if, like me, your path is different and you didn't begin acting as a child or in theater, you're probably still focused on preparing for auditions. Both theater work and audition preparation provide an actor a similar benefit: NOT being interrupted in the throughline of our work.

However, when we work in film and television, we usually have to do multiple takes in a row. The audible and visual distraction of ten to forty crew members running around can create quite the challenge. Perhaps the scene has explosions, or you're in a car chase, or working with animals or small children. There's a long list of potential distractions you don't find on a theater stage, in an audition room, or during a self-tape audition.

Additionally, in film and television we're commonly acting out of order, meaning on your first day of work you may be performing the last scene of the script. All of this is both the beauty and artistic challenge of acting in the exciting world of film and television.

"Aaaaaaaand back to one!" the First A.D. (Assistant Director) barks, meaning, "Let's start that take over from the beginning of the scene."

When we act, there is a natural desire to 'get it right', or, in some circumstances, just 'get it in the can', meaning, just get it done.

Now let's go back and hear the Director say, "Let's do it again a little faster."

The acting challenge is, what type of 'faster' does the director want, within the context of the show, script, scene, and your character?

What I created way back in the early '90s, inspired somewhat by my acting coach at the time, David LeGrant, was building a 'Rolodex' in my mind, a catalogue of what was my most natural mood, essence, and pace in different situations and environments in my life.

On a daily basis, I carried around a notepad – yes, we did that before Smartphones – and logged my responses to different circumstances and emotional triggers. What evolved from that concept over a few years was what I now call Kevin's Ten Questions, and here they are:

1. What happened five seconds before the scene started?
2. Where am I? Public, private or public-private? (Public-private might be in a restaurant where you're sitting at a table with someone

– your scene partner – but other patrons might be able to overhear your conversation.)
3. What time is it, exactly? AM or PM?
4. What is my relationship with the other character(s)?
5. What do I need/want?
6. What am I afraid of?
7. What do I know, that the other character doesn't know that I know?
8. What is the consequence if I fail?
9. Why do you stay? Not just leave or hang up?
10. Where am I going or what am I going to do five seconds after the scene ends?

For the purposes of learning how to quickly make a truthful artistic adjustment, based on your director's result-oriented request, "Let's do it again a little faster," I only want you to focus on numbers two and three: *Where Am I - public, private or public-private location?* and, *What time is it exactly?*

As human beings, it's amazing how quickly and naturally our entire demeanor, energy, pace, and physical presence change, based purely on the exact time of day and where we are. We all know this, but we don't really pay attention to it much throughout our normal lives. Yet our entire job as an actor is to take someone else's words and scenario and truthfully manifest a performance that the television and movie-watching public believes.

When you begin to become instinctively aware in your mind, with a transference to your body, how certain locations and times of day can create an instant artistic direction, you will not only become a better actor, you'll avoid the trap of just thinking about going "faster" per the director's request.

Why? Simple, there are a hundred different reasons in life that make us suddenly move or speak faster or slower, more gently or forcefully, or softer or louder, and another thousand reasons why we feel scared, cautious, excited, happy, sad, and the list goes on and on. Human beings have a massive assortment of paces and presences based on time and location.

I have no desire to intellectually overwhelm you, so I'm going to present four basic scenarios, because, unfortunately, many directors are not taught to speak to actors in terms of why or how, but rather just, "Give me a result," such as, "Faster."

For the record, I am not blaming directors at all, I'm merely sharing with you a real-world problem, and I'm a solution-oriented guy (artist.) ☺

Now I'd like to share a few technique solutions I've created over the course of my career. Wishing you success and my professional best!

PREPARATION

Scenario #1

The director says, "Okay, let's do this at a whisper level, but don't whisper."

A scene with this type of direction could be in almost any setting, but let's put us in what I call a public-private location.

Initially you performed it in a normal voice, but for the next take you need to follow the direction. While it may feel easy to lower your voice by thinking, *Just lower it*, what if you were to quickly say to yourself, *I'm in a library*. There is your quickie form of processing direction, but organically. You do not "substitute" putting yourself in a library, but instead infuse yourself with a location trigger.

Within those thirty to ninety seconds that you have to make the adjustment, close your eyes and recall having a muted, not whispered, conversation in a library. Yes, think of being in a library, and just let that library conversation filter through your body.

Then do the scene again.

Scenario #2

The director says, "I need you to be a lot more uncomfortable on this take."

The feeling of being uncomfortable, and why, can be as individual as we are, but what we do as performers, far too often, is try to be uncomfortable by, again, just thinking about the word.

I like to keep my direction processing triggers simple. One of the most common uncomfortable feelings we've all had is when we're in an elevator and a slightly odd or creepy person gets on. You have to look down and desperately wait for your floor, or for them to exit first. We want that feeling to flow through your veins so you can quickly and naturally achieve the 'uncomfortable-ness' the director desires.

Scenario #3

The director says, "We need to bring the pace down, so go slower."

Once again, pace in acting is massively important, and all too commonly the genesis of result-oriented direction, which can feel and appear as "bad" acting. Why?

Because in the interest of a fast turn-around time from take to take, most actors just mechanically think about going slower. While a talented actor can sometimes pull this off, it usually renders as false on camera.

A quick solution trigger is choosing an exact time of day. My acting coach used to ask actors at what time of day the scene took place, and most would say morning, noon or night.

I strongly recommend you do not use any of those three. All of us know a common moment of the day, based on our individual lives, when we move slower. When our minds are just tired, be it four pm, two am or six am matters not. Quickly put yourself in the exact time of day that will help you trigger a tired mind, and then perform the scene. This way you create an organic performance of slowing down.

Scenario #4

The director says, "That was great. Now let's go again, but do it faster."

Throughout my career, I've always found "do it faster" to be the worst non-creative and lazy effort by a director, but we typically nod our heads and proceed to think about going faster.

The good news is that there are several simple and organic triggers for speaking or performing at a naturally faster pace. One of my favorites is the reality of having to go to the bathroom, but trying to hide it while talking. Your pace quickens automatically.

You might try having a need to quicken your conversational pace so you can get off a call because you're about to miss something you urgently want to watch, like your child's dance recital, or something is burning on the stove, or you're expecting another important call.

Finally, you might want to generate an internal urge to finish up your discussion because you're transitioning to get out of the house and to your car before you're late to an appointment.

The choice for the above scenario that works best for you is individual, but these feelings of quiet urgency are a wonderful acting trigger to pick up your pace organically, not just mentally.

I assure you, whether it's a live audition, Zoom-type audition, or working on set, organic but simple triggers (not substitutions) make you a far better actor and working professional when faced with poor, result-oriented directing.

These few options I've discussed are just a fraction of the possibilities. There are hundreds and hundreds of potential triggers you can assemble in your 'Actor Rolodex.' Take notice of them when you know you feel them, track them, practice them, and then use them in your work.

Of course, these triggers are something you can use in addition to your overall preferred acting technique and not meant to replace it.

Chapter 13.

Be Safe and Take Care

"There is a need for aloneness, which I don't think most people realize for an actor. It's almost having certain kinds of secrets for yourself that you'll let the whole world in on only for a moment, when you're acting."

- MARILYN MONROE

BRIONNE DAVIS DAVEL

Agreements

Brionne Davis Davel is an actor, educator and life-transformation mentor. Feature films include co-starring in the multi-award-winning MOONGARDEN, and a leading role in the Oscar-nominated EMBRACE OF THE SERPENT (Alfred P. Sloan Award and Cannes Directors Fortnight winner.) Television guest star appearances include *Ray Donovan, Castle Rock,* and *Narcos: Mexico.* Stage work includes the Los Angeles revival of *Bent* at the Mark Taper Forum, the role of Hedwig in a San Francisco revival of *Hedwig and the Angry Inch*, the role of Lee in the Off-Broadway revival of *True West,* and the one-man shows *A Noble Exile* (based on his own memoir) and *Shame.* He has taught acting, theater history, and production at the Studio Institute Global, and been a guest instructor at the Anthony Gilardi Acting Studio. Brionne has led numerous leadership workshops designed to empower personal responsibility, compassion, and generosity as a way to achieve goals.

Understand that care for self is part of the movement forward in telling the story.

I can do burpees and push-ups and running and fight sequences. But I can't do all of that with fourteen-hour days, three or four days in a row. It's not going to serve the story, because I'm going to be wiped out after the second day. Being in care of myself is part of that contributing factor of knowing how much I can do.

You have to care for yourself. As an actor on the set, your body is your tool and you might be very vulnerable under certain working conditions. That's why SAG provides rules for eight-hour days. You need to honor your own health and wellness.

I'm pro-union and I'm a big fan of contracts. Everything in writing before you start work. You have a contract before you open a script. You can open the script for the audition, read the entire script, sure. But once they agree to hire you, before you do anything... before you step into a table read or a rehearsal, whether it's a union or non-union project, have a contract.

If you have an agent or manager, involve them in the process, that's what they're there for. For a non-union situation, you can look at what the SAG contract states and use it as a reference point for your stipulations.

"You don't have to pay me SAG rate, but these are the terms under which I will work." Things like meals provided, no abuse of overtime. Are they going to pay overtime? I always request, and get, a 12-hour turnaround.

If the production isn't paying you, or they're paying very little, you can request a percentage of revenue after the film's release (profit rarely happens, so ask for a small percentage of revenue.) And/or ask for an additional credit on the film. If you're playing a main character, you can ask for a producer credit. Once the film is in post-production, you'll want to be active and support the release anyhow, so why not get a credit?

Even if they are your best friend, you need a contract. Make a written agreement, however simple, just so there's clarity between you. It's all in black and white. Of course, your contract might change over the course of a production, but based only on mutual agreement.

I have a relationship with myself, I honor myself, I respect myself. That self-respect and awareness of being generous with self, what does that do? It draws people to you, people will respect you, include you in their decision-making, and be generous with you.

If I am generous, I generate abundance. If I am courageous, I generate empowerment.

If I am joyful, I generate joy. If I am creative, I generate creativity.

The reverse is true as well.

If I am victimizing myself, I will always be the victim. If I am selfish, I will generate loneliness. If I am greedy, I will generate scarcity.

Like attracts like. When you look out for yourself with healthy self-awareness, you'll attract people who are also self-aware, respect themselves, and respect others. And people like that don't want drama.

I mean, they want drama on camera. Unspoken expectations work well in scenes, as subtext, but they don't work so well in life. Unexpressed expectations are limiting, and prevent possibilities, and ultimately create drama and conflict.

The vision for the story is bigger than any behind-the-scenes petty drama. I'm committed to creating this film, this play, or whatever the project is. If I allow arguments back and forth, or I "need to be right" in a situation, that's just blocking the thing from moving forward.

The vision for the project is bigger than all of us. We're all contributing and, ideally, working harmoniously together. If so, the project has a much better chance of moving forward, being executed creatively, and fulfilling its own potential. Whereas it can get all-too-easily derailed when those things are not in place.

I once collaborated with a producer for two years to develop a movie project. It was on the verge of getting made and we were all very excited. But then this producer, for whatever reason, pretty much hijacked the film, and it fell apart.

About a year later, a writer/script supervisor asked me about my work experience with this producer. I said, "I can't say anything about specifics. But walk away, walk away quickly."

If you're seeing red flags, and the behavior of the people around the script doesn't align with you... I'm sorry, but it's probably not worth it. Your time and energy may be better invested elsewhere. Trust your instincts, and also, do your research. Find out who they've worked with before, what their relationships are like, what is their reputation? It's a small world; you'll find out quickly. And that leads me to what you want your reputation to be.

I remember when I was very young, there was a magazine cover with Tom Hanks that proclaimed, "Nice Guys do Finish First."

I read the article and still remember thinking, *That's what I want people to say about me.* I want people to say, "He's a nice guy. He's committed, he's generous. He's contributing. He's a visionary."

Those are the things that I want people to see in me. So in order for people to see me as all that, I get to be all that, and I can be that right now, regardless of where I am in my career.

My personal contract is like a mission statement that I first wrote years ago. It begins with, "I am committed to creating global unity."

Awesome. Wonderful. I'm committed to creating global unity. That's an awfully big statement, right? How the heck do I do that?

It started with recognizing that I'm either contributing to global unity, or I'm not. This vision actually supports every moment of my life. I frequently check in with myself and ask, *Am I being in a way that is serving my vision of global unity right now? Or am I needing to be right about something? Am I arguing? Am I trying to prove somebody wrong?* That's not unity.

If I find that I'm thinking or behaving in a way that doesn't support unity, I shift.

I've served as a mentor and coach for leadership courses, and one of my favorite quotes from those experiences is, "I can either be right, or I can be free." Personally, I'll take the latter.

I'm also committed to being responsible. I want to be courageous. I want to be loving. I want to be generous. What is the result of these agreements with myself?

While EMBRACE OF THE SERPENT and MOON GARDEN are perhaps my most successful movies to penetrate the commercial world, I did both of those films solely based on their content and the people involved in the projects. I did them because I loved the story, and the creators.

Still, we had an agreement – there was a contract in place before we started work. I never had to track down payments, I enjoyed being on set, and the films are incredible. I'm certain I attracted these experiences because of who I was being – a result of the agreements I have with myself.

My contract with myself isn't static, it evolves over time. For example, I'm not going to do a film for free anymore, I'm not going to be a production assistant, I'm not going to do non-union extra work. I'm very glad I did all of those things, because I was able to build relationships and a career from studying everything I could study, volunteering my time, and writing and performing a one-man show. I just don't want to do those things anymore, so I have updated my contract with myself.

PREPARATION

Write a contract with yourself right now.

This is what I'm agreeing to, with myself. This is who I'm going to be in my career.

How do you want to be seen in the world? Don't focus on actions you plan to take, but rather a way of being that will generate what you want in the world.

Explore what is missing in your life right now. If you're missing respect in your relationships, then YOU get to be respectful. If you're missing excitement, then YOU get to be exciting. If you're in scarcity, then YOU get to go be generous.

Be sure that this contract includes: *I am committed to being this person in every arena of my life, whether it be waiting tables, in all my relationships, with my family members, and with my environment.*

As your career evolves over time, there will be things you don't want to do anymore. You'll outgrow some things, like I did, and that's great. Your priorities will shift as your career evolves, giving you an opportunity to update your contract with yourself.

Your contract with yourself can lay the groundwork for a wonderful career, and a wonderful life.

BENJAMIN EASTERDAY

Making Space for Safety

Benjamin Easterday is a seasoned veteran with over 30 years in film and television, and has broadened his horizons to encompass development and mixed reality. His expertise includes roles in front of and behind the camera as well as significant contributions to script development, financing, and the logistical aspects of film production. As an independent producer and founder of The EV Entertainment & Production Group, as well as Scripts2Screen, he has played pivotal roles in fostering independent talent, securing investments, and generating educational content, notably a web series for Discovery Education. His diverse career spans from acting and producing to stunt-action safety coordination, participating in productions like FAST AND FURIOUS, SG-1, the series *Smallville*, and various independent films for distribution platforms such as Mar Vista, Tubi and Lifetime.

"How you do anything is how you do everything."
- UNKNOWN (ATTRIBUTED TO ZEN BUDDHISM)

Is this a statement, a failure, or a goal? Every actor finds themselves at a crossroads. Many of us perform a cycle of self-analysis or actualization, wondering daily, *What is my approach and preparation for life?* And on stage, or as the camera is about to roll, *How do I approach and perform this scene?*

Whether you are the actor in the scene or the stunt double, the audience only sees the end result. They don't see the hours used to prepare for each scene, to match yourself to the storyline, your character's inner life, the character arc, to each moment of each scene. They don't see you work for hours to rehearse the dialogue and physical movements. Preparing for safety is a part of that.

Why Safety?

Safety in how you perform is key in any situation. The world screams, "Make smart decisions!"

This applies to the decisions you as a performer make, as you bring a scene to life. With big stunts, weapons, driving vehicles, safety is often overlooked because of time, the talent's ability, financial limitations, and ego. Yes, ego. Some will forego safety in order to prove something, to themselves or others.

When you are on set and eager, ready to go, even a seasoned professional can jump past what has been rehearsed or is expected, or not on that day's call sheet. This can lead to costly errors and can even be a recipe for disaster.

We saw poor safety choices on the RUST production. While final judgement has come down to juries' opinions, the very foundation of established safety measures for how we work on a film set was violated.

We hire an Armorer for one and only one reason: safety (not to help with other props.) It is supposed to be the Armorer's sole responsibility to secure all weapons, to check all ammunition, to teach actors safe handling of weapons, and to confirm each hand off is done safely. Gun blanks and dummy rounds are dangerous enough, live ammunition has no place on a movie set. It's also mandatory that a weapon be handled only by approved individuals; this could include an axe, a knife, or any other object that could cause harm if handled unsafely.

In the RUST example, a lack of care for safety was also demonstrated by the First A.D., as Safety Officer, for allowing negligent procedures in general, and especially for handing off a weapon without a full safety check. The talent, from extras to the lead actor, Alec Baldwin, contributed to an unsafe set, as they neglected to handle and operate the weapons with standard gun safety protocols.

Finally, the lack of safety in maintaining an obstruction-free line of sight (aim) down range caused a fatal accident. Had it been observed, the weapon would still have fired a live round, but the projectile may not have hit anyone.

When fundamentals are stepped over or treated as insignificant, the result can be a senseless tragedy, like the cinematographer on the set of RUST being shot to death with a live bullet, or the 2014

MIDNIGHT RIDER incident, where a disregard for the safety of the location on a live train track led to a young camera assistant losing her life.

We often don't even notice that safety is being overlooked. I urge you to pay attention to your own safety, as well as the safety of others.

With the following principles, you can be more in control of both your creative decisions and physical movements, while keeping yourself and everyone around you safe.

PREPARATION

Next time you step on to a set, explore and know the space, especially as it relates to who and what shares your space. That is, pay attention, so you can be aware of everyone and everything in the space with you.

Any major physical movement must be discussed and blocked before shooting. Then, stand by what you have committed to in the scene. If you are meant to handle any weapons, make sure you are trained properly, and follow all protocols.

When there is a lot of physical action, take your time to prepare, practice, and never rush to a finish. If you don't feel certain of what you're supposed to do, don't just say, "I'm ready."

Take a moment to ask the director or stunt coordinator for more detail and clarity.

Less is often more. Trust the camera will find what it needs to in your performance.

GIOVANNI TRIMBLE, PHD

Navigating Intimacy in Acting – The Importance of Intimacy Coordination

Dr. Giovanni Trimble is an LMFT, Certified Autism Spectrum Disorder Clinical Specialist who holds a Ph.D. in human sexuality. They are a published author, Organizational Consultant and Intimacy Coordinator, and published the quantitative dissertation, *Reddit Users' Sexual and Romantic Orientations: A Split Attraction Model Study on Branchedness*. Giovanni gained intimacy coordinating experience working for queer independent erotic film companies based in San Francisco and Oakland, California. Their approach to supporting actors with intimate scenes is gender affirming, culturally sensitive, kink aware, and accommodating of disabilities.

The spontaneity of improvising intimacy with a stranger on set can resemble a gamble, fraught with potential pitfalls. Scenes intended to evoke tenderness can quickly devolve into discomfort, awkwardness, or even regrettable instances of violence. Such deviations from the script often arise from a lack of clearly defined boundaries, leaving actors vulnerable to unexpected touches and reactions.

When I have worked as an Intimacy Coordinator with actors on film sets during intimate scenes, I have observed that for some, when the camera focuses on them, they appear invincible. It's as if they possess limitless capabilities and boundless energy. The lens' attention and the lights' radiance fuel an adrenaline rush that propels them into a state of heightened awareness and performance. Occasionally, the intensity of the moment seems to overwhelm them, and I have witnessed actors lose themselves in their characters' emotions.

When working on a film set, I am habitually attuned to the cast and crew's well-being. I watch for signs when they are pushing themselves too far and check in on them when needed. One sign that I look for is when a scene doesn't require the level of emotion and intensity that the actor has brought to it.

The Role of the Intimacy Coordinator

As an intimacy coordinator, I am a crucial presence on set, tasked with preempting such challenges and safeguarding actors' well-being. A primary goal is to foster an environment where actors can engage in intimate scenes confidently, free from coercion or trauma.

Intimacy coordinators play a pivotal role in creating safe and respectful environments for intimate scenes. They work closely with directors, producers, and actors to ensure that boundaries are established, communication is clear, and consent is paramount. By choreographing intimate moments and providing guidance on physical and emotional safety, intimacy coordinators help actors navigate potentially sensitive material with confidence and professionalism.

The Importance of Boundaries and Consent

In the entertainment industry, discussions surrounding personal boundaries and consent frequently take a back seat. Many actors find themselves ill-equipped to set their limits or express discomfort, especially amid the relentless demands of production schedules. The pressure to "go along", combined with the production's financial constraints, can further discourage individuals from advocating for their own needs.

Empowering actors to set their boundaries and advocate for themselves on set is paramount.

In essence, the principle of enthusiastic consent should underpin all interactions, ensuring that every intimate encounter on screen is rooted in mutual respect and affirmation. By fostering a culture of empowerment and accountability, the art of coordinating intimacy becomes not only a safeguard but also a beacon of integrity within the realm of acting.

NAVIGATING INTIMACY IN ACTING – THE IMPORTANCE OF
INTIMACY COORDINATION

PREPARATION

1. Create a Supportive Community

Cultivating a supportive community outside of work can serve as a crucial buffer against the challenges of the industry. Having trusted friends, colleagues, or mentors to lean on, can provide actors with much-needed emotional support and guidance. Additionally, participating in support groups or workshops focused on intimacy coordination and consent can help actors build confidence and strengthen their self-advocacy skills.

2. Understand Your Rights, and Diversify Your Income Streams

Understanding your rights as an actor is essential to navigating the complexities of intimate scenes on set. Actors should familiarize themselves with industry standards and guidelines regarding nudity, simulated sex, and other intimate content. Additionally, exploring additional income streams can help reduce the pressure to compromise boundaries for the sake of employment.

3. Approach Intimate Scenes with Care

Advocating for intimate scenes to be approached with the same level of meticulous planning and choreography as fight sequences is crucial. Clear communication and mutual consent should reign paramount, with actors and intimacy coordinators working together to ensure everyone feels safe and respected on set.

4. Listen to Your Instincts

Listening to your body can also be instrumental in navigating intimacy on set. Physical discomfort often serves as an early warning sign of emotional distress, ideally prompting actors to honor their instincts and assert their boundaries unequivocally.

Remember that "No" is a complete sentence, and any violation of boundaries warrants immediate attention.

ALI CHEFF

Mantras For Actors

Ali Cheff is an actor, documentary filmmaker, and humanitarian clown who works and plays in different areas of storytelling, including stage, screen and voice over. They have appeared in short films, the feature comedy A LOOK IN THE REAR VIEW, the series *Hellbound* and *Deadly Affairs* and will be voicing Ionah in Netflix's animated series *Maid Chronicles*. Ali has performed as a Humanitarian Clown with Patch Adams for over fourteen years. They also spent three years documenting the ratification of the Equal Rights Amendment in Virginia. Ali believes in compassion, love and authentic choices on camera, on stage, in the booth, and in life. Their other piece in this book is "Click In, Click Out" in Chapter 8.

MANTRA definition:
- A sacred verbal formula repeated in prayer, meditation, or incantation, such as an invocation of a god, a magic spell, or a portion of a scripture containing mystical potentialities.
- A commonly repeated word or phrase, especially in advocacy or for motivation.
- A concept or fact that is mentioned repeatedly, especially in advocacy.

First, a Rant About Myths
    There are a lot of myths and stories told to actors about who you have to be, what sort of side hustles you have to have, what makes you a legitimate talent, etc. I think my early childhood was making sure I checked off all the essential myths. *Get a restaurant job at thirteen.* Check. *Do every job known to humans, so that I have experience to substitute and pull from.* Check. *Don't take roles for the money, do struggle to pay rent, since artists must starve.* Check. *Artists must have*

a certain body. Check and fail. Actors must look this way visually, look that way, speak this way, don't do that type of play, only certain performances are worthy art to perform, etc., etc. My head and heart are spinning with it all.

What I have learned to combat these myths is to find a team. Not just the manager and coach and agents, people whom you care about and who care about you. Friends who remind you this is a job of play. Of switching in and out of personalities and experiences. It is made up of a team and crew of people.

Every set or stage is a ship with many workings. The smoother we can make it for everyone we're working with, the more enjoyable we become to be around. That leads to those folks wanting to hire us again, because they can trust us to do our job: helping the whole production, being on the team, doing our part to create and bring stories to life.

I learned to just do the job. Show up knowing your character and knowing you as the character. Have an opinion. Your character likes lemons or they don't. They have insecurities and hopes and dreams. And they have their own job to do within each scene.

A Pep Talk, Because I Need One Too

The more I talk with coaches and other actors, the more I realize how much is physiological, to stay in the play of performance. We are like surfers riding waves. It is having focus, willingness to tumble, to paddle back out to catch the next wave, or crash into the sand. There's also missing the wave, heading out too soon, or hesitating and lifting too late.

We are in vulnerable spaces in an industry with many ups and downs. The dream is that forty-foot wave. The thing is, there are all the little waves before and after. And there's not just one forty-foot wave... there will be more. Sometimes it's calm waters, and sometimes you get to ride. It is keeping the mind steady and aware. That it is going to be tiring, and thrilling, and spread joy across your face.

There will be days you feel like a fraud or not good enough. Those days, think of a surfer. When they paddle out, they can't think about anything else. It's the same when you step on that stage or set, or into the recording booth. Know you are there to play, perform, and let all of the nonsense go crashing down under that ocean, deep below the water, where it doesn't affect you.

We are in a job that asks us to be vulnerable, but doesn't provide safety, nor the understanding for recovery. We have to create these things for ourselves. (See also "Click In, Click Out" in Chapter 8.)

My acting coach told me to write for five minutes on why I love acting, then to laminate it and carry it with me in my pocket. Through that exercise, I realized one of the things I most relish and most respect, is union with the audience. It saves time and reminds me why I am an actor.

My other acting coach told me to have five statements (mantras) of my goals, and to say them five times daily. Every time we tell ourselves we're not good enough, it's like a mantra. All the things we tell ourselves repeatedly tell our brains they are reality. So why not give your brain a reality that will help you manifest the mindset to act?

PREPARATION

1. Spend five minutes free-writing about why you love acting, what you love about it, what is fun about it, why you want to do it.

2. Come back to what you wrote, and circle or highlight five affirmative statements, such as:
I want to…
I love…
I appreciate…

3. If you had to pick only one of these five, which is the most meaningful and resonant to your soul? Your top priority?
Note: a common practice for working with affirmations is to write them in present time, as if they're already happening, such as:
I am so happy now that…
I'm earning a great living doing what I love.
I'm so grateful now that…
I have a new agent who is getting me a lot of great work.
I'm thrilled to be working with…. (favorite actor/s or director)
I'm so excited I've been cast in…

4. Chose a mix of four or five from the above two lists to use as mantras. Start with what you love about acting, your primary reason/s for being an actor, then include a few of the affirmations of your goals. Have it laminated to carry around as my teacher recommended.

5. Recite your statements with feeling five times each morning. Read them right before bedtime. They will become your mantras and influence your mindset. (Of course, you can always change them up and make a new list.)

Here are some things I say to myself when I'm nervous on set. Feel free to adopt them or come up with your own:
I am here not to be liked, but to help things run smoothly.
Which often leads to being liked.
I am going to have fun.

Which often leads to having fun!

"I just love being part of creating cool art."

- ANGUS CLOUD

PERMISSIONS

NOW ACT!
Vol. 1
Insight, Advice, and Preparation Processes from Actors, Coaches, and Casting Directors

"Preparing a Character for the Stage" by Jennifer Allen © 2025 by Jennifer Allen

"An Actor Prepares – The Boy Scout Approach" by Thaine H. Allison, Jr. © 2025 by Thaine H. Allison, Jr.

"How Acting Can Help You Help Others" Alan Angelo © 2025 by Alan Angelo

"Craft, Career and Content" and "Acting is Technical" by Christopher M. Allport © 2025 by Christopher M. Allport

"Talk to Yourself" by Mackenzie Barmen © 2025 by Mackenzie Barmen

"Stage vs Screen" by Paul Barry © 2025 by Paul Barry

"How Could You Play That Part?!" by Jayce Bartok © 2025 by Jayce Bartok

"So What?" by Winter Bassett © 2025 by Winter Bassett

"Methods and Strategies for Learning Your Lines" by Allison Bergman © 2025 by Allison Bergman

"Embracing the Moment: Techniques for Presence in Acting" by Bruna Bertossi © 2025 by Bruna Bertossi

"What I Learned from Martin Sheen" by Lynne Burnett © 2025 by Lynne Burnett

"Choosing Material" by Tim Carr © 2025 by Tim Carr

"Learning Lines by Heart" and "No Schm-Acting, Please" by Crystal Carson © 2025 by Crystal Carson

"Click In, Click Out" and "Mantras for Actors" by Ali Cheff © 2025 by Ali Cheff

"Acting is Living Truthfully Under Imaginary Circumstances" by Bryan Chesters © 2025 by Bryan Chesters

PERMISSIONS

"Dueling Animal Opposites... Creating the Electric Moment on Stage or Screen" by Devorah Cutler © 2025 by Devorah Cutler

"Do It Because You Love to Act" by Cindy D'Andrea © 2025 by Cindy D'Andrea

"Agreements" by Brionne Davis Davel © 2025 by Brionne Davis Davel

"What Would It Be Like if You Really Meant It?" by Clea DeCrane © 2025 by Clea DeCrane

"Making Space for Safety" by Benjamin Easterday © 2025 by Benjamin Easterday

"Casting Directors Do Care" by Danielle Eskinazi © 2025 by Danielle Eskinazi

"Master Classes, Tony Bennett, and How Many Levels Have You Got?" by Michael Genet © 2025 by Michael Genet

"Audition Notes" by Paul Guay © 2025 by Paul Guay

"How to Read a Script" by Thomas Gumede © 2025 by Thomas Gumede

"Subtext" by Price Hall © 2025 by Price Hall

"Emotional Personal Touchstones" by Diana Jordan © 2025 by Diana Jordan

"Save It for the Camera" by Kim Krizan © 2025 by Kim Krizan

"A Writer's Perspective for Actors" by Laurie Lamson © 2025 by Laurie Lamson

"But They Don't Make Movies Where I Live!" by Vinnie Langdon III © 2025 by Vinnie Langdon III

"Casting with Diversity and Authenticity - I'm Looking for You, So Be You!" by Roxanna Lewis © 2025 by Roxanna Lewis

"Let's Get Physical" by Josh Margulies © 2025 by Josh Margulies

"Eleven Memorizing Tricks and Tips" by Cindy Marinangel © 2025 by Cindy Marinangel

"Creative Collaboration" by Mara McCann © 2025 by Mara McCann

"The Art of Getting Out of Your Own Way" by Leigh McCloskey © 2025 by Leigh McCloskey

"Yes, I'm Acting – Believe Me Anyway" by Malcolm McDowell © 2025 by Malcolm McDowell

"Relax and Be Yourself" by Jack O'Halloran © 2025 by Jack O'Halloran

PERMISSIONS

"Let It Go" by Joy Osmanski © 2025 by Joy Osmanski

"Life, Luck, Law, and Logic in Art" by Mark Pellegrino © 2025 by Mark Pellegrino

"The Hill of Embarrassment" and "Comedy Is a Necessity" by Stanzi Potenza © 2025 by Stanzi Potenza

"The Six Audition Tools" by Holly Powell © 2014 updated © 2025 by Holly Powell

"The Little Brain in Your Heart" by Kimmy Robertson © 2025 by Kimmy Robertson

"How to Create a Showcase for Your Acting Through Collaboration" by Caryn Ruby © 2025 by Caryn Ruby

"Memorization and Stage Direction" by Sarah Rush © 2025 by Sarah Rush

"Real-Life Preparation" by Michael Savage aka Sirtony © 2025 by Michael Savage aka Sirtony

"How to Cope with Difficult Personalities" by Lisa Sawicki © 2025 by Lisa Sawicki

"Make It Work with Five W's" by Stephen H. Snyder © 2025 by Stephen H. Snyder

"Being in the Present Moment" by Donn Swaby © 2025 by Donn Swaby

"Mind, Body, Emotion & Spirit" by Leandro Taub © 2025 by Leandro Taub

"Navigating Intimacy in Acting" by Giovanni Trimble, PhD © 2025 by Giovanni Trimble, PhD

"Diversity in Hollywood" by Dioncio Virvez © 2025 by Dioncio Virvez

"Learn Your Character's Skills" by Katherine Waddell © 2025 by Katherine Waddell

"Processing Direction" by Kevin E. West © 2025 by Kevin E. West

QUOTES

The quotes throughout are included under the fair use doctrine of the U.S. copyright statute: "It is permissible to use limited portions of a work including quotes, for purposes such as commentary, criticism, news reporting, and scholarly reports."

ABOUT THE AUTHOR / EDITOR

Laurie Lamson

An award-winning screenwriter with a filmmaking background, Laurie has written well over one hundred produced film, video, and audio scripts. She often collaborates with production companies on education, entertainment, and marketing projects for corporate and government clientele.

Dedicated to supporting creativity and positive impact, she offers writing workshops and consultations to fellow writers and creators.

Laurie served as the editor or co-editor for three anthologies in the *Now Write!* creative writing series started by her aunt, Sherry Ellis. Working on the series inspired her to create this compilation for actors.

OTHER BOOKS BY LAURIE

Nonfiction
2026 Datebook/Planner for Artists, Writers, Creatives
Inner Yoga: 25 Simple Self-Care Tools for Creative People
Now Write! Screenwriting (anthology co-Editor)
Now Write! Mysteries (anthology co-Editor)
Now Write! Science Fiction, Fantasy, and Horror (anthology Editor)

Fiction
The Second Big Bang (sci-fi/fantasy comic novella adapted from original screenplay by Laurie Lamson and Sandra de Fontanes)

jazzymaemedia.com
nowwrite.net
creativefreedomnow.com

www.ingramcontent.com/pod-product-compliance
Lightning Source LLC
Chambersburg PA
CBHW020732160426
43192CB00006B/206